EXPERIMENTAL PSYCHOLOGY

EXPERIMENTAL PSYCHOLOGY

Edited by

A.K. Sharan

ANMOL PUBLICATIONS PVT. LTD.

NEW DELHI - 110 002 (INDIA)

ANMOL PUBLICATIONS PVT. LTD.
4374/4B, Ansari Road, Daryaganj
New Delhi - 110 002
Ph.: 3261597, 3278000
Visit us at: www.anmolbooks.com

Experimental Psychology

First Edition, 2003

ISBN 81-261-1416-9

PRINTED IN INDIA

Published by J.L. Kumar for Anmol Publications Pvt. Ltd., New Delhi - 110 002 and Printed at Tarun Offset Press, Delhi.

Contents

Preface

Etymologically, the scientific study of all forms of human and animal behaviour, sometimes concerned with the methods through which behaviour can be modified is named psychology. "Study of mind", psychology is intimately related to the biological and social sciences. Some divisions of psychology are applied fields, while others are more experimental in nature. One of the important of these is clinical psychology which is concerned with the diagnosis and treatment of mental disorders. Experimental psychology is the broad field, which includes specialisations in child educational, social, developmental, physiological and comparative psychology.

The present book consists of Twentysix chapters highlighting major problems in the field. Case studies are also given. The material contained herein will be useful for one and all.

In compiling the information, various standard books, reports and journals are consulted. I am beholden to all those scholars whose opinions, and research findings are borrowed herein—partially or substantially. I am also thankful to my friends, colleagues and family members for their moral support and constant inspiration. Equally, I am indebted to my publishers for publishing my work within shortest possible time.

—**A.K.S.**

1

The Relevance of Psychology and Psychologists to Health for All

Introduction

The role of psychologists with regard to health and mental health is rather different in different parts of the world and so is the organisational status and nature of psychology as an academic and professional discipline. At the one extreme we have countries like the United States with over 100,000 psychologists who often have prestige and influence comparable to that of medical doctors. At the other extreme, there is the People's Republic of China with a much bigger population, but only about 2000 psychologists.

It is not only on a global scale, but also in Europe that international differences are considerable. Greece, for example, has very few psychologists and no university provides a Master's or Ph.D. programme in psychology, while countries like Holland, United Kingdom and Sweden count themselves among the most densely psych-populated nations in the world with a considerable number of universities providing Ph.D. curricula and carrying out extensive research programmes. But even in these latter countries the status and role of psychologists in the health field is often subordinate to that of medical doctors and their organisation is weaker and more diffuse.

This situation co-determines the involvement of psychologists in WHO programmes, because that involvement is decided upon by national governments and authorities, to whom the comparative status of relevant professional organisations plays an important role, despite the quality and relevance of the knowledge they have to offer.

Psychological Aspects of HFA/2000

When the Thirtieth World Health Assembly in May (1977) accepted HFA/2000, it decided upon a fundamental change in member states' health policies and in international cooperation in health.

This becomes clear from the major themes that the European region of WHO has adopted in her strategy for attaining HFA/2000. These themes are:

(i) equal opportunities to health and health care;

(ii) health promotion and prevention of ill-health or disease;

(iii) community participation;

(iv) multisectorial cooperation;

(v) primary health care;

(vi) international cooperation.

The major categories of change that are supposed to bring about such improvements in health care are:

(i) changes in lifestyle;

(ii) changes in the environment;

(iii) changes in the care system.

The General Programme of Work (GPW) for the present period (1984-1989) cites four major activities in which psychologists can play a central role:

1. The development of mental health policies and the promotion, coordination, evaluation and support of programmes throughout the world.
2. The improved understanding and utilisation of psycho- logical factors in the promotion of health and human development.
3. Prevention of alcohol and drug abuse.
4. Prevention and treatment of mental and neurological disorders (WHO, 1983).

The World Health Assembly recently voted for a resolution that underlines the importance of this part of the GPW by stating that: "use of mental health knowledge and skills can improve health care in general" (WHO, 1984).

Consequently the target document on HFA/2000 of WHO/EURO speaks for the necessity of application of "psychological and biobehavioural principles in preventing, managing and controlling mental health problems and promoting mental health: (WHO, 1983).

In this document 38 specific targets in support of the Regional Strategy for Health for All are stated. A working group of the European Federation of Professional Psychologists Associations (EFPPA) recently concluded that psychology and psychologists have a substantial bearing on at least twenty of these targets.

From the target descriptions it becomes clear that the knowledge needed to implement HFA/2000 includes:

(i) description of indicators of health in all its facets;

(ii) methods of reliably and validly measuring/monitoring these indicators;

(iii) determination of the ways in which physical and social factors influence health and health (risk) behaviour of individuals and population;

(iv) determination of the separate and combined effects of specific types of (covert and/or overt) behaviour on health and of the factors determining each type;

(v) methods of intervention and of evaluation of interventions at individual as well as population level.

Psychologists, especially those working in the subspecialties designated as clinical and health psychology, will readily recognise these desiderata as precisely those that traditionally have been considered as characteristic or their own field and can point to a vast body of knowledge accumulated in these areas. In the following some examples will be presented to illustrate this claim.

Accident Prevention

Target 11 refers to the field of accident prevention in which considerable progress has already been made, but in which further progress can be made as the results of psychological research have shown. Consider the case of accidents involving motor vehicles and child pedestrians (McPherson, 1984).

The peak incidence of these accidents is between the ages of 5 and 7 years, and the generally accepted explanation, even by the children themselves, is that children of this age tend to be inattentive to oncoming traffic and attempt to cross streets at inappropriate times and places, giving drivers insufficient opportunity to take effective avoiding action. Preventive methods have therefore concentrated on the children themselves, e.g. by educating them in the dangers of traffic, in the 'stop and look' procedure before crossing, and by providing protected crossing places. However, when behavioural analyses were carried out, based on systematic observations of children among traffic, it was shown that whereas children were clearly anticipating the possibility of an accident, and were taking appropriate avoiding action, drivers were not. Drivers did not appear to anticipate the possibility that a child might step on to the road. For example, when they saw children at the kerb, they did not slacken speed or move further from the kerb, and when an accident did threaten, they usually took action too late to have avoided it, had not the child done so. In other words, the entire responsibility for avoiding such accidents was being taken by the child of 5 or 7 years, and not by the driver. These observations thus suggest that further reductions in this type of accident will occur only if the focus of intervention shifts from the child to the driver. This approach to the investigation of accidents is typical of the 'applied behavioural analysis' approach which is widely used in contemporary applied psychology.

Suicide Prevention

Target 12 refers to the field of suicide prevention. Over the past two decades psychologists have extensively investigated the causes of suicidal acts and of the rising trends in these acts. The influence of psychological and social factors on suicidal behaviour is well documented (Diekstra, 1981). However, despite intensive efforts the results of suicide prevention programmes in general have been disappointing. This has led to the conclusion that it is unlikely that further significant improvement will result from merely applying existing methods more extensively or vigorously. Instead, a reconceptualisation of the problem is required. To illustrate this point, the case of suicide prevention in schools can be considered. Both in the United States and in Holland so-called Adolescent Suicide Awareness Programme (ASAP) have recently been set up (Diekstra and Hawton, 1987). Such programmes are carried out and coordinated by staff of community mental health centres.

ASAP is directed at influencing the attitudes and behaviours of three target groups, namely pupils, parents and teachers, by holding meetings and mini-workshops for each of these groups on a regular basis. Information on suicidal behaviour, the extent of the problem, its causes, signals and how to react in case one is confronted with a severely depressed or suicidal youngster, is provided. Listening and communication skills and adequate methods for motivating such youngsters to accept required help and for referring them appropriately are also learned.

Although the effect of these programmes on rates of suicide and attempted suicide among the young has not yet been established, due to the fact that they are of such recent date, it has already been shown in two centres that the rate of referrals of high risk adolescents, by teachers, parents and fellow students, has gone up dramatically.

Coined in WHO terminology, programmes like ASAP are community-based, preventive of ill-health or disability, a form of primary mental health care and multi-sectorial.

Developing and Supporting Health Lifestyles

The HFA/2000 target document clarifies this target, by stating that "The skills that enable people to control and direct their lives, and thus to live in a healthy way, include the capacity to formulate problems, find solutions, communicate effectively and question and intervene actively on their own behalf when necessary. These skills are more easily learned in childhood and youth."

What the target document does not say is that developmental psychologists in different parts of the world have found in longitudinal studies that early parent-child interactions are highly consistant over time and situations and that some well-defined patterns of interactions are closely related to behaviour problems and coping styles of children in puberty and adolescence (no longitudinal studies are available yet that have followed children for more that 14 years (ISSBD,1982).

Home based intervention (parent centred) may therefore produce substantial initial and continuing gains in the child's development. Studies suggest that the effects tend to be maintained for years after intervention is terminated. The critical activity promoted is parent, especially mother-child interaction around common activities. Para-professional workers, suitably trained, can act very affectively as home visitors/parent educators.

The Emergence of Health Psychology

From the three examples described above, to which a legion of others can easily be added, it becomes clear that it is not just clinical or medical psychology but psychology in general, including social, developmental, industrial and personality psychology, that is of utmost relevance to present WHO programmes. All the subdivisions or sub-disciplines of psychology have produced and will produce knowledge that is applicable to health and health care. The growing awareness of this fact both among psychologists and in other disciplines in the health field is probably one of the main reaons for the emergence of a new speciality of psychological research and professional practice presently called health psychology.

The designation signifies the broadening of psychology to include the general health of the individual in a social, community and ecological setting. More than ever before psychologists are becoming involved in health promotion, in the relationship between health and environment, in prevention and control of chronic illnesses, and in questions of use of and access to health care by different social groups. They are rapidly accumulating knowledge that is of high relevance in these areas.

Other examples worth mentioning are: the development of procedures for systematic citizen input into decision making with regard to health care; the development of methods of evaluation and procedures for promoting change in community settings, as well as instruments to measure aspects of city readiness for social action (Moos, 1984). A beautiful example of this is the work of Levine (1982) in organising the citizens of Love Canal, a neighbourhood near a toxic waste dump, to take appropriate social action for improving public health.

The Dissemination of Psychological Knowledge

Clearly there is a great deal of knowledge within psychology that awaits broader application. One of the reasons why the available knowledge is not translated into action is that applied psychologists themselves are often not fully aware of what their own field has to offer. Improving training standards, one of the main functions that EFPPA in cooperation with WHO could fulfil, is an important tool in amending this situation. There are, however, other reasons why the public has not benefitted enough from what psychology has to offer.

Important political, social, economic and organisational constraints on the application of available knowledge are present. For example, vested interest groups may gain social, inter-political and economic benefits from the status quo and may lobby against the application of new knowledge.

Another reasons is that there is still, in many countries, very little systematic review by policy-makers of new knowledge arising from research projects — knowledge which could influence health policies and programmes. This lack of coordination is often the result of weak organisational links between the research community and policy makers both within and among countries. Such links are, however, better established by some academic disciplines, such as the medical sciences, than by others.

Therefore, it is relevant to point out that the expanding of the number of points on which the substantial corpus of psychological knowledge and techniques is brought to bear on human health problems depends on how much better psychologists learn to work with policy makers and community leaders as consultants and participants in the design, implementation and evaluation of health and health care programmes (Holtzmann, in preparation).

Recommendations

What psychology as a body should strive for in relationship with WHO, in particular with WHO/EURO, is:

(i) The recognition of organisations like EFPPA as non-governmental organisations collaborating with WHO;

(ii) The establishment within the WHO/EURO organisation of an advisory committee on health psychology;

(iii) Membership of programme advisory committees where health psychologists could make a significant contribution;

(iv) Use of (health) psychologists in designing and evaluating research programmes, studies and applications;

(v) The establishment of a clearing house through which (a) names, interests and specialist skills of health psychologists working in the region and (b) the nature of relevant projects being carried out in countries of the region, specifying topic, design, methods, staff and timetable, could be made know to WHO;

(vi) The establishment of WHO-collaborating centres for health psychology throughout the region.

Finally, it would be desirable if WHO/EURO would agree to reserve a special issue of Public Health in Europe for a directory and review of European health psychology.

Table 1 : Targets in support of the regional strategy HFA/2000 of special relevance to psychology.

Target 3	By the year 2000, disabled persons should have the physical, social and economic opportunities that allow at least for a socially and economically fulfilling and mentally creative life.

Target 4 By the year 2000, the average number of years that people live free from major disease and disability should be increased by at least 10%.

Target 9 By the year 2000, mortality in the region from diseases of the circulatory system in people under 65 should be reduced by at least 15%.

Target 10 By the year 2000, mortality in the region from cancer in people under 65 should be reduced by at least 15%.

Target 11 By the year 2000, deaths from accidents in the region should be reduced by at least 25% through an intensified effort to reduce traffic, home and occupational accidents.

Target 12 By the year 2000, the current rising trend in suicides and attempted suicides in the region should be reversed.

Target 13 By 1990, national policies in all member states should ensure that legislative, administrative and economic mechanisms provide broad intersectoral support and resources for the promotion of health lifestyles and ensure effective participation of the people at all levels of such policy-making.

Target 14 By 1990, all member states should have specific programmes which enhance the major roles of the family and other social groups developing and supporting healthy life-styles.

Target 15 By 1990, educational programmes in all member states should enhance the knowledge, motivation and skills of people to acquire and maintain health.

Target 16 By 1995, in all member states, there should be significant increase in positive health behaviour, such as balanced nutrition, non-smoking, appropriate physical activity and good stress management.

Target 17 By 1995, in all member states, there should be significant decreases in health-damaging behaviour, such as overuse of alcohol and pharmaceutical products, use of illicit drugs and dangerous chemical substances, dangerous driving and violent social behaviour.

Target 24 By the year 2000, all people of the region should have a better opportunity of living in houses and settlements which provide a healthy and safe environment.

Target 25 By the year 1995, people of the region should be effectively protected against work-related health risks.

Target 28 By 1990, the primary health care system of all member states should provide a wide range of health-promotive, curative, rehabilitataive and supportive services to meet the needs of vulnerable and under-served individuals and groups.

Target 29 By 1990, in all member states, primary health care systems should be based on cooperation and teamwork between health care personnel, individuals, families and community groups.

Target 31 By 1990, all member states should have built effective mechanisms for ensuring quality of patient care within their health care systems.

Target 32 Before 1990, all member states should have formulated research strategies to stimulate investigations which improve the application and expansion of knowledge needed to support their health for all developments.

Target 36 Before 1990, in all member states, the planning, training and use of health personnel should be in accordance with health for all policies, with emphasis on the primary health care approach.

Target 37 Before 1990, in all member states, education should provide personnel in sections related to health with adequate information on the country's health for all policies and programmes and their practical application to their own sectors.

Target 38 Before 1990, all member states should have established a formal mechanism for the systematic assessment of the appropriate use of health technologies and of their effectiveness, efficiency, safety and acceptability, as well as reflecting national health policies and economic restraints.

Developing A Psychological Contribution to HFA 2000: Smoking Prevention

This paper begins with a brief review of previous actions against smoking before suggesting contributions that psychologists should make.

What have clinical psychologists done about smoking?

The main contribution of clinical psychologists to action against smoking has been developing, providing and evaluating treatments to help people stop smoking (Bernstein & Glasgow, 1979). These treatments have mainly been offered to groups rather than individuals. Most have been intensive, time-consuming and therefore expensive. Associated with them has been research evaluating and comparing their outcomes. This research has shown a concern with percentage success rates. There has been little attention to the applicability of the methods evaluated and scant concern with the absolute numbers rather than percentages of people who might be helped. A third characteristic has been the isolated of our work from that of other agencies.

Much less work has concerned preventing the onset of smoking (Botvin, 1982). Recent work may be summarised as teaching "lifeskills". It involves teaching young people decision-making, resisting social pressure, and developing awareness of other influences, such as advertising, which tend to promote smoking.

What else has been done?

Psychologists sometimes seem unaware that many groups helping people to stop smoking have been run by professionals other than ourselves. Raw and Heller (1984) reported that only 9% of smoking clinics in the UK were run by clinical psychologists. Sixty two per cent were run by Health Education Officers, 13% by medical staff, 11% by Health Visitors and 5% by others.

A second, and very widespread, activity has been health education about smoking.

Thirdly, most District Health Authorities in the UK have or are developing policies against smoking. Most involve increased restrictions on smoking in Health Authority premises publicity about the policy, offering help in the form of support groups for employees who wish to stop smoking and advice or suggestions to local employers and other organisations that they too should develop policies against smoking.

A fourth kind of action concerns cigarette advertising. Cigarettes may not now be advertised on television in the UK. However, this is a ban in name only. Sponsorship of sporting events by tobacco companies results in massive television exposure of cigarette brand names. Later we shall see that taxation is another powerful but underused means of influencing cigarette consumption.

What have we learned about smoking and its prevention?

We have learned that there is no single reason why people smoke (Ashton & Stepney, 1982). Smoking may serve a range of different functions at different times and under different circumstances. Similarly we no longer expect that a single form of help will be effective for everybody (Lichtenstein, 1982).

However, in contrast to the pessimism of some reviewers in the 1970s we now know that some methods are more effective than others. So far as psychological help is concerned we know that skill-based methods are better than, say, educational or aversive techniques.

We also know that very brief interventions can help some people to stop smoking (Russell et al, 1979). These workers showed a small but significant percentage increase in people stopping smoking after brief advice and information were provided routinely by General Practitioners (GPs). The importance of this finding is that it could be repeated on a very large scale.

We are more aware and accepting of smokers' motives. We know that smoking cannot be dismissed simply as nicotine addiction, but that it is maintained by a number of factors. Related to this it seems that giving up smoking is not one change but the end result of a series of stages and processes (Prochaska & Diclemente, 1983).

We know that most help is unsuccessful. Twenty per cent is often spoken of as an average long-term success rate for a smoking treatment service, but this may be an overestimate. Hunt et al (1971), reviewing a large number of American smoking clinics, reported that around 20% of people who stopped smoking originally were still abstinent at one year. Bradshaw (1973), also reviewing the results of a large number of clinics, reported a median end of treatment success rate of 37%. If these two results are taken as representative, putting them together we could expect only around 8% of people entering treatment to be abstinent a year after the end of treatment.

Against this pessimism it is helpful to remember that there are currently estimated to be 10 million former smokers in Britain. We may not be good at helping people stop smoking but many smokers themselves know how it is done.

Finally, we know that increasing taxation on tobacco is

effective in helping some smokers to give up the habit. Russell (1973) plotted consumption of cigarettes against real price for the years 1946 to 1971, and showed a striking inverse correlation. Substantial price increases led to marked reductions in consumption.

What has been achieved?

Although the percentage of smokers in the population is failing, successive chancellors of the Exchange have failed to seize the opportunity to accelerate this downward trend by increasing taxation markedly. Similarly, the failure to regulate sponsorship of the sports and arts by tobacco companies has meant that there is still a vast amount of cigarette advertising.

Furthermore, there is an inconsistancy between the government's initiation, coordination, and funding of action against illicit drugs, tranquillisers and solvent misuse, and the shortage of such actions against smoking.

It is difficult to evaluate the success of Health Authority policies against smoking as most are very new. However, I am pessimistic. I do not know of any British Health Authority which included actions and achievements concerning smoking in the objectives against which the performances of its General Managers will be evaluate. The climate of opinion within Health Authorities does not seem to me to be against smoking. In this context, climate of opinion is not a woolly notion. A General Manager who makes no secret of his view that the anti-smoking lobby is making a fuss about nothing is unlikely to promote or support action against smoking. In short, Health Authority policies against smoking are unlikely to achieve their intended effects because they are not well incorporated within the current management arrangements, and in many cases are not supported by the General Managers whose job it is to implement them.

Clinical psychologists have made little progress in reducing the number of people smoking. Moreover, the work we have done has been less in response to perceived health care needs than to our own professional interests and priorities. We have run and evaluated relatively small treatment groups. There are many other actions we could have taken. How many of us assessed the options before embarking on treatment groups? How many of us asked smokers whether they wished to join treatment groups, or perhaps receive some other sort of help? In addition to all this, our work has usually shown little coordination with other action.

The Health Costs of Smoking

To put this lack of achievement into perspective, consider the health costs of smoking. Around one smoker in four eventually dies from his or her smoking. This amounts to about 100,000 deaths each year in the UK, or about 700 deaths in an average District Health Authority. Smoking is the largest single preventable cause of death in Britain (Roya College of Physicians, 1983). Action against smoking should therefore be central to some of the main aims of Health For All 2000 — promoting lifestyles conducive to health and reducing preventable conditions.

Towards a Psychological Contribution

If psychologists are to be more responsive and effective in smoking prevention we must first shift the current emphasis in our work from helping people to stop smoking towards preventing young people from starting. Research on skill-based methods of primary prevention was mentioned earlier and some of it is used in schools. We should use our clinical and evaluation skills to promote, improve and evaluate this work, and we should do so in a planned and coordinated way with the other professionals concerned.

Secondly, the study referred to earlier (Russell et al, 1979) showing the effectiveness of General Practitioners advice against smoking is often cited but rarely applied. We should draw the attention of Health Authority managers and GPs to the method and its implications, and help to implement and evaluate work of the same kind in many localities.

Thirdly, although there are difficulties (Kozlowski et al, 1980), there are also many needs and opportunities for consumer research in smoking prevention. Reports of smokers themselves being asked what help they would like or find useful are rare.

Fourth, and most important, we should take action on a wider scale, and at different levels. A logical place to start is with and within the Health Authorities by whom most of us are employed. It is helpful and right that Health Authorities should serve as exemplars to their consumers and to other organisations and employers.

Our results have been disappointing so far but negative results may be used positively. So far, psychologists, as well as most Health Authorities in Britain and the British Government, have done little more than tinker with smoking prevention. Tinkering has not been effective. We should use the evidence of past failures to arague for wider and more effective action.

One kind of wider action could be pressure within the Health Authorities to include smoking prevention targets in the objectives given to General Managers. Another step would be to propose particular smoking prevention objectives. In doing this we must learn from past mistakes by listening to the people we wish to influence in order to suggest a programme of actions which will be acceptable and achieveable. With this in mind a suggested first task for General Managers might be to involve Health Authority staff and managers in proposing actions designed to get people thinking about smoking as a problem about which something should be done. The same wide range of people could be asked to propose restrictions on smoking, and to state how adherence to the restrictions is to be monitored and maintained. Actions of this kind should be the first in a progressive series formulated by us in cooperation and consultation with other colleagues. Again we can learn from past mistakes. Most action against smoking in the past has been one-off.

Lastly, an important part of our contribution is that all proposals should include plans for evaluation and opportunities to modify the action subsequently.

Conclusions

The proposals here contain little detail, but that is inevitable. One of the main lessons to draw from previous work on smoking is not to assume that we know what is needed, but to ask the consumers and look closely at the problems we wish to help with. A second general point is that future actions should be better coordinated with other agencies' plans and not carried out in isolation. Thirdly, we should think more of absolute numbers of people and their needs, and less of maximising percentage success rates.

If these conclusions sound familiar I suggest it is because the failings of much of our previous work on smoking have characterised a good deal of our work with other problems and client groups. As a profession I believe we are beginning to acknowledge and respond to these mistakes.

2

Clinical Psychology in USA

Clinical psychology in the United States is generally thought to have begun with the work of Lightner Witmer. Witmer, after receiving his Ph.D. degree under Wundt in 1892, was appointed director of the laboratory of psychology at the University of Pennsylvania. Four years later, in 1896, Witmer founded the first psycholgical clinic in the US, and gave the first course in clinical psychology. In fact, it was Witmer who named this area of psychology 'clinical psychology'. It would seem, therefore, that he is rightfully viewed as the founder of clinical psychology. A more detailed description of Witmer's contributions can be found elsewhere (Garfield, 1965, 1974). Howevever, it is worth mentioning also that Witmer founded, edited, and wrote for the journal, *The Psychological Clinic,* from 1907 to 1935, at which time the publication of the journal ceased.

In spite of Witmer's contributions, his impact was surprisingly limited. Psychology was still in its infancy and there did not appear to be strong demands for psychological services. A more significant development, however, was also occurring around the turn of the century which was to have a greater impact on clinical psychology. This was the development of the mental age scale by Binet and his colleague, Simon, in France. The availability of a potentially worthwhile test of mental ability was of some consequence for those working with a variety of children's problems. The American psychologist,

Henry Goddard, revised the scale for use in the US in 1908 and helped to popularize it. The first child guidance clinic was founded in Chicago in 1909, and the director, the psychiatrist William Healy, was much interested in the appraisal of mental abilities. The use of psychological tests was thus associated quite early with the development of clinical psychology.

A few other early developments can be mentioned before going on to more recent history. Although the first child guidance clinic in Chicago employed a psychologist, Grace Fernald, and thus provided a model for the employment of clinical psychologists, the number of such clinics increased very slowly. In a similar fashion, the development of the mental hygiene movement in the US and of psychoanalysis abroad had little immediate impact on the growth of clinical psychology in this early period, although they did at later periods. The Stanford-Revision of the Binet-Simon Scale by Lewis Terman and his colleagues at Stanford University in 1916 was an event of some importance. It was for many years the most recognized psychological test, and the hallmark of the clinical psychologist.

Thus, during the first three decades of this century and continuing through the fourth decade, clinical psychology was a very small and slowly developing field within psychology. Clinical psychologists were employed in child guidance clinics, institutions for the mentally retarded, a small number of state mental hospitals, and in universities. There were no legal standards or requirements in order to function as a clinical psychologist, and there were no special or organized training programmes in clinical psychology in the universities. The primary duties of the clinical psychologist centred around the administration of psychological tests, with a major emphasis on Stanford-Binet Scale of Intelligence. A survey by Louttit (1939) of 111 psychologists in child guidance clinics indicated that 'psychometrics' was their most frequent activity, with over 86 per cent of the group engaged in this activity. Educational guidance and vocational guidance were the next most frequent activities. Psychotherapy, the currently most popular activity of psychologists in the US, was listed as the sixth most frequent activity. It should be noted also that clinical psychologists during this period were to a large extent professionally involved in working with children.

The advent of the Second World War changed matters drastically. There was an initial need for psychologists to help in the screening and selection of men for the armed forces. As the war continued and the battle casualties increased, there was a shortage of trained psychiatrists to provide the necessary diagnostic and treatment services. As a result, clinical psychologists were offered commissions as officers in the US Army in 1944, a special five-week course of training was provided, and clinical psychologists were assigned to military hospitals and medical units. Of importance here was the opportunity for a number of clinical psychologists to participate in a wider variety of activities with patients than previously, particularly individual and group psychotherapy.

When the war was over, the Veterans Administration (VA) had to deal with a large number of emotionally disturbed individuals who required a variety of in-patient and out-patient services. This agency, like the army, also sought the help of clinical psychologists. Positions were set up for clinical psychologists which, patterned after the military, mentioned such primary functions as diagnostic testing, research, and psychotherapy with appropriate supervision. This, therefore, provided a number of new and relatively well-paid positions for clinical psychologists. At first, positions were available for psychologists without the doctorate. However, in the latter part of 1951, the VA in line with other developments to be discussed shortly, decided to require the Ph.D. degree for all clinical psychology staff positions.

Although there was a great need for clinical psychologists at this time, there were too few trained psychologists available for employment. The VA, therefore, in co-operation with qualified universities, set up a collaborative training programme. The essence of the programme was as follows: Graduate students admitted to the programme would spend approximately half a week at various VA installations. This would provide them with a stipend to defray the costs of graduate training as well as with clinical experience under supervision in VA hospitals and clinics. University faculty members would serve as consultants to provide instruction and liaison with the field settings. On the whole, the programme was successful and helped train a large number of clinical psychologists, a significant percentage of whom later took positions with the VA. For many years, over 700 students per year participated in the programme and the VA became the largest single employer of clinical psychologists.

At least three other developments during the immediate post-war period also deserve mention. Because of the shortage of personnel in the basic mental health professions — psychiatry, clinical psychology, psychiatric social work, and psychiatric nursing — the US Public Health Service and its National Institute of Mental Health also provided substantial support for graduate training in clinical psychology. Fellowships for students were provided, as well as funds for faculty salaries, equipment, and the like.

The other two developments pertain to events within the American Psychological Association (APA). The first was a decision in 1945 that both applied and scientific psychology should be in one organizataion with special divisions to reflect the various interests. Consequently, the American Association of Applied Psychology, formed in 1937, was disbanded and incorporated into APA, and the former's journal, the *Journal of Consulting Psychology* eventually became the clinical journal of the APA.

The other development of importance pertains to decisions reached concerning the training of clinical psychologists. In part, because of the demand from governmental agencies to indicate acceptable university programmes for possible support, the APA decided to implement a programme of accrediting doctoral programmes in clinical psychology. Also, in order to provide adequate guidelines for training, a Committee on Training in Clinical Psychology was appointed and an important report was issued in 1947 (American Psychological Association, 1947). The recommendations were subsequently discussed at a major conference on training held in Boulder, Colorado, in 1949 (Raimy, 1950). The conference provided a general definition and framework for clinical psychology in the US, as well as general guidelines for graduate training which have been of great importance in the subsequent development of clinical psychology.

Very briefly, the significant recommendations of the Boulder Conference were as follows. It was decided that the training programme would be a Ph.D. programme and that the clinical psychologist would be trained both as a scientist and as a practitioner. He was to be a psychologist first, and a clinician second. His training and expertise in research would constitute the unique contribution of the clinical psychologist to the mental health field. For the first time, also, a one-year internship was to become a required part of the programme.

By 1950, therefore, the situation as regards clinical psychology had changed rather markedly from what it had been in the pre-war period. Clinical psychology was recognized more clearly as a distinct speciality within psychology with specific training requirements; training for clinical psychologists had expanded greatly and was being partially supported by agencies of the federal government; there were abundant job opportunities available; and many individuals were interested in becoming clinical psychologists.

Functions And Activities

Deriving from the developments described earlier, the main professional functions of the clinical psychologist became crystallized as 'Diagnostic Testing, Psychotherapy, and Research'. Of these, diagnostic testing and research had links with traditional aspects of psychology, even though the approach to diagnostic testing was very different from what it had been in the past. Psychotherapy, however, was a relatively more recent activity and the one activity that led to conflicts with organized psychiatry — however, more about this later.

The diagnostic testing which became popular in the post-war era was influenced greatly by the work of David Rapaport and his colleagues. (Rapaport *et al.*, 1945), and differed noticeably from the earlier emphasis on psychometrics. A comprehensive battery of tests was used which included the Wechsler-Bellevue Scale, the Rorschach, and several others. Not only was the test battery lengthy and complex, but the responses of the client or patient were viewed and interpreted within a framework of psychodynamic theory. This type of diagnostic testing was perceived as a highly skilled professional activity by both clinical psychologists and psychiatrists and was the primary activity of the clinical psychologist during this period. Projective techniques, regarded as a means of securing cues to unconscious conflicts and personality processes, were highly valued techniques and basic courses on the Rorschach method were introduced in most universities with graduate clinical programmes.

In the immediate post-war period, psychologists also participated to some extent in psychotherapeutic activities. The extent of this participation varied from setting to setting depending upon local ground rules and the particular participants involved. In some settings clinical psychologists did not engage in psychotherapy and the latter was reserved for psychiatrists. In others, 'selected' cases might be assigned to the psychologists, and in some instances, certain psychologists might be allowed to engage in psychotherapy and others not. The official policy in the VA at that time was that clinical psychologists were qualified to work with less severe cases under psychiatric supervision.

However, this policy was not followed very strictly in a large number of settings.

The third primary function of the clinical psychologist, research, has tended not to be engaged in as much by clinical psychologists as the other two functions. The possible reasons for this are undoubtedly varied, and in the absence of adequate data, can only be speculated upon. It would appear that a large number of clinical psychologists were primarily interested in clinical activities and much less interested in research endeavours, spite of the importance attached to research in the scientist-practitioner model and in the training universities. Many students expressed interest in research to conform to university expectations, but once their doctoral research was completed, they were essentially not very much involved with it. In some instances, complaints were made by clinical psychologists that their training in research emphasized laboratory procedures, was divorced from clinical concerns, and was viewed mainly as a hurdle to be overcome. A number of others said that the demands of their clinical duties were such that there was no time available for any research endeavours. Whatever the reasons, it seems clear that research was engaged in correspondingly less than diagnostic and psychotherapeutic activities (Kelly, 1961; Garfield and Kurtz, 1976).

The three functions mentioned, however, remained as the more or less recognized functions of the clinical psychologist. Over the year, there did appear to a number of other functions which also were engaged in by clinical psychologists. These included consultation to agencies, teaching of various kinds, supervision of psychologists and other professionals and non-professionals, and administration. As clinical psychology grew and developed in the post-war period, changes also occurred in the amount of time devoted to the various functions and to their relative importance.

As mentioned earlier, diagnostic testing and assessment was the primary activity of clinical psychologists in the 1940s and 1950s. However, by 1960, such activities had decreased in relative importance and psychotherapy had become the dominant activity (Kelly, 1961). This trend has continued as indicated in a survey of 855 members of the Division of Clinical Psychology of the APA conducted in the mid-1970s (Garfield and Kurtz 1976). In this survey, the percentage of time devoted by this sample of clinical psychologists to individual psychotherapy, was 25.07 per cent. An additional 4.35 per cent of time was given over to group psychotherapy, and behaviour modification was listed by 2 per cent. Thus, over 31 per cent of the professional time of clinical psychologists was devoted to psychotherapeutic activities. The next two most frequent activities were teaching with 13.82 per cent and administration with 13.21 per cent. Diagnostic and assessment activities constituted the fourth most frequent activity with 9.79 per cent. Other areas which can be mentioned were: clinical supervision, 7.78 per cent; research, 7.04 per cent; community consultation, 5.23 per cent; scholarly writing, 3.77 per cent; and research supervision, 2.71 per cent.

As the foregoing indicates, there has been a decided shift in the time devoted to various professional activities by clinical psychologists over the past few decades. Psychotherapy, a field dominated to the past by psychiatrists and not a prime activity of psychologists historically, has become the major involvement of clinical psychologists. In fact, probably a very large number of individuals enter the field of clinical psychology in order to become psychotherapists. Testing, however, which has been a unique activity of psychologists, has diminished in relative importance. Accompanying the latter development has been what appears to be a gradual decrease in the emphasis on projective techniques and in the use of lengthy batteries of tests for diagnostic purposes. Thus, in a relatively short period of time, there has been an important reording of the value hierarchy of activities in clinical psychology. These changes have also been reflected in graduate training programmes which have been modified accordingly. Courses in projective testing have been reduced, and courses and practical in psychotherapy have been introduced and expanded.

Work Settings

Clinical psychologists have been employed in a variety of settings. In earlier periods of development, they were primarily involved with children in school settings, child guidance clinics, and institutions for the retarded. In more recent times, clinical psychologists have become more heavily involved in working with adults in psychiatric hospitals and out-patient clinics, in medical schools, in general hospitals, in community mental health centres, and in private practice. The institutional affiliation of the sample of clinical psychologists surveyed by Garfield and Kurtz (1976) is presented in Table 2.1. As can be noted there, approximately 35 per cent were employed in such institutional settings as psychiatric or general hospitals, out-patient clinics, or medical schools. An additional 30 per cent were employed in university settings, and just over 23 per cent were in private practice. A little over 11 per cent of the sample were employed in such settings as public schools, the federal government, juvenile correction centres, rehabilitation centres, state departments of mental health, and private corporations. It can be mentioned also that there were no significant differences between men and women in terms of institutional affiliation, and almost half of the sample indicated some part-time engagement in private practice.

Although the great demand for clinical psychologists and other mental health professionals has diminished in recent years, with the exception of academic positions, there are still a variety of job opportunities available.

Current Developments in Training

As indicated earlier, American clinical psychology adhered exclusively to the scientist-practitioner model of training until around 1970. All graduate students were trained in both research and clinical skills. However, there was a certain amount

Table 2.1

Primary institutional affiliations. Garfield and Kurtz, *American Psychologist*, 1976, 31, p. 2. Copyright (1976) by the American Psychological Association, Reprinted by permission of the author.

Primary affilitation	*N*	%
None	10	1.17
Mental hospital	72	8.42
General hospital	51	5.97
Out-patient clinic	44	5.15
Community mental health centre	64	7.48
Medical school	68	7.95
Private practice	199	23.27
University psychology department	188	21.99
University, other	60	7.02
Other	99	11.58
Total	855	100.00

of discontent expressed from time to time concerning this model by some clinicians who felt that their clinical training was inadequate, and by others who felt that their research training was also inadequate. There was an obvious conflict between scientific-research values and clinical ones that became more pronounced as the number of practising clinical psychologists increased in the post-war period. Some critics of the scientist-practitioner model claimed the model was an unrealistic one and that such conflicting or disparate goals could not be obtained. Others, however, argued that the model was a desirable one which had not been adequately implemented (Garfield, 1966).

The above mentioned concerns were reflected in the appointment of a special APA committee to evaluate professional training (Committee on the Scientific and Professional Aims of Psychology, 1965), and in discussions held at a national conference on the professional preparation of psychologists in Chicago in 1965 (Hoch et al., 1966). The report of the committee recommended consideration of alternative models such as more professionally oriented programmes leading to a Doctor of Psychology degree (Psy.D.) or to a Doctor of Psychotherapy degree. At the Chicago Conference several alternative models were introduced including the Psy.D. programme. However, the conference participants overwhelmingly reaffirmed their support for the scientist-practitioner model. Nevertheless, representatives from the University of Illinois stated their intention to seek university approval for setting up a Psy.D. programme in addition to their existing Ph.D. programme. Students would thus have a choice of models from which to choose. This actually did occur in a few years and a competing model was thus available (Peterson, 1968).

Not many universities have tended to follow the Illinois model. However, several other developments in training have occurred. Within a short time after the Psy.D. programme at Illinois was begun, a group of psychologists in the State of California, with the support of that state's psychological association, formed the California School of Professional Psychology. Unlike the Illinois programme, the school was a 'free standing' school and was not part of a department of psychology or affiliated with a university. The majority of the faculty were recruited on a part-time basis from practitioners in the community. Because of the demand on the part of prospective students for training in clinical psychology, and the fact that the approved university programmes can accept only a small percentage of those who apply, the California School has expanded rapidly to include four campuses in different parts of the state. It can be noted, too, that although the emphasis in on professional training, the degree awarded is the Ph.D.

At the present time there has been evident a decided growth

in these non-traditional programmes. Three different patterns are discernible. The initial development of a Psy.D. programme along with the Ph.D. programme in a university department of psychology has not shown much growth or development. The Psy.D. programme at Illinois is actually being terminated since it apparently began to resemble increasingly the Ph.D. programme. a second pattern, currently evident at a few institutions is the professional school of psychology which is part of a university system and which is headed by a dean. These schools generally offer a Psy.D. degree in one or more professional areas of psychology with the Ph.D. given in a separate department of psychology, although there are variations in this pattern.

The third pattern of development is the most rapidly growing and potentially the most important of these recent developments. This is the marked increase in free standing schools of professional psychology. Such schools appear to be springing up all over the US. In California, alone, there were reported to be twenty-four such schools (Perry, 1979). Besides the increase in the number of such schools, the number admitted in many instances in much larger than that admitted to the university programmes. For example, the California School, may admit 100 new students at some of its campuses each year, whereas the average university programme admits eight to twelve new students. Such a development would appear to pose some potential problems with regard to the quality of training provided and to the definition and unity of clinical psychology in the US. Such concerns have been voiced in journal articles (Ericksen, 1966; Perry, 1979; Wollersheim, 1974) and at recent professional meetings. It is worth discussing some of these concerns.

Although professional programmes and schools were advocated and developed because of supposed limitations in professional training in academic programmes (Pottharst, 1970), a major concern expressed at present about these new programmes is precisely the same — concern over the quality of these programmes. These schools depend on students' tuition for practically all of their income, and this conceivably can influence standards for admission and retrention in the programme. Part-time faculty are selected on a different basis than are full-time university faculty and are not as dependent on the programme as regular faculty since their main income is derived from their private practice or regular occupational setting.Undoubtedly, the standards among these schools vary considerably since local educational charters and accreditation procedures also vary. Since most of these schools have not sought or been granted accreditation by the APA, the actual data on the quality of the training programmes are lacking. This absence also causes concerns.

Another major concern, expressed by the writer during a debate at a recent convention of the APA (Garfield, 1980a), pertains to the impact of these professional schools on the traditional definition of clinical psychology and what this may portend for the future of clinical psychology. As already indicated, clinical psychology under the scientist-practitioner model has gorwn and expanded enormously. In the last thirty-five years, the membership of the Division of Clinical Psychology in the APA has increased sevenfold and the number of approved training universities has quadrupled. During this period clinical psychology has become recognized as a vital profession in the mental health field. All of these developments would appear to be due at least in great part to the research oriented programmes of training received by clinical psychologists in the past. The development of non-university based professional programmes lacking the research training and emphases of traditional programmes is seen as posing a distinct threat to the acknowledge definition and uniqueness of clinical psychology as it has developed over the years. The development of purely professional schools has the clear potential of splitting the areas of research and practice within the field and of creating two different types of clinical psychologists with very different value systems. The existence of rival factions with opposite views could thus lead to the setting up of separate organizations and to some confusion concerning the definition of clinical psychology.

The present status of clinical psychology training in the US is thus in a state of flux which could have significant consequences for the future development of the field. It is also a reflection of a larger conflict in American psychology between scientifically and experimentally oriented psychologists on one hand, and practitioners, largely clinical psychologists in private practice on the other (Chein, 1966; Perry, 1979). This conflict, which has become intensified in recent years, will be discussed in more detail later.

Theoretical Orientations

Although clinical psychologists have indicated interests in a variety of theoretical views, certain orientations have been more preferred than others, and this also has varied over time. During the late 1940s and into the 1960s psychoanalytic and psychodynamic theories were the most influential, and this emphasis was also manifested in university training programmes. This influential both diagnostic and therapeutic practices. Psychodynamic long-term psychotherapy was highly valued as the most important and intensive form of therapy, whereas briefer and less evocative forms of therapy were viewed as alliative and supportive. In a similar fashion, projective techniques were considered a most important part of the psychologist's diagnostic testing battery since they were a means of tapping unconscious drives and conflicts. Even the more objective tests, such as the Wechsler Scales, could be interpreted from a psychodynamic orientation (Rapaport *et al.*, 1945).

In the survey of clinical psychologists reported by Kelly in 1961, a psychoanalytric orientation was indicated by 19 per cent, a neo-Freudian by 13 per cent, and a Sullivanian by 9 per cent. Thus, 41 per cent of the sample clearly indicated a psychodynamic orientation. A preference for a learning theory orientation was expressed by approximately nine per cent, with four per cent expressing a preference for a Rogerian view. However, almost forty per cent of the sample identified themselves as eclectics.

In a more recent survey, the pattern of theoretical preferences appears to have undergone some change (Garfield and Kurtz, 1976). The total of the three psychodynamic preferences mentioned above was found to be 19 per cent in the later survey, thus indicating a noticeable decline. The preference for a learning theory orientation had increased slightly to approximately ten per cent. The preference for an electric orientation, however, has become the dominant one with almost fifty-five per cent of the sample indicating such a preference. Even some behaviour therapists are viewed, or view themselves, as electric behaviour therapists (Swan, 1979).

Thus, it appears the psychodynamic orientations among clinical psychologists have decreased over the past 15 or 20 years and that electric views appear to be the preference of slightly over half of the clinical psychologists surveyed. Although behaviour and learning theory oriented therapists are an exceedingly active and productive group of psychologists, they still are a relatively small group. However, some of their emphases and procedures undoubtedly have been utilized by other more electrically oriented psychologists.

Another more recent development which can also be mentioned in the relative popularity of cognitive emphases in psychotherapy. Although Ellis's Rational-Emotive Therapy was listed by slightly less than two per cent of the sample in the survey by Garfield and Kurtz (1976), a number of other cognitive approaches and emphases have made their appearance in the recent literature 1977; Beck, 1976; Goldfried and Goldfried, 1975; Meichenbaum, 1977). There has also been evident a tendency on the part of some behaviour therapists to combine cognitive and behavioural components of therapy (Ke and Hollon, 1979; Mahoney, 1974).

Recently, there have appeared also several books and

articles which have discussed a *rapprochement* between psychodynamic and behavioural views (Birk and Brinkley-Birk, 1974; Feather and Rhoads, 1972; Marmor, 1971; Marmor and Woods, 1980; Wachtel, 1977). Whether or not such divergent theoretical systems can be reconciled and integrated remains a debatable issue (Messer and Winokur, 1980). However, as previously noted there does appear to be a decided tendency toward espousing an electric perspective with correspondingly less reliance on more doctrinaire approaches (Garfield and Kurtz, 1976). It is perhaps no coincidence that two books with electric psychotherapy in their titles have appeared in 1980 (Garfield, 1980b; Palmer, 1980).

Although there has been evident a decided preference for an eclectic position in terms of the sample of clinical psychologists surveyed, the precise meaning or intrpretation of the electric position is not at all clear. Although the term eclectic signifies that the person holding such a view does not adhere to one specific theoretical orientation, it does not allow us to know what views or practices eclectic clinical psychologists actually utilize. A study of 154 clinical psychologists, self-designated as eclectics in a previous survey, did indeed indicate they held a wide variety of views. (Garfield and Kurtz, 1977). This was evident when they were asked to select the two theoretical orientations most characteristic of their eclectic views and the two orientations least characteristic of their views. These responses are presented in Table 2.2. In this analysis learning theory was selected most frequently as a positive orientation, followed by psychonalytic and neo-freudian orientations.

In terms of negative reactions, the rational-emotive, existentialist, and psychoanalytic views received the most negataive responses.

In the above mentioned study, it was also of interest to see what were the most frequent combinations of the two orientations indicated by the respondents. As can be seen in Table 2.3, a number of combinations were selected, even though only those selected by five or more respondents are listed. Actually thirty-

Table 2.2

Positive and negative responses to selected theoretical orientations.Garfield and Kurtz. *The Journal of Consulting and Clinical Psychology,* 1967, 45. p. 79. Copyright (1977) by the American Psychological Association. Reprinted by permission of the author

Orientation	*Positive*	*Negative*
Psychoanalytic	46	41
Neo-Freudian	43	21
Sullivanian	24	16
Rogerian	36	25
Learning theory	72	26
Existentialist	17	44
Humanistic	29	16
Rational-emotive	18	57

number of combinations were selected, even though only those selected by five or more respondents are listed. Actually thirty-
two combinations were listed by the 145 respondents. The relative popularity of learning theory and the lack of popularity for the national-emotive orientation in this sample is apparent.

The designation, eclectic, thus covers a wide variety of views and, by implication, of clinical practices. Two self-designated eclectics may actually hold somewhat opposing views. Nevertheless, the preference for an eclectic view does indicate a possible dissatisfaction with adhering solely to one theoretical orientation and with the desire to select theories and methods which seem best for particular clients. Clearly, it represents a significant view in American clinical psychology.

Table 2.3

Combinations of theoretical orientations selected by five or more respondents. Garfield and Kurtz, *The Journal of Consulting and Clinical Psychologists, 1977* 45, p. 79. Copyright (1977) by the American Psychological Association. Reprinted by permission of the author

Orientation	*n*
Psychoanalytic and learning theory	21
Neo-Freudain and learning theory	16
Neo-Freudian and Rogerian	9
Learning theory and humanistic	8
Rogerian and learning theory	8
Psychoanalytic and Rogerian	7
Sullivanian and learning theory	7
Learning theory and rational-emotive	7
Psychoanalytic and neo-Freudian	6
Rogerian and humanistic	5
Sullivanian and humanistic	5
Psychoanalytic and humanistic	5

Professional Issues and Problems

As clinical psychology in the US has grown and developed, particularly in the last thirty five years or so, a variety of professional issues and problems have been encountered. Among the most important have been relationships with organized medicine and psychiatry, setting standards for professional practice, legislative efforts for certification and licensing, and value conflicts and power struggles within the APA and within clinical psychology itself. Because of space, only some of the most important items will be discussed.

As mentioned earlier, there was an association organized in

1937 to meet the needs of applied psychologists, the American Association of Applied Psychology (AAAP). It consisted of four sections, one of which was devoted to clinical psychology. Thus, there were two organizations, one for the science of psychology, and the other for the application of psychology. However, in 1945, the AAAP agreed to become incorporated into the APA as a sign of unity within American psychology, and thus both scientific and professional interests were henceforth to be represented by the APA. The latter in turn was to include divisions which would represent the various and diverse interests of psychologists in the US. Also, because of the growth of the APA, a central office was established in Washington, DC, with a full-time executive officer.

With the continued growth in the size of the APA and with the increase in professional concerns, the role and size of the central office has increased greatly. This expansion has also led to various types of conflicts. Clearly, there were differences in values between the traditional scientific and research emphases of psychology and the newer professional concerns for adequate training in clinical skills, for legislative activities, and for the less scientific and more intuitive emphases of the clinician. Such conflicts were evident in university departments of psychology as well as within the APA and state psychological associations. As the number of clinical psychologists increased more rapidly than did the number in other scientific specialities, various concerns were raised and there were skirmishes for power evident between the two groups. There were also verbal indications on the part of some psychologists of possible secession from the national organization. A group of experimental psychologists, for example, formed their own organization, the Psychonomic Society, in 1960. This group is still active today, has its own meetings, and publishes its own journals. The issues and conflicts are still apparent today and a resolution remains for the future. However, let us now proceed to some other developments which also were of some importance.

With the increase in professional activities, there was an obvious need to establish standards and codes of professional practice. Three important activities can be noted very briefly here. A profession or a speciality within a profession can set up some types of certification to specify competency in certain areas. Thus, following the model of medical specialities, an American Board of Professional Psychology (ABPP) was organized in 1947 to examine and certify psychologists in three areas of psychology — clinical psychology, counselling psychology, and industrial psychology. More recently, school psychoology was added. Individuals with a Ph.D. and five years of experience are eligible to take the written and oral examination for the diploma in their speciality.

The ABPP diploma in clinical psychology, although a means of certifying a high level of competence in clinical psychology, was still a form of self-certification. Psychologists were also interested in legislation at the state level which would restrict the title of psychologist to those who reached at least a minimal level of training and experience. Securing state certification or licensure, however, was a more difficult goal to reach than was certification by the profession. In addition to the normal difficulties and hurdles usually encountered in getting bills enacted through the state legislatures and the governors' offices, there was strong opposition manifested by organized medical groups at the state and national levels. Most of the opposition appeared to be directed at the independent practice of psychotherapy, which the medical groups wanted to be under the control or supervision of physicians. Before discussing this problem further, however, it would be worthwhile to mention psychology's concerns and efforts with regard to ethical practice.

The APA, while insisting on the rights of its members to pursue their profession, devoted considerable thought to the issues involved in matters of independent practice. In 1953, a rather detailed code of ethics was finally published to guide professional practice and to ensure that adequate safeguards were observed in the practice of psychotherapy (American Psychological Association, 1953). For example, sections of the ethical code pertinent to these issues included the following:

> In clinical or consulting practice the psychologist must refer his client to an appropriate specialist when there is evidence of a difficulty with which the psychologist is not competent to deal (pp. 78-79).
>
> The psychologist who engages in psychotherapy is obliged to assist his client in obtaining professional help for all important aspects of his problem which fall outside the boundaries of the psychologist's competence. Most frequently this principle will require that adequate provision be made for the diagnosis and treatment of medical problems.
>
> To this end, psychologists doing psychotherapy may be expected to establish and maintain effective inter-communication with a psychologically-oriented physician. The usual and most desirable interpretation of this principle is that the clinical psychologist will establish an effective working relationship with a psychiatrist. However, the principle is worded in more general terms in recognition of the fact that a psychiatrist may not be available, or that a physician with another speciality, such as pediatrics, may be more helpful in treating the medical problems of a particular client (pp. 799-80).

Psychologists thus took their new role and responsibilities seriously and did attempt to set up appropriate standards and safeguards. However, as indicated, there was decidedly strong opposition from medical groups. For example, a joint resolution was issued in 1954 by the American Medical Association, the American Psychiatric Association, and the American Psychoanalytic Association. This statement, among other things, emphasized the role of the physician in the diagnosis and treatment of 'illness that has chiefly mental symptoms'. They also stated that, 'Psychotherapy is a form of medical treatment and does not form the basis for a separate profession'.

Because of such opposition, certification and licensure proceeded slowly. By the end of 1955, only nine states had enacted such legislation. In New York State, a licensing bill for psychologists was passed by both house of the legislature, but was vetoed by the Governor, primarily because of medical opposition. A certification act in New York finally was passed in 1956.

There is no need to retell the story of these conflicts and the struggle to secure legislative recognition for psychologists. It can simply be mentioned that by 1978, all fifty states in the US had enacted some type of legislation pertaining to psychology. Thus, approximately thirty-five years was required for legislation of this type to be secured. On the other hand, once this level of success was attained, a new problem emerged, namely, 'sunset laws'. In two states where the legislature recently reviewed existing legislation, the laws pertaining to the regulation of psychologists were rescinded. Concern has been expressed by psychologists in other states about the possibility of such legislative action in their states, but it is too early to know if such a pattern will occur elsewhere.

Although over the past thirty-five years there have been competitive skirmishes between psychology and psychiatry, and such incidents continue to occur with varying degrees of intensity, the relationship between the two professions is 'relatively' amicable. During this period of time, clinical psychology has not only grown and matured as a profession, but its stature as a significant profession in the mental health field has been increasingly recognized by governmental agencies and the public alike. Particularly in the area of mental health research clinical psychologists have played an increasingly significant role, and in the opinion of the author, this has given them a role which is not available to a purely service oriented profession.

In the preceding pages, the author has attempted to provide an overview of clinical psychology as it has developed in the

US.Because the field has developed so rapidly since the Second World War, the greatest emphasis has been devoted to this period. Attention was given to programmes of training, primary functions, theoretical orientations, work settings, and to professional problems and issues. The field of clinical psychology has experienced many changes and has faced a number of difficulties. Most of the latter have been successfully resolved, but new challenges and issues always appear to emerge. Currently, the issue concerning models of training appears to be an important one for the future of clinical psychology. How this will be resolved and in what directions clinical psychology in the US will move in the future cannot now be foretold.

3

The Health Beliefs of The Health Professionals

Health Psychology is concerned with all aspects of behaviour pertaining to health, disease, prevention and treatment. Many aspects of behaviour have been studied including uptake of medical screening, behavioural factors in the aetiology of coronary heart disease, adherence to medical regimens, distress caused by medical procedures and coping with chronic disease. This work has been applied in a variety of settings, including hospitals, health centres, schools and worksites and has resulted in improvements in health outcomes for patients. A major focus has been the beliefs that people, including patients, hold about their health, their symptoms and about their medical treatment (see for example Johnston & Marteau, 1987 in press).

The behaviour and beliefs of politicians, planners, administrators, receptionists, doctors, nurses and therapists may all influence health outcomes for the individual. However, research to date has focused on the patient, largely ignoring these other sources of variance. In this paper, the belief of health professionals, those providing clinical care directly to patients, are examined.

The relative neglect of the study of health professionals may be due to an implicit assumption that their behaviour and beliefs are based directly and invariantly on medical care, an empirically derived set of shared beliefs. We have argued that the invariance assumption is false, there being numerous published examples of diverse approaches to identical clinical situations (Marteau & Johnston, 1986b). One explanation put forward to explain these differences is that they stem from differences in medical knowledge. However many of the situations concern events for which there is no knowledge.

Beliefs can be characterised by their empirical status and by consensus (Figure 3.1). Using this categorisation, knowledge refers to those beliefs which have been verified; they may be shared (box a) or unshared (box d). Where knowledge exists, a belief can be categorised as erroneous and labelled as adherence to a myth (box b) or personal ignorance (box e), depending on whether it is shared or unshared.

The majority of clinical situations require decisions based on untested beliefs (boxes c and f), untested either because the evidence has not been collected or because they are untestable. For example, until recently, the treatment of mild hypertension with anti-hypertensive medication was based on a working hypothesis (box c) from the shared generalisation from data on the treatment of severe hypertension. Frequently, pataients present with symptoms which resemble but do not exactly fit the textbook descriptions of a disease and the clinician will then prescribe treatment based on a personal belief that the symptoms are compatible with that diagnosis (box f).

Health professionals spend much of their time dealing with data that are untested, hence decisions are taken on the basis of individual beliefs for which there is no necessary consensus. Thus psychological models that consider beliefs as well as knowledge are more applicable in explaining health professionals' behaviour than models that consider knowledge as the sole determinant of behaviour.

Elsewhere we have demonstrated that various cognitive and behavioural models can explain some of the variance in the

Figure 3.1

Categorisation of Beliefs According to Verification and Consensus

		Empirical Status of Belief		
		tested		untested
		verified	unverified	verifiable or unverifiable
CONSENSUS	shared	KNOWLEDGE based on accessible data a	ERROR —myth b	WORKING HYPOTHESIS c
	unshared	KNOWLEDGE based on new or private data d	ERROR —ignorance e	PERSONAL BELIEF f

behaviour of health professionals (Marteau & Johnston, 1987). In this paper we will review evidence concerning the extent to which the Health Belief Model (HBM), a model of health-related behaviour (Backer et al., 1979), may be applied to the behaviour of health professionals by considering whether the health beliefs of the health professionals vary in accordance with the main parameters of the HBM.

The HBM includes four main dimensions of belief: the individual's perceptions of seriousness, vulnerability, benefits of and costs or barriers to health related behaviours. It also postulates that prior to a health action there is a cue or trigger to act.

Perceived Seriousness of a Condition

Physicians dealing with the same condition (diabetes) have been shown to have quite different perceptions of the disease depending on whether they work with children or with adults (Marteau & Baum, 1984). Paediatricians viewed the condition to be significantly less serious than did general physicians.

There is further evidence of inter-professional differences in seriousness estimates from work on nurses' and physiotherapists' assessments of patients whose care they shared. The nurses rated the patients' pain to be more serious and their disabilities to be more severe than the patients did (Johnston et al., 1987 in press).

Perceived Vulnerability

Marteau & Baum (1984) also found that the paediatricians working with children with diabetes rated the likelihood of a patient with diabetes developing compliations of the disease to be lower than did the general physicians, the difference being significant for 7 out of 8 complications.

Physicians' estimates of disease mortality have been shown to have some of the characteristics of personal beliefs. Deviations from true rates were in part related to the frequency with which the physician had encountered people with that illness and in part related to journal coverage of the disease in the preceding six months: the more encounters and the more column inches devoted to an illness in the New England Journal of Medicine, the higher the mortality estimate (Christensen-Szalanski et al, 1983).

Perceived Benefits of a Health Action

Health professionals may vary in their beliefs about the likely effectiveness of treatments they administer. In a recent study of the resuscitation skills of trained nurses, we found widely differing views of the effectiveness of resuscitation: it was rated to be effective in from 2% to 90% of cases, the median being 40% (Wynne et al, 1987).

In the study of physicians' perceptions of diabetes, paediatricians were less likely to believe that reducing blood glucose levels would be beneficial in reducing diabetic complications (Marteau & Baum, 1984). Weinberger et al (1984) found similar differences in belief. Physicians who were successful in achieving glycaemic control in their patients were more likely to perceive glycaemic control to be effective in reducing the likelihood of diabetic complications than were physicians who were unsuccessful.

Perceived Barriers to a Health Action

Health professionals may perceive barriers which prevent them from carrying out appropriate health care actions. Asking the patient's permission to take blood for routine monitoring of diabetes in childhood appeared to act as a barrier to taking the blood. When the barrier was reduced, by sending an advance letter explaining that a blood sample would be required, the rate of sample collection rose from 30% to approximately 70% (Marteau & Johnston, 1986).

Cohen (1983) found that clothing might be a barrier to appropriate patient examination. Physicians looking after patients with diabetes examined the feet of 98% of patients who entered the consultation barefoot but only 52% of those who entered wearing shoes and socks.

Beliefs and Behaviours

Whether these differences in beliefs relate systematically to differences in how health professionals manage the care and treatment of patients is a further question. There are certainly indications from some of the studies in this area that beliefs are related to behaviours. For example Marteau & Baum (1984) found different beliefs about diabetes associated with different treatment goals; Wynne et al, (1987) found different beliefs about the effectiveness of resuscitation associated with different levels of success in performing the skill: Weinberger et al (1984) found different beliefs about the effectiveness of diabetic control associated with different levels of success in achieving diabetic control.

Conclusions

In neglecting the systematic study of the beliefs of the

health professionals, Health Psychology may ignore an important source of variance in patients' health outcomes. Psychological models which assume knowledge as the basis of beliefs are inadequate to accounts for the beliefs held by health professionals. Models that consider personal as well as shared beliefs, such as the HBM, illustrate some of the important dimensions of professionals' beliefs in the context of uncertainty, the context in which many health judgements are made. Given that there is some evidence that the beliefs of the health professionals are related to their behaviours which in turn are related to health outcomes for patients, the beliefs of the health professionals may prove to be an appropriate target for interventions.

4

Clinical Psychology in Europe

Continental Europe is far from a unity; it embraces many different countries all of which have their own history and culture as well as separate social, economic, and political systems. The disparities in the educational systems and in the organization of the professions involved in the health and social services of these countries contribute to the confusion. In view of this, the current status and activities of clinical psychologists practising in various continental European countries need to be related to each country's tradition in psychology and to its individual evolution of professional training.

The main focus of this chapter will be on the Scandinavian countries of Norway and Sweden. These countries have witnessed the most progressive legislative development concerning the professionalization of psychology in Europe (Fichter and Wittchen, 1980). The other countries of Scandinavia will be viewed in relation to the above and from this northern perspective other countries, both in Western Europe and in the socialist countries of eastern Europe, will be highlighted.

Scandinavia

Norway

The first psychological institute at the University of Oslo was founded in 1909. The first professor of psychiatry, Ragnar

Vogt, later got the honour to be referred to by Sigmund Freud who stated that the first mention made of psychoanalysis in a textbook of psychiatry was made in the Norwegian language. Professor Vogt's interest in psychoanalytic theories had an important impact on the development of Norwegian psychology. However, it was left to Harald Schjelderup, the first professor of psychology, to go beyond Vogt's theoretical interest into practically oriented psychoanalytic research. The first textbook of psychology to combine experimental and psychoanalytical thinking was Schjelderup's *Psykologi* published in 1927. This book is still considered relevant today. In the 1930s, Norwegian psychology received valuable inspiration from the country's refugees. Perhaps the one to have had the greatest influence was Wilhelm Reich with his character analysis. Otto Fenichel was also to be found amongst many other well known personalities who lived in Norway for a while.

In the 1920s a heated debate regarding psychoanalytic theory and practice had been conducted and it was to reach its height during Reich's stay. This debate culminated in a royal resolution that limited the right to use psychoanalytic methods for diagnosis and psychotherapy. Four psychologists were among those who got the authorization, and with this it was stated that those other than medical doctors were qualified to practise psychoanalysis (Suard, 1959). During the Second World War the University was closed (1943-45); nevertheless, plans for a new and more practically oriented discipline were developed and progress in this direction continued until the present day.

Education and training. The training of psychologists is carried out at the Psychological Institute of the University of Oslo and in the Faculty of Psychology of the University of Bergen. Both universities have similar systems but their training is slightly different. Training programmes are frequently revised to take into account the requirements of the Psychology Act.

A national professionhal council for psychology, which includes representatives from all institutions teaching psychology at university level, has worked out standard criteria for the Norwegian degree in psychology (embetseksamen). These criteria serve as common guidelines for the university programmes. The following areas must be studied by the prospective psychologist:

1. factors (biological, intrapsychic, social, and economic) which regulate feelings, contact and communication between individuals and groups and those which prevent normal growth and adjustment;
2. certain professional skills and assessment techniques and their relevant application in various forms of psychological practice;
3. the set of rules and regulations regarding professional practice and personal conduct;
4. the basis of the psychologist's work for his/her function in society.

At the University of Bergen, the student of arts with *grunfageksamen* (2-3 terms) which is a general theoretical introduction to psychology. This stage does not qualify individuals for professional practice.

The psychological *embetsstudium* has two parts, which normally talling two and half years of studied of each part is evaluated by a written report. The activity it covers further theoretical and methodological to study in the basic areas of psychology and in its most important supporting disciplines. Required Laboratory courses or some form of field work complement. The theoretical activity supporting the view that theory divorced from practice of limited value. All teachers responsible for training in the first part of the course are specialist and carry out research in their respective fields. It is therefore left to them to decide the essential knowledge and experience which is useful to the students. The second part of the course is a generally oriented practical training which prepares students for professional work. This applied part is subdivided into five terms which cover both academic teaching and clinical experience:

Term 1. Teaching is given on clinical diagnosis and other professional skills, partly in psychiatric hospitals and partly at the university psychological clinics. Teaching regarding special education is also given along with two weeks' experience in a residential setting for special education.

Term 2. In addition to those in the first term, the students are given courses in learning problems, educational-psychological diagnosis and counselling. During this term, students are given a three-week practicum in a school psychology department.

Term 3. As the course progresses the students are introduced to clients which they treat under the supervision of qualified staff. Academic teaching covers psycho-pharmacology, milieu therapy, clinical neuro-psychology, industrial and organizational psychology; practical experience involves training in a psychiatric out-patient or in-patient setting (9 weeks).

Term 4. Teaching in clinical community psychology, in research in psychotherapy, organizational psychology, and in school sociology is provided; practical experience is obtained at a neuropsychological clinic.

Term 5. There is no formal course work during this stage; the students finish a dissertation and prepare themselves for the final examination.

All psychologists thus qualified are allowed to do clinical and psychotherapeutic work. Trainees working in health institutions receive supervision of their initial work (two hours per week) during their first two years. The Norwegian Psychological Association arranges different seminars as part of postgraduate training but the clinical training takes place partly in psychiatric institutions in psychothrapeutic and psychoanalytic institutions or associations. The Norwegian Psychoanalytic Institute and the Institute of Psychotherapy receive late support for their postgraduate programmes.

The Norwegian Psychological Association accredits specialists in clinical psychology. The requirements for the specializations are five years of clinical practice in at least two different institutions, with at least two of the five years spent as a full time employee in the same institution. Furthermore, a minimum of two years must be spent and or the supervision of a specialist with compulsory attendance at several postgraduate seminars.

The professional role. As a result of the Psychology Act of 9th March 1973, professional psychology in Norway entered a new era. In accordance with the Act a degree from a Norwegian university (cand, psychol) became the basic qualification for a psychologist. The universities are now legally bound to implement the minimum standards required by the Act in their psychology training programmes. They must develop curricula and types of evaluation which enable their graduates to fulfil the role legalized by the Act. The Act also protects the use of the professional title 'psychologist', and theoretically enables restrictions to be placed on the use of various psychological methods and treatments and legislates on the limits of confidentiality.

Sweden

In Sweden the development from an almost pure academic position to an acknowledged profession occurred very rapidly. As late as 1958, a plan for the educational of psychologists was implemented. This programme was on two levels, *fil, cand* and *fil. lic.* the latter being a preparation for teaching and research. *Fil. cand,* did not qualify for independent psychological practice; it only allowed the graduate to carry out restricted psychological tasks such as assessment, which was the main psychological function at that time. Actually the *fil. lic.* was not a practical training either, and in order to develop as a clinician the *fil. cand.s* had to work independently and continue their own education in different ways, by practising and taking various courses of study.

In its 25 years of existence the Swedish Psychological Association had continually worked for better standards of education and for the legal recognition of psychologists. A new plan for the education of psychologists is currently in operation. There are still two levels of training; a basic education of three years in the university which was introduced in 1969, and two further years instituted in 1972. This training leads to *psykologexamen*. Theoretical courses are combined with practical sessions giving experience in assessment, treatment and prevention. After a further year's work in an agency decided on by the *Socialstyrelsen* (Social Department), trainees are officially recognized as *Legitimerad Psykolog*. The fully qualified psychologist is then part of medical personnel and is responsible for his/her professional work to the *Socialistyrelsen*.

Clinical tradition and development. Sweden does not have the same psychotherapeutic traditions as Norway. Its psychotherapeutic developments can be described as waves that washed over the country and changed the landscape commencing with group psychotherapy in the 1960s (Sigrell, 1980). Perhaps because of the lack of established individual psychotherapeutic traditions, group psychotherapy based on psychodynamic theory was enormously popular. A group psychotherapy association was founded and group psychotherapy training was started. The next wave was a milieu therapeutic one, and in its wake a family-therapy wave emerged, followed by approaches based on communication and systems theories. Later, other psychotherapeutic approaches made their appearance — psychodrama, *Gestalt* therapy, behaviour therapy, bioenergetics, and so on. In recent years Scandinavian associations representing the latter two movements were created.

Thus at the beginning of the 1970s psychotherapy predominated in Sweden. Still more separate associations started to organize their own training in therapy, not only in group and family therapies but also in individual therapy. Teachers were recruited from Stockholm as well as from the UK and the USA.

In some of these years, Scandinavia found itself almost overflowing with American therapists offering seminars and different therapy training programmes. This led, especially in Sweden, to a concern about family therapy and politics. The apolitical stance of American therapists, whose ideas and methods were having such a strong impact on Scandinavians, was criticized. A politically-aware family therapy was demanded (Kjellquist, 1977).

Postgraduate training in psychotherapy by the State. In 1978 a proposal for postgraduate training in psychotherapy was accepted by the Swedish State. This training is open to all professions working with psychological problems. Requirements regarding former education, professional practice, and actual capacity to do psychotherapeutic work were specified. The training is organized in two stages: *Stage One* is an independent training of professionals who wish to broaden their knowledge and skills in their own field in order to include psychotherapeutic activities. In addition, it is the basic training for those who wish to continue to *Stage Two* which provides a thorough training in psychotherapy.

Stage One training is carried out over three terms and consists of seminars (240 hours), individual and/or group supervision (60 and 120 hours respectively), and personal therapy (group 120 hours, individual 50 hours). The candidates must have had three years clinical experience and have had the opportunity to practise therapy between *Stage One* and *Stage Two* training.

Stage Two prepares the students not only to practise but also to direct therapeutic activities and act as consultants in psychosocial activities and preventive work. The training in *Stage Two* lasts six terms and includes seminars (460 hours), individual supervision (100 hours) or supervision in group (200 hours), individual personal therapy (75 hours) or personal therapy in groups (160 hours). The students must be exposed to both forms of these activities.

The aim of this programme is to provide such a calibre of knowledge that is viewed, especially in *Stage Two* as equivalent to advance theoretical university education (Sylvander, 1980). Psychologists are the only professionals whose basic university course is accepted in place of *Stage One* education. All other existing training programmes in psychotherapy which are administered by the different groups and associations (some 50 programmes are in existence) are validated against this state programme.

Denmark

Denmark has the oldest psychological institute in the Nordic countries. The psychological laboratory was founded in 1894. Professor Lehman was the first professor of psychology (1910). A special version of phenomenological psychology developed by Professor Rubin has traditionally had a strong impact on clinical theory and thinking in Denmark. Three different university examinations prepare psychologists to practise. The training for psykologisk kandidatexamen (cand.psych.) aims to provide a background for independent psychological work; its emphasis is on breadth of subject matter and its duration five and a half years.

Magisterkonferensen i psykologi is primarily a training in research methods and few students take this examination. *Pedagogisk Kandidateksamen i psykologi* (cand. paed.) aims to train teachers to solve the problem of shortage of school psychologists. It normaly takes 3½ to 4 years after qualifying as a teacher with a minimum of two years' teaching experience.

In the last years the Danish Psychological Association has established a postgraduate training programme. The programme is organized around the concept of basic groups of up to ten members. These groups aim to provide, under experienced leadership, peer supervision of clinical practice, discussion to plan clinical activities, and group directed academic tutorials. The participants in this scheme also receive at least six general courses, more formal teaching and five specialist courses (*Dansk Psykolognytt, 1980*). The training does not qualify for any recognized title or status. The Danish Psychological Association has approximately 1,500 members. One-third of the membership is employed in clinical psychology, as school psychologists, in hospitals, or in residential treatment homes. Since 1973 a new group of psychologists has emerged, namely psychologists without employment; 82 psychologists are unemployed and 193 occupy part-time posts (Bakdal, 1980).

Finland

This country did not produce special plans for the education of psychologists until 1980. Academically, psychology is placed as both a natural science and a humanistic and philosophical science. The Finish Psychological Association exercises some sort of quality control by giving approval only to members who fulfil their requirements which is *fil. kand. examen* or an equivalent academic degree (similar to a Master's) this being the highest degree in psychology. In addition a minimum of three years' professional practice must be completed with between five and six special courses approved by the Association.

From 1980 a decree regarding psychological examination came into force. In accordance with this decree psychologists are required to follow 180 weeks of study which include 10 weeks in a practical setting. All Finish universities follow the same framework for the education of psychologists and requirements are clearly specified. This new pattern of education appears less theoretical than previously but the more advanced parts of the programme still rely heavily on methods of psychological research and both practitioners and researchers are trained similarly.

Iceland

The University of Reykjavik provides only an undergraduate programme in psychology. To obtain a higher degree the students have to go abroad, usually to Denmark. In 1979, the Nordic Psychological Congress was held in Reykjavik with Iceland's 50 psychologists acting as hosts. The congresses have been held every three years since 1947.

Nordic Co-operation

The Nordic Council (*Nordisk Rad*) approved as early as 1958, a recommendation regarding the legal recognition of psychologists. The governments of the countries involved were asked to consider such recognition, and the co-ordination of the guidelines regulating psychologists in all Nordic countries with a view to establishing a common labour market. In response to the Council's recommendation both Denmark and Sweden eventually concluded that problems relating to the standardization of training had to be solved before recognition was put forward. In Finland the registration of psychologists and the protection of the title Psychologist was proposed in the *Riksdagen* (Parliament) in 1969. The proposal was rejected but it was agreed that some legal regulation of the psychological profession was needed.

In 1980 a working party, appointed in 1976, reported back to the Council on the question of a common labour market for the social and medical professions. It was agreed that Norwegian and Swedish psychologists had equivalent qualifications as well as those Danes who have obtained the *cand. psych.* The question regarding Finnish training was postponed because it was difficult to assess the implications of their new plan mentioned above (Nu. 1979).

Activities of the Clinical Psychologist in the Nordic Countries

In Sweden, as in Norway and many other countries, the pioneer clinical psychologists were found in child guidance clinics or similar settings. Hertzman-Ericson(1980) pointed out that in the 1940s the psychologist was primarily involved in testing and diagnosis, in the appraisal of the patients' degree of psychic disturbance and in the evaluation of their potential resources. The clinics were run with enthusiasm by psychologists who constituted a new group that was eager to learn and understand more about psychic disturbance. Early in this development, they were seen to introduce some form of supervision of their own group. In the 1950s alternative forms of treatments became the focus of their activities — play therapy, individual or group therapy as well as parent groups. The outstanding features of the 1960s were a great expansion of intern education and training along with the development of various methods and evaluation procedures. A shift occurred from out-patient treatment to milieu-therapy in kindergartens, in special therapeutic schools, or in treatment homes. The clinical psychologists were leading in this development. In the last decade family therapy has dominated, especially in Sweden where its many immigrants have presented new problems to be tackled.

The different psychiatric institutions were and are still partly dominated by medical thinking, with its consequent emphasis on diagnosis. The psychologist operating in that system offered a service to the medical doctors and to the psychiatrists in particular by assisting in the diagnosis of the disturbance. From the 1960s onwards this picture has gradually changed and psychologists are accepted as taking part in treatment; psychotherapy both individual and group, now constitutes an important part of the psychologist's work. Another important aspect is the training and supervision of ward personnel of the institution which appoints them. Evaluation and research, where these activities are carried out, are most often performed by psychologists and psychiatrists. Participation in administration and planning is also more common and more attractive for psychologists today than it was a few years ago.

Most of the psychologists holding clinical positions in the Nordic countries work in psychiatric institutions for children, adolescents and adults, and in multidisciplinary teams both outside and within these institutions. Increasingly more emphasis is laid on out-patient treatment. In Norway, the psychologist who has specialized in clinical psychology may head a psychiatric out-patient clinic for children and adolescents. Denmark has had a long tradition of psychologists as heads of treatment homes for children and adolescents.

In the Nordic countries all health services are free and under government control. It is possible to have private treatment but it is only in Norway that the psychologists (with a clinical speciality) are reimbursed by the national health insurance scheme when referral has been made by a medical doctor. The general political trend is to invest in preventive work and out-patient treatment, trying to keep people out of institutions. The old institutions with hundreds of patients are gradually being run down and the psychiatric health services are organized in smaller units. This trend implies a broadened perspective on psychiatric problems and demands a change in the various professional roles. The clinically trained psychologist seems very well equipped for this development. For example, in a large scale Swedish project, *Nackaprosjektet,* three psychiatric teams were established in an area of 70,000 inhabitants, outside Stockholm. This well funded project aimed to organize the complete adult psychiatric services, keeping to a minimum the need for hospitalization by developing various types of community support systems. The report of this work (Hoffman, 1978) showed that by virtue of both their theoretical and practical training the clinical psychologists adjusted easily to the different professional role required of them.

With the aforementioned development in psychiatric services, it is evident that there is no longer any definite demarcation between psychiatric services and preventive work, and psychiatry has gradually been redefined in psychological and social terms as much as in medical terms. Nevertheless, when decision-making and final responsibility are at issue, the medical perspective is still dominant in Norway, as well as in the other countries.

Clinically trained psychologists work in various institutions and services for handicapped children. In addition to the more traditional functions, they are also engaged in the integration of services for these individuals in the local community as well as being concerned with the political implication of these problems. Clinical psychologists are important contributors in family consultation centres as therapists, consultants, and as supervisors to other professional groups. Child welfare centres have a responsibility not only for the physical, but also the mental health of the children. Therefore, clinical psychologists aid the early detection of disturbances and the planning of preventive activities at different levels. Hitherto they were mostly part-time consultants, but new posts are being established. The same trend is found in general hospitals, in maternity clinics, in paediatric and many other wards. The contribution of the clinical psychologist is looked upon as a valuable one. Clinical neuropsychology is a relatively new subject, butit is expanding rapidly. Research in clinical psychology needs to be strengthened and the universities of Oslo and Bergen have established two institutes to stimulate and train in clinical psychological research.

In practice, many psychologists start their professional career, not as a supervised psychologists in a protected professional milieu, but more often as the only psychologist in a district (primarily as a school psychologist), or as the only psychologist in an institution, or in Norway, as an isolated community psychologist. This trend, together with the investment in preventive psychiatric work in the community has, esxpecially in Norway, led to a heated debate regarding the concept of clinical psychology and the demands for clinical specialization. The concept 'clinical' is a medical one. A specialization in psychological treatment is proposed to replace that in clinical psychology. In some ways this entails loosening the ties with medical tradition and hospital treatment, and establishing psychology on its own two feet as an independent discipline which offers alternative treatment outside hospital.

In conclusion, the university education offered in the Nordic countries includes both academic and professional training. Very briefly, it seems that Finland emphasizes basic research and theoretical training, while Denmark stresses practical professional work. In Sweden and Norway there seems to be a better balance between the two aspects of training.

Other Continental European Countries

When looking at the rest of continental Europe, the picture is less clear and generalizations are more difficult to make in view of the great diversities already mentioned. The Council of Europe published a report in 1978 about the role of the psychologist as a member of a medical team caring for adults, children, and adolescents (Study Report, European Public Health Committee, 1978).

A questionnaire was sent to the health authorities of the member states, but the data did not provide a clear picture. The number of psychologists actually employed in these services differed enormously. It is obvious that the statistics thus obtained must be related to the population of the countries, development of their services, training and experience of the psychologists, and whether in full or part-time employment. However, the general trend was that the demand for psychologists was higher than the number presently employed. The minimum period of formal training for registration or recognition as a psychologist ranged from 4 years in Luxembourg to 6½ to 7 years in Norway. Some countries (e.g. Cyprus, Malta) do not provide university training for psychologists and students need to go abroad, either to other European countries or to the USA and Canada. Nevertheless, most countries appear to have post-graduate programmes for clinical psychologists.

Psychologists are seen to carry out different functions depending on the position held. Assessment, different forms of therapy, counselling, consultation, education, and research are the main functions of the practising psychologists. Generally, psychologists have great autonomy within a multidisciplinary team.

The report from the Council of Europe ended with a resolution which was adopted by the Committee of Ministers in November 1978 at the 296th meeting of the Ministers' Deputies and was later approved by the member states. It was recommended that the governments concerned consider the principles mentioned in the appendix to the report (Resolution (78) 61) when adopting national legislation, regulation, and practices. The governments of the member states were also invited to inform the Secretary General of the Council of Europe, at five-yearly intervals, what action had been carried out in accordance with the resolution. This resolution and its approval should be seen at the first step towards standardizing training and the professional status of psychologists in Europe.

What was not apparent from the Council of Europe Study Report was the growth in the activities of some psychotherapeutic groups who adhere to more or less restricted theoretical systems. These groups arrange seminars within private associations and institutions that provide training programmes. Many of these 'missionary' therapists coming from the USA (in particular California seemed to have moved from country to country in Europe after shortened successes. On the other hand, some therapeutic approaches have shown more stability. The Swedish psychologist Bo Sigrell (1980) has speculated than such approaches endure, (1) when the psychotherapeutic method is theoretically well-founded (i.e. documented research exists), (2) when there is well established international organization with its own journals which public both research and discussions on training, and (3) when the host country had prominent psychotherapists who wish to encourage technical and expansion of their activities.

Then training is properly established approval is sought for official status as postgraduate specialization by the various national psychological associations; following this legal recognition is sought. As yet very few countries have achieved legal recognition; in many countries the psychological association has granted approval. For example, in Holland, psychologists wishing to work as psychotherapists must belong to their national psychological association; there the title 'psychologist' has been protected since 1971. Protection was granted in East Germany in 1967, in Portugal in 1972, and in Norway and Sweden in 1973 and 1978 respectively. Certification is being prepared in West Germany and Poland. Austria has had legislation regarding the function of psychologists since 1978 (Fichter and Wittchen, 1980).

West Germany

Almost all expertise in psychology and psychiatry disappeared in Germany with the Second World War. Few of the psychologists have returned, for the war represented a complete break, especially for the dynamic approach to psychology.

West Germany is a federation of lands which accords great autonomy both to its school system and to the health services. Psychology as a subject in its own right was not fully introduced in German universities until 1950. This education varies a great deal in content, being partly dependent on the availability of teachers. It takes five years to get a postgraduate qualification (*Diplom Psycholog*). Schools of psychotherapy have developed postgraduate programmes of training lasting three years but these give no formal qualifications. Seen through Norwegian eyes (Ekern, 1980) psychologists who have received therapeutic training in Germany appear to be well educated at the theoretical level they choose, but they do not appear so flexible and skilled in practice. The Psychological Association suffers from psychologists identifying and working for their own interest groups rather than for the Association. The situation varies so much from one part of the country to the other that it is difficult for psychologists to work in a unified manner towards future registration and approval of training programmes. It is, however, expected that new legislation regulating therapeutic activities will be put forward in a few years' time. Until then, psychologists are allowed to carry out assessment and provide counselling but it is tacitly accepted that many of them practise therapy as well.

France

In France, the university training of clinical psychologists takes five years. The specialization which is formally defined relates almost exclusively to psycho-diagnostics. The qualification required for employment as a clinical psychologist in public hospitals or related institutions is laid down in Articles 2 and 3 of a Decree December 1971 and by an Order of February 1972. The qualification of psychologist is awarded by the Secretariat of State for Universities.

The health authorities indicated to the Council of Europe that the number of psychologists on the labour market exceeds current demand. However, compared with Norway and Sweden, France actually has a smaller proportion of psychologists employed in psychiatric services per 100,000 inhabitants (2.5 and 2.6 compared to 2.3 respectively), and there is no reason to believe that the incidence of psychological problems is fewer. One explanation may be that psychologists in France are not allowed to be involved in treatment. However, it was acknowledged by many institutions that psychologists did practise psychotherapy. This is another example of the discrepancy between the official position regarding the function of psychologists and what in practice they do by obtaining qualifications through privately organized and financed post-graduate training.

Belgium

To obtain employment as a psychologist, a university degree in psychology is usually sufficient. However, as the number of psychologists seeking employment increases, additional qualification (further specialize training) is required.

The university qualification is usually a *licencie* in psychology and/or education involving four or five years of study. It is the basis for further specialization in clinical psychology without the granting of a special title. Rules governing psycho-medico-social centres and the School and Vocational Guidance Bureaux are more specific with respect to qualifications that can be reasonably required. In institutions certified by the Department of Public Health psychologists take an active part in examination (psychometric and clinical), in discussion of diagnoses with the team and in the therapeutic provisions. Moreover, teams in which psychologists play a therapeutic role are becoming increasingly numerous. It often happen that the psychologist is better trained than the doctor for certain specialized forms of therapy. The psychologist may also contribute a therapeutic role in residential institutions where a group appoach to treatment is prominent (Council of Europe, Working Paper, 1976).

Italy

Traditionally, in Italy, psychology has either been a branch of philosophy or has belonged to the institute of education when related to children. Psychologists do not have a tradition in therapeutic work and have not achieved registration or protection of their interests. University training is similar to that of France; for this reason many students go to that country to pursue their education. In 1968, legislation provided for the incorporation of psychologists in psychiatric hospitals as well as mental health centre teams.

East Germany

The German Democratic Republic was founded in 1949 and during the first half of the 1950s psychology was introduced at university level (Kossakowski, 1980). It planned to give particular weight to a solid theoretical and methodological basis for the training of students in professional work, chiefly in education, clinical work, and industry. The total period of study is five years and it is possible to specialize in clinical psychology during the last three years. This specialization is then acknowledged on the diploma. Advanced training in psychotherapy is also available to psychologists; behaviour therapy and client-centred therapy are the most important theoretical orientations of the university training programme (Fichter and Wittchen, 1980). The overall aims were to promote the development of psychology in theory and practice, to raise standards and support the development of human psychology at an international level. When the activities of the clinical psychologists practising in the GDR are examined, they reflect the development of the society in general. As Kossakowski stated, psychologists are involved with many others in the promotion of mental and physical health. In the health service system, psychologists deal with varied forms of diagnosis and carry out therapeutic work. In the last years, the preventive aspects of the psychologist's role have gained prominence when compared to psychotherapy. In addition, within the health service system and out-patients centres, clinical psychology is given a great part to play. What is less well known and different from Western European countries is the fact that clinical psychologists in East Germany along with engineering and industrial psychologists work directly in industry and the transport system. Their activities extend from participating in the construction of industrial plants and other work settings, through the creation of effective communication and management channels within the firm, analysis of problems dealying production (including those relating to strain and tiredness), and their solution up to advising the management regarding personnel selection. Psychologists are also gaining more influence in the forensic area by assessment, and involvement in the re-education and reintegration of offenders in society.

5

Health Beliefs And Health Behaviour: An Analysis

Introduction

The purpose of this paper is to explore the relationships between health beliefs and health behaviour. The behaviour in question is breast self-examination (BSE) and the framework for our analysis is the Health Belief Model of Becker and his colleagues (Becker, 1974; Becker et al. 1977). According to the most recent formulation of the model, by Janz & Becker (1984), preventive health behaviour can be predicted from three sets of beliefs: perceived susceptibility to the disorder; perceived severity of the disorder; and the perceived benefits and barriers of doing the particular behaviour. In the case of BSE, women most likely to carry out the behaviour are those who believe they are especially vulnerable to breast cancer, that breast cancer is a severe disorder, and that the benefits of the behaviour outweigh the costs. The purpose of our analysis is to test those predictions.

The study from which the data are taken (Calnan & Rutter, 1986a) was part of an extensive British investigation into BSE (UK Trial of the Early Detection of Breast Cancer Group, 1981). The data were collected prospectively over twelve months, from two cities, and the subjects were selected at random from all women aged 45-64 who were registered with general practitioners in the two locations. In the first, the "BSE city", subjects were invited to attend a BSE class, and those who accepted (278) were compared with those who declined (262). In the second city, there was no such invitation, and subjects acted as controls (594). Beliefs were measured at the beginning of the year and again at the end for all three groups of subjects, and self-reports of BSE were collected at the same time. Since the severity of breast cancer is doubted by few (Stillman, 1977) the second of Becker's dimensions was omitted and just two sets of beliefs were tapped: perceived vulnerability to breast cancer (PVC), and perceived value of BSE (BSEVAL). The measures of behaviour were Frequency and Technique.

Method

The first stage of data collection consisted of a home interview, during which questions about many health issues were asked, including the following: PVC (5-point scale); BSEVAL (5 points); frequency of self-examination (10 points, from less than yearly to daily); and techniques of self-examination (6 points), where a score of six denoted full compliance with the "ideal" techniques which were to be recommended in the class. One month after the interview, every woman in the BSE district received a postal invitation to attend a class on BSE at her local city hospital. The class was to consist of a short instructional film and a talk by a nurse, followed by a group discussion. The invitation had not been mentioned by the interviewer, and there was, of course, no provision for classes in the control city. One year after the first interview, the interviewer returned, and the same four measures were taken. The design thus allowed a comparison of three groups — attenders, non-attenders and controls — on two occasions, before the classes began and a year later.

Results

The main findings from our preliminary analyses were as follows. First, there were small but significant differences between attenders' and non-attenders' beliefs at Time 1, in that, for both PVC and BSEVAL, attenders had slightly higher scores. In part, perhaps, that is why they accepted the invitation to attend the class in the first place, and our analyses bear that out. Sixty-four per cent of attenders and 52% of non-attenders were correctly assigned to their group by a discriminant analysis using just PVC and BSEVAL at Time 1, PVC was the more important of the two.

The second finding was that there were marked changes in both beliefs and behaviour from Time 1 to Time 2. They were strongest for the attenders and they were more noticeable for behaviour than beliefs. Non-attenders and controls, however, also made significant changes, and at least part of the apparent success of the campaign, therefore, was probably due to the publicity it received and to the "cueing" effect of the initial interview. Finally, in all three groups of subjects, there were reliable positive relationships between beliefs and behaviour. The women most likely to do BSE frequently and well were those with high scores on both PVC and BSEVAL, and those most likely to do it infrequently and badly were those with low scores on both measures. "High" and "low" were defined by the median. Together, however, BSEVAL and PVC accunted for no more than 25% of the variance in any of the multiple regression analyses we conducted. BSEVAL was consistently the more powerful predictor of the two, for Frequency and Technique alike.

Those, then, were our preliminary findings, but there remains one final result, which, for the purpoose of the present paper, is the most revealing. In the literature on beliefs and behaviour in general - that is, outside health — one of the most valuable contributions of late has been the Theory of Reasoned Action of Fishbein (Fishbein & Ajzen, 1975; Ajzen & Fishbein, 1980). Behaviour, Fishbein argues, is predicted by two measures; the subject's "private" beliefs about the consequences of doing the behaviour; and her perceptions of how those who are important to her believe she should act. Recently, however, it has been suggested that a third predictor might be added to the model, namely how the subject has behaved in the past (Bentler & Speckart, 1979; Fredericks & Dassett, 1983). Since our design was prospective, we had an ideal opportunity to examine the suggestion ourselves, and we did so in a further series of multiple regression analyses.

The results are given in Table 5.1. For all three groups, it emerged, behaviour at Time 1 did predict behaviour at Time 2, and it was a much stronger predictor than either BSEVAL or PVC. The most marked effects were for the control group — where there had been relatively little change in either beliefs or behaviour from Time 1 to Time 2 — and the proportion of variance explained by the three measures was now around 50%, against 25% before behaviour at Time 1 was included. Beliefs, in other words, did predict behaviour, but behaviour predicted behaviour even better.

Discussion

Taken together, our findings lead to perhaps three main questions, and the first is whether the Health Belief Model is supported. The data confirm that beliefs do predict behaviour, for both perceived benefits/barriers and perceived susceptibility made significant contributions to the belief-behaviour equations and the relationships were generally highly reliable statistically. To that extent the model was supporfted. However, the evidence also suggests that the relationship between behaviour and the dimensions of belief which the model stresses was neither strong nor linear.

There were two pieces of evidence in particular. First, only a small proportion of the variance was explained in the analyses, a common place finding in studies using the Health Belief Model (Langlie, 1977). The figure was never more than 25%, and it was generally much lower. It was also noticeable that the greatest variance was explained in the control group, where the least behaviour change was found. Second, the strongest predictor of

Table 5.1

Beliefs at Times 1 and 2 and Behaviour at Time 1 as Predictors of Behaviour at Time 2

			CUM.MR²	*BETA*	*r*
ATTENDERS (N=278)					
FREQ 2	Step 1	$FREQ_1$	0.11	0.22**	0.34***
	Step 2	$BSEVAL_2$	0.18	0.28***	0.34***
TECH 2	Step 1	$TECH_1$	0.15	0.34***	0.38***
	Step 2	$BSEVAL_2$	0.19	0.22***	0.31***
	Step 3	PVC_2	0.20	0.16*	0.21***
NON-ATTENDERS (N=262)					
FREQ 2	Step 1	$FREQ_1$	0.30	0.36***	0.55***
	Step 2	$BSEVAL_2$	0.35	0.21***	0.40***
TECH 2	Step 1	$TECH_1$	0.35	0.49***	0.59***
	Step 2	$BSEVAL_2$	0.38	0.14***	0.35***
CONTROLS (N=594)					
FREQ 2	Step 1	$FREQ_1$	0.46	0.57***	0.68***
	Step 2	$BSEVAL_2$	0.51	0.26***	0.47***
TECH 2	Step 1	$TECH_1$	0.41	0.50***	0.64***
	Step 2	$BSEVAL_2$	0.46	0.25***	0.45***
	Step 3	PVC_2	0.46	0.12**	0.30***

Note: The subscripts 1 and 2 indicate the times at which the measures are taken.
*p<0.05 **p<0.01 ***p<0.001

all was prior behaviour. Prior behaviour plays no part, apparently, in the Health Belief Model — or, indeed, in rival models such as Fishbein's - but from now on, we suggest, it should.

The second issue to discuss is how to improve upon the Health Belief Model. The modest relationship between beliefs and behaviour suggests at least two directions for future research. First, it might be worthwhile to incorporate other belief dimensions. In addition to specific beliefs, more general beliefs might be introduced, such as the value placed on health (where health is often only one of many competing values), the way health is defined, beliefs about the extent to which the individual feels responsible for her health and in control of it, and beliefs about the value of disease prevention and health promotion.

Alternatively, it may be even more useful to focus on the dimensions of belief included in Fishbein's Theory of Reasoned Action. According to this model, as we have seen, behaviour which is under conscious control is predicted by our "private" beliefs about the consequences of performing the behaviour and our "normataive" beliefs about the behaviour, which are the perceptions we have of how people who are salient for us believe we should behave. Private beliefs about the consequences of performing the behaviour are exactly what BSEVAL measures - and it is important to note that BSEVAL was consistgently a better predictor than PVC. But, and this is the crucial point, *normative* beliefs play no part in the Health Belief Model, even though it is known that they may sometimes be more important than private beliefs (Ajzen & Fishbein, 1980). Fishbein's model, in other words, already includes the most powerful predictor from the Health Belief Model — the perceived value of the behaviour - and we still have normative beliefs to add to the equation. The Theory of Reasoned Action, we suggest, will be well worth pursuing.

A further direction for research might be to move away from beliefs and to concentrate instead on the structural factors which modify beliefs, and the circumstantial factors which enable or constrain intended or preferred courses of action. In a recent analysis, for example, marked social class differences emerged in a variety of health behaviours among middle-aged women (Calnan, 1985, Calnan & Rutter, 1986b), and the differences remained even when a range of other measures, including beliefs, had been taken into account. What matters now is to find out the *mechanisms* by which social class — and structural factors in general - have their affects. Do they *shape* beliefs from the outset, or do they merely influence the ways in which beliefs are translated into intentions and behaviour?

The third and final issue raised by our findings is the practical implications for people who plan programmes for the early detection of breast cancer — and for health education in general. The evidence from our study shows that even a single class on self-examination is valuable, particularly for improving technique, though further evidence is needed on how long the effects last and what, if anything, is needed to maintain the improvement. The results also indicate that health education might be more effective in encouraging women to practise self-examination if it focused on changing beliefs about the value of the behaviour rather than beliefs about susceptibility to breast cancer. The latter is the more important for the decision to attend the class in the first place — and it is gaining that attendance which probably matters more than anything else - but BSEVAL then takes over as the underpinning for BSE itself. The first stage in any campaign must therefore be to find out the targets salient beliefs — and then tooo persuade them to take notice of the campaign, to attend the classes which are offered, and to carry out and maintain the behaviour which is recommended. If those beliefs are not discovered, and they are not attacked, the campaign will fail.

A Study of Renal Dialysis Patients

This paper examines the relationship between several psychosocial variables and the processes and outcomes involved in the management of patients in renal failure. There is considerable recognition now that the onset of renal failure and its treatment are stressful phenomena (Kaplan de Nour, 1983; Nichols and Springford, 1984; Hardiker et al, 1986). The psychosocial aims of renal care can therefore perhaps be summarised as the attempts to help patients cope with these stresses and to maximise the quality of life for them. It is also equally important to maximise the likelihood of informed compliance with the requirements of therapy in order to achieve the first two aims.

Patients in end-stage renal failure lose the function of their own kidneys. This, if they are to survive, has to be replaced. The current available therapies are dialysis and transplantation. Some patients may undergo dialysis while awaiting a suitable matching transplant. Others may not be medically suited for transplantation and for them dialysis is the only option. There are two major types of renal dialysis. Haemodialysis (HD) necessitates the use of an "artificial kidney machine" to which the patient is physically attached in either the hospital or home setting, usually for three 4-6 hour sessions ina week. Strict dietary and fluid restrictions are necessary to control blood biochemistry between dialyses. Considerable amounts of new learning and comprehension of the processes involved are required for home based dialysis. The more recent continuous Ambulatory Peritoneal Dialysis (CAPD) presents a seemingly different physical and psychological set of experience for the patient. Fluid is drained into the peritoneum via a catheter from an attached bag which is worn under the patient's clothing. Waste products pass into the fluid which is subsequently drained into the same bag 4-6 hours later. The old bag is then disconnected and a new bag drained in. This procedure is undertaken 3-4 times daily. No external machine is required. This exchange procedure is a cognitively simpler task for the patient than is haemodialysis. Hygiene is essential to reduce the risk of peritonitis but there are less stringent dietary and fluid restrictions.

A number of psychosocial variables have been identified as relevant to coping with the above processes. The present study examined several of these in relatiion to each other and a number of clinical parameters, particularly the existence of physical or psychosocial "risk factors" among patients.

Method

A sample of 159 adult renal dialysis patients, all on treatment for at least six months, were studied using a structured self-report interview and questionnaire approach. Patients came from two renal units in England. Mean age was 50 years (range 18-73 years). Fifty-five were aged over 60 and 104 were aged under 60 years; 94 were male and 65 female; with 81 CAPD and 78 HD patients.

Measures on which data are reported in this paper were as follows:-

1. The Multi-Dimensional Health Locus of Control Scale (MHLC) devised by Wallston et al (1978).
2. A renal care quality of life semantic differential adapted from Johnson et al (1982).
3. The Life Satisfaction Self-Anchoring Ladder Scale of Cantril (1965).
4. A scale to assess perceived renal treatment stresses adapted from Conley et al (1981).

Results

Mean scores for the three dimensions of the MHLC for the current sample were compared with the composite data from Wallston and Wallston (1981) for varaied samples of healthy adults or patients. These data are presented in Table 5.1a.

From Table 5.1a it can be seen that the mean Internal score was very similar to that of the various Wallston samples. The mean Chance score for the sample was higher than all of the Wallston samples, including the "chronic patients". Most notably the Powerful Others score was considerably higher than those of each of the Wallston groups. In the absence of reported standard deviations for the Wallstons' data formal comparisons of statistical significance could not be undertaken but the above does suggest that, particularly for the Powerful Others dimension, the renal patients scored significantly differently from other clinical populations.

Table 5.1a

Comparison of MHLC mean scores with those from other populations (Wallston and Wallston, 1981)

Combined Samples	*N*	*Internal*	*Chance*	*Powerful Others*
Chronic patients	609	25.78	17.64	22.54
College students	749	26.68	16.72	17.87
Healthy adults	1287	25.55	16.21	19.16
Persons engaged in preventative health behaviours	720	27.38	15.52	18.44
Current study	159	25.43	20.47	26.88

The three MHLC dimensions were examined in relation to a number of clinical variables. Results were interestingly predominantly negative. None of the MHLC dimensions were significantly related to type of treatment (HD versus CAPD), or to length of time on treatment, to Treatment Unit in which care was provided or to presence or absence of "risk factors" such as medical risks, e.g. diabetes, cardiovascular disease, or social risks. The only significant relationship with clinical variables was that the over 60 group showed higher scores on the Powerful others dimension than patients under 60.

The inter-relationships between the various psychosocial parameters were, however, statistically and theoretically significant in several ways. These data are presented in summary in Table b.

Table 5.1b

Relationships between life satisfaction, treatment stress, renal semantic differential and MHLC dimensions (Spearman)

	Life Satiisfaction	*Renal Semantic Differential*	*Treatment Stress*	*MHLC Internal*	*MHLC Chance*	*MHLC Powerful Others*
Life Satisfaction	-	.660**	-.451**	.201*	-.072	.194*
Renal Semantic Differential	-	-	-.517**	.178*	-.105	.049
Treatment Stress			-	-.143	.119	-.078

* p<0.05

** p<0.01

From Table 5.1b it can be seen that level of Life Satisfaction correlated positively with high Internal and with high Powerful Others scores on the MHLC. Positive quality of life as assessed by the Renal SD was significantly related to high Internal scores but, surprisingly, high Treatment Stress was not significantly related to any of the MHLC dimensions. The Chance dimension was unrelated to any of these three others variables. Not surprisingly the Life Satisfaction and Renal SD correlated significantly and positively (.660). The extent of perceived Treatment Stress correlated significantly negatively with both Life Satisfaction (-.451) and the Renal SD (-.517).

The strategy adopted in the study was to use the three previously established MHLC dimensions in the above analyses. As a check on the relevance of this factor structure in the renal dialysis patient sample the three dimensions were inter-correlated and a factor analysis from the raw data of the MHLC undertaken. The Internal dimension did not correlate significantly with Chance (-.019) but showed a small significant positive correlation with Powerful Others (.209). The Chance and Powerful Others dimensions inter-correlated positively more significantly (.348). The factor analysis based on an oblique factor structure after rotation with Kaiser normalisation produced three factors accounting for a total of 70.7% of the variance. Factor 1 accounted for 31.2% with its three highest loading items all being Powerful Other items from the original scale. Factor 2 accounted for 25.1% of the variance with the three highest loading items all being Internal. Factor 3 accounted for 14.4% of the variance with highest loadings from three Chance items from the scale. Although statistically rather crude these checks suggest that the multi-dimensional nature of the MHLC is confirmed, at least in general terms, for this sample.

The mean score for the population on the Life Satisfaction Ladder scale was 6.62 (SD = 2.35), a score virtually identical to the Cantril general population USA normative data. The distribution was not completely normal and other specific satisfacation and happiness questions not reported here showed some differences from general population norms. Interestingly and importantly this result suggests that the renal dialysis patients' level of life satisfaction was not overall significantly lower than that of the general polulation. Closer examination of subgroups of the sample reported in Stout et al (1987a) suggests that male patients aged under 60 with risk factors have the lowest life satisfaction but that older dialysis patients do not intrinsically have lower life satisfaction on dialysis than younger patients.

Discussion

In summary the above data seem to confirm the factor structure of the MHLC dimension among this sample. They show that although these dimensions are not related in a simple way to the type of treatment, despite seeming differences in the degree of control perceptions under haemodialysis and CAPD, the MHLC is related in a non-random way to other psychosocial variables, of particular importance perhaps is the finding that life satisfaction is positively related not only to high Internal control but also to high Powerful Other control scores. Given the importance of adequate treatment self-care behaviours for physical survival as well as psychological well-being, the relationship between Internal control and life satisfaction is understandable. It is unclear whether the more satisfied patients had high Powerful Other scores prior to illness and treatment or whether, as is perhaps more likely, these scores reflect the dependency of patients in this situation and the fact that they value the expert support of the renal care team looking after them such that in a causal way this increases life satisfaction. The absence of a relationship between treatment stress and control dimensions is surprising and might be a function of either the measuring instruments used or the failure to identify the subtleties of treatment stress perception among patients, if such a relationship does really exist.

It seems likely that there are complex relationships in several directions of casuality between MHLC, measures of quality of life, compliance behaviours, and mood state variables, an issue also addressed in a different setting by Wright (1985). These latter two classes of data were not examined in the present study. It is also important to remember that allocation to treatment type was non-random and the absence of differences between the treatment types therefore must be interpretated with caution. Treatment decisions and physical health outcomes could both be causes and effects of locus of control characteristics of patients. Finally, from other data obtained by the team undertaking this research, it seems likely that the patients' perceptions of sexual and marital satisfaction (Stout et al, 1987) and of dependency (Simon et al, 1984) are also related in quite complex ways to the various social and medical aspects of renal care.

It is suggested, therefore, that closer examination of the locus of control dimension is warranted, both at the level of individual patient treatment decisions and in terms of group comparisons as in the present study.

6

Encounters Between Doctors and Parents

Introduction

There is an extensive literature concerned with informing parents of a child's diagnosis of severe mental or physical impairment (Ward, 1982). Several studies have viewed it as a crisis production grief followed by stages of shock and disbelief, denial, anger, adaptation and adjustment similar to the phases identified in the bereavement literature. It has been suggested that the way in which parents are told of a child's impairment may affect both the way they adjust to the situation and their early treatment of the child.

There are many ways in which the encounter can go wrong. The doctor may feel that she or he has been both sympathetic and informative and may be dismayed when, at their next meeting, parents seem to remember little of what they have been told. Parents may experience severe shock and anger, and their feelings about how the news was broken may make them suspicious of professionals in general for a long time to come. While at once level we are concerned with an encounter between individuals, at another level we need to understand the broader structural context in which the encounter takes place. In this paper we shall consider some of the factors which seem to be associated with parents feeling dissatisfied with how they were told about their child's impairment.

Methodology

The data presented here were obtained from interviews with a stratified random sample of two hundred mothers of severelly mentally handicapped children aged 0-16 in two health districts. The sample was chosen with proportional allocation for age and sex so that it was representative of the population from which it was drawn — the total population of severely mentally handicapped children in the two health districts. The main findings of the study are published elsewhere (Pahl & Quine, 1984; Quine & Pahl, 1986).

For more than one third of the children, the cause of their impairment was unknown: in some of these cases parents attributed their child's problems to a pre-natal injury to a difficult birth, to vaccine damage of an infection, but for many the lack of a clear diagnosis contributed to their distress. Thirty-three per cent of the children had Down's Syndrome. Fourteen per cent of the children had cerebral palsy. Among the other known conditions (18% of children) were primary genetic or chromosomal abnormalities, metabolic disorders, developmental defects such as spina bifida, and foetal environmental syndromes such as Foetal Rubella Syndrome. Twelve per cent of the sample had siblings who were also mentally handicapped. The children were mostly living at home with their natural mother and father and other children, although a few were fostered and a few were in community homes. The findings are based on the 190 cases where the parent had known the child from birth. Parents were asked a number of questions about the time they first learned about the child's impairment and were asked to give an account of the encounter.

Findings

In our study 29% of parents were told of the impairment at birth or within the first seven days. Thirty-three per cent were told in the first year, 15% in the second and 22% were not told until during or after the child's third year of life. Three quarters of parents were told by a hospital doctor. In some cases the doctor involved was summoned soon after the birth by the midwifery staff who had delivered the baby. In others, it was the paediatrician to whom the child had been referred once developmental delay or other problems had been noted at the clinic.

As other studies have shown, there were high levels of dissatisfaction (Cunningham, 1984). Nearly two thirds (60%) of parents were dissatisfied with the way they were first told about the child's impairment. Why should this be so? One explanation might be that satisfaction is determined by interest factors, by the psychology and personality of the mother, which might lead to a general attitude of dissatisfaction with services. However, there was no correlation between general satisfaction with services and satisfaction with learning about the handicap. Nor was there a significant association between the mother's stress rating, using the Malaise Inventory (Rutter et al, 1970) and satisfaction with learning about the handicap. However, parental satisfaction was found to be significantly related to the time at which the parents were told about the child's handicap. Forty-nine per cent of mothers who were told at the child's birth were dissatisfied compared with 67% of parents who were told during the first year, and 72.5% of parents who were told during the second year or later ($x^2 = 7.57$ df.2 $p<0.05$), so a greater proportion of parents who had the impairment confirmed early in the child's life were satisfied than were those who found out later.

Next, satisfaction with the first information regarding the handicap was broken down by the presence of an aetiological factor. In conditions where a definite cause could be identified, such as in chromosomal or metabolic disorders or recessive genes, a significantly higher proportion of mothers were satisfied ($x^2 = 4.22$ df.1 $p < 0.05$). The remaining groups are 'non-specific mental handicap' and 'cerebral palsy' for which a cause often cannot be ascribed (Kirman & Bicknell, 1975). Significantly more mothers of children in this group were dissatisfied with the way they were told (70%). It has been suggested that it is much more difficult to come to terms with mental handicap of unknown origin (Hunter, 19980). As one might expect there was an association between the nature of the diagnosis and the age of the child when the parents were first told that the child was mentally handicapped. Nowadays, Down's Syndrome is usually recognised at birth and can be confirmed by a blood test a few days latter. Children suffering from non-specific handicap are usually identified much later and parents have often been anxious about the development of their child for a considerable time. Table 6.1 shows that parents of Down's Syndrome children were more likely to be told of the impairment at birth than were parents of children in other diagnostic groups. Of the Down's Syndrome children, 63% were identified at birth or within the first seven days and 100% had been identified by one year. By contrast only 32% of the children with non-specific handicap had been identified by the end of the first year, and only 52% by the end of the second year. About half of the parents in this group had been seriously concerned about their child's development for many months before the diagnosis of severe mental handicap was made. Most noticed developmental delay. Sleeping, feeding and behavioural problems and screaming bouts were also a cause for concern. Some parents were worried when children began to have fits. Many parents in this group were critical of the *process* by which impairment was identified in their child, and by the lapse of time which occurred between their expression of anxiety and receiving a diagnosis. Parents spoke of long battles with the authorities to get recognition of their child's impairment and of frustration when their anxieties about their child's development appeared to be disregarded by the general practitioner. Thus, it seems that satisfaction may be linked both with early information and with the existence of a possible cause for the impairment. The dissatisfaction may have its roots in the waiting and worrying parents have gone through, and their heart-searching about the cause of the handicap.

Table 6.1

Date when Parents were First Told of Impairment by Diagnostic Category

	Diagnosis			
	Down's Syndrome	*Other known conditions*	*Cerebral palsy*	*Cause unknown*
	%	%	%	%
Parents were told:				
At birth	63	26	19	5
First year	37	23	52	27
Second year or later	-	51	30	68
Total	100	100	100	100
Number:	62	35	27	66
$x^2 = 85.86$; df 6. Highly significant, $p<0.001$				

Discussion

1. Early Acknowlegement of the Problem

Much of parental dissatisfaction in this study stemmed from the timing of the first identification and diagnosis of mental handicap. In the Down's Syndrome group the parents who were dissatisfied had often faced delay, denial and evasion before the diagnosis was made. Babies were taken away immediately after birth with no explanation, and put in special care nurseries. Nursing staff behaved oddly toward the mother. The mother's questions were evaded or ignored. Even though the time between the mother's suspicions being aroused and diagnosis being made was of comparatively short duration, it was sufficient to raise parental anxiety and anger.

The mothers of children identified as suffering from mental impairment of no known cause were generally told even later about the impairment. In addition, there was often a lapse of time between parents becoming seriously concerned about their child's development, and diagnosis of impairment.

It was apparent from the comments of mothers in this study that they would have preferred to have been told that something was wrong as soon as possible, even though doctors might have been uncertain of the exact nature of the impairment. Delay and uncertainty simply led to additional distress for parents, and may have had a lasting effect on the relationship between doctors and parents.

2. The Importance of a Sympathetic Approach

The findings of this study showed that there was a strong relationship between parental satisfaction with information at first identification and the parents' feelings that the person who communicated the information had a sympathetic approach. Sixty-seven per cent of the dissatisfied parents in our study mentiioned the unsympathetic manner of the doctor. Korsch et al (1968) reported some similar findings, showing that satisfaction with information at a walk-in Emergency Clinic at a Children's Hospital was positively related to three parental ratings of doctor's behaviour: being friendly rather than business-like, seeming to understand the mother's concern, rather than not understanding, and being a good rather than a poor communicator. These writers believe that if these ingredients are missing from doctor-pataient interaction, patients will be dissatisfied.

3. Sharing Information and Uncertainty

A large number of parents in our study said that they had not received enough information about their child's condition. Overall, 74% of parents said that it had been hard to get information about their child's condition, and, at another point in the interview, 74% said they wanted more information. A number of studies confirm that patients/parents do want information. Even if the illness is cancer or the patient is dying, the majority of patients want to be told. Surveys of patient satisfaction show high levels of dissatisfaction with information, which is in sharp contrast to the generally high levels of satisfaction with other aspects of health care.

Ley, in a review of theory and experiment in the field of doctor-patient communication, showed that sometimes patients are dissatisfied even when doctors have made special efforts to give them adequate information (Ley, 1977). He advanced a cognitive explanation for this: that for communication to be effective the message it contains must be understood and remembered. The significance of the failure to understand and remember is that if patients do not understand what they are told, they are likely to be dissatisfied. Ley et al (1976) were able to increase patient satisfaction with communication by increasing understanding and recall.

Intervention

As a result of this study of parental satisfaction and consideration of the literature in the field of doctor-patient communication, we have producd a model of the ingredients which we feel are important in the encounter between doctors and parents when mental handicap is suspected. This 'model procedure' is to be carried out by doctors in one health district when a child is born with a congenital impairment or when developmental delay or other factors make mental handicap a suspected diagnosis. A similar model procedure carried out in Manchester with Down's Syndrome infants has been shown to be extremely successful in improving the way in which parents are told (Cunningham et al, 1984). In particular, we hope to be able to improve levels of satisfaction in parents of children with non-specific mental handicap.

7

Genetic Counselling Service

Introduction

"Genetic Counselling is the process whereby an individual or family obtains information about a real or possible genetic problem." (Hsia and Hirschhorn, 1979).

Originally, the practice of genetic counselling reflected a predominantly content-oriented approach with the provision of medical information and genetic facts (Kessler, 1979). This approach assumed that the human decision-making process was inherently rational. However, the development of a more person-centred approach was prompted through recognition that genetic informatiion is not received in an emotionally neutral manner. It also became accepted that the psychological responses of counsellees are often necessary steps in comprehending, integrating and acting upon the content material of counselling.

In genetic counselling, susceptibility to genetic disease is provided via genetic risks given to counsellees. Interpretation of risks is highly subjective (Pearn, 1973). Risks can be perceived differently by different people and also differently by the same person on different occasions. Modifying factors such as intellegence, presentation of risks and nature of outcome play a crucial role.

Evaluation of genetic counselling services is difficult when the aims of counselling are not coherently defined. Several studies examine the level of knowledge obtained following counselling and some review options taken, but relatively few include consumer assessment as part of their evaluation, particularly in terms of the match between the service delivered and clients' expectations. Of those reporting on knowledge gained, the results paint a somewhat poor picture (Shaw, 1977).

The present study attempted to redress the balance by directly assessing counsellee perceptions in a pilot survey as a means of evaluating a genetic counselling service. Counsellees were Duchenne Muscular Dystrophy Carriers who had received a service from the Genetic Counselling Clinic. Duchenne Muscular Dystrophy (DMD) is a severe X-linked, genetically lethal condition that affects boys, usually before the age of 5. It is transmitted by a female who is apparently perfectly normal and shows no sign of the disease, i.e. a female carrier. The son of a known female carrier has a 50% chance of being affected, any daughter has a 50% chance of being a carrier. In two thirds of cases there is a family history of the disorder; the remainder are spontaneous mutations. DMD is the commonest form of Muscular Dystrophy with an incidence approaching 1 in 3000 male births. It is a severe and relentless disease with boys first noticing difficulty in walking culminating in the necessity of a wheelchair at approximately age 8 to 10. Death usually occurs between the ages of 16 and 25 and at present there is no effective treatment. Carrier status is calculated from the combination of genetic risk from family history and from an estimation of biochemical risk. In carriers there is a reported raised level of the enzyme creatine phosphokinase (CPK). However, only 70% of carriers can be defined accurately as the range of CPK activity overlaps with normals. A woman is a definite carrier if she has an affected son and a family history. A possible carrier is a woman who is related to a definite carrier. As yet there is no parental diagnosis available, so information regarding carrier status is important in genetic counselling in order to help couples make reproductive decisions. In addition, options open to couples need to be delineated. The understanding of risks to DMD is important as there is no definite test for carrier status or for the disease itself. Results presented are equivocal in terms of understanding gained (e.g. Emery et al, 1972).

Families' responses to DMD are also important if counselling follows the birth of an affected son. Many clients do not remember information given at diagnosis and would like further follow-up. Many workers now feel counselling should broaden to cover counselling and support of families with an affected child (Frith, 1983).

On the basis of a 1975 report, in which Bundey (1981) assessed the incidence of DMD in the West Midlands, a register for high risk women was set up. The aims of the register were to confirm initial diagnosis, assess genetic risks, to present risks in a comprehensible form to counsellees and to present options regarding families' decisions in accordance with clients' own wishes and goals. In order to evaluate these aims, it seemed necessary to obtain clients' own views and perceptions.

Method

Genetic Counselling for DMD

Families can be seen at the clinic or at home where they are visited by a field worker. The field worker aims to visit each family on the Register, every 2 to 3 years, and also to visit every female at risk for being a carrier soon after she has reached the age of 16 years.

Objectives

The aims of the study were to compare clients' expectations of the service with the actual service delivered. In addition, it aimed to test differences in these expectations between high and low risk carriers of DMD in order to assess the need for a selective register for high risk carriers. Satisfaction, knowledge of genetic facts, decisions made and clients' own concept of counselling were assessed using a questionnaire designed to encompass these variables. The questionnaire was utilised in a structured interview format, carried out within the clients' own homes, and was designed in liaison with the Genetics Department.

Sample

In view of one of the aims of this study both low and high risk carriers of DMD were included. Specifically, a low risk carrier was defined as having a 1 in 20 or lower risk for carrying DMD. These women were not put on to the Genetic Register. A high risk carrier was defined as 1 in 10 or worse risk for carrying DMD, women with risks in between were placed in one of the two groups depending on their family history and pedigree, e.g. a woman with a risk of 1 in 15 may be placed on the Register if there is a family history of DMD or she has a son who suffers from the disorder.

Women on the register who were of child bearing age (not over 45 years) and of independent status (i.e. 18 or above) as known to the Genetics Clinic were to be included in the sample (N=30).

Women defined as low risk who were of child-bearing age and independent status as known to the Genetic Clinic were also included in the sample (N=18).

Results

Twelve women in each group were interviewed. Each group included one woman who reported receiving no genetic counselling. Neither woman was included in the analysis. Thirty women from the Register were contacted initially by the Genetics Clinic. Of this group, 6 did not wish to take part in the study, 6 had moved from the area and 6 were not visited on geographical grounds. Eighteen low risk women were initially written to by the Genetics Clinic and of these 6 were not visited on geographical grounds.

There were only 3 statistically significant differences between the high risk and low risk carrier groups. These were as follows:

age - high risk women were on average 3 years older than low risk women;

directiveness - high risk women would prefer a less directive approach to counselling than the low risk group;

awareness of religious beliefs — the high risk women felt the counsellor was more aware of their religious beliefs than the low risk group.

For the remainder of the results, the rating given by both high and low risk carriers are pooled.

Satisfaction

Eighteen out of 22 women were satisfied with when and where counselling took place. A greater degree of satisfaction was noted if counselling took place within the client's own home. Fourteen out of 22 women, however, felt they received too little counselling.

Knowledge

Twelve out of 22 women gave incorrect risk figures for their carrier status. In addition, over half of these women gave incorrect answers for the risk of a future son being affected and the risk of a future daughter being a carrier (13/22; 17/22 respectively). Significantly, when asked how women perceived their carrier risk, no woman reported that she saw herself at low risk. Sixteen out of 22 women felt they were at high risk for carrying DMD, despite the objective data given them. When asked how well they remembered the information given to them by the counsellor, the majority rated "averagely". Only 5 felt they remembered the information very well; 17 out of 22 believed that this information was not given to them in written form.

Women were asked to rate from a number of variables those which they considered to be part of counselling. They then rated which of these variables they had actually received in the genetic counselling given to them.

What do you think counselling involves ?

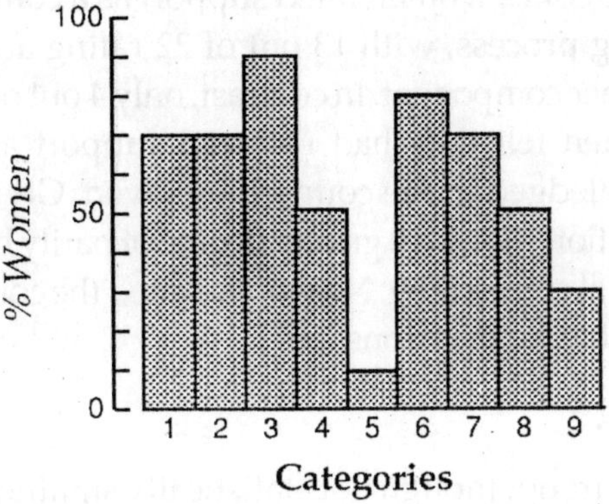

Key :

1. Giving information
2. Receiving information
3. Advice
4. Client responsible for decisions
5. Counseller responsible for decisions
6. Support
7. Accepting emotions
8. Client as part of a family
9. Client as an individual

What did you actually receive ?

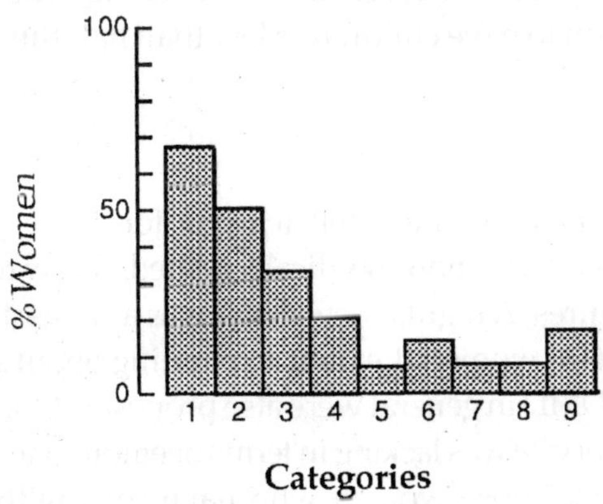

Fig. 7.1 Concept of counselling

Figure 7.1 shows the mismatch in some factors between women's own concept of counselling and counselling received. Specifically, 16 out of 22 women rated support as a component of the counselling process, with 13 out of 22 rating accepting emotions as another component. In contrast, only 4 out of 22 and 2 out of 22 women felt they had received support and had emotions acknowledged in the counselling given. Giving and receiving information showed a greater degree of parity between expected and actual counselling. No woman rated the counsellor as being responsible for decisions.

Decision Making

There was a trend, though not statistically significant, for high risk carriers to have had more pregnancies than low risk women. Whilst pregnant women tended to contact the genetics clinic, 17 out of 22 women stated that they would have a termination of pregnancy should they be carrying a male foetus, irrespective of their carrier status. Factors influencing decisions about further procreation most commonly included women's experience of DMD, their age and the number of children they had already. However, decisions regarding children were discussed in only 48% of cases and counselling would only affect the decision to have children in less than half the women interviewed.

Improvements

The majority of women felt a need for more general information plus information specifically related to new research and new procedures. A regular newsletter was a suggestion put forward by several women. Leaflets explaining about genetic risks and about DMD in general were also proposed. One or two women felt the service was lacking in terms of emotional support offered to clients. Those women who have sons with DMD proposed that the clinic should take steps to follow them up more closely. Five women felt they could make no suggestions toward improving the service as they found it completely adequate.

These women also felt they had received an adequate amount of counselling.

Discussion

The results presented suggest that several issues need to be addressed by the service offered by the Genetic Counselling Clinic. These include reviewing the actual counselling process itself and what it offers clients through acknowledging the dimensions stated by the clients themselves. Many women count support and accepting emotions as part of counselling but believed they had not received this. Knowledge about carrier status and genetic risk was poor and often confused, with women perceiving their risk differently from the objective risk figure given (see Pearn, 1973).

However, results need to be seen within the context of the assessment carried out. The assessment was a pilot assessment and needs to be validated and tested for reliability. The small sample size and large number of variables employed in this design reduce the power of the study. However, certain significant differences and trends in the data were observed. Moreover, this investigation did not aim to provide a comprehensive evaluation but sought rather to draw attention to some relevant features worthy of further exploration.

Lastly, the study made no attempt to compare the results obtained from DMD families with other groups. This was largely because of the difficulty in finding valid and appropriate controls. Comparing families with a DMD family history who had not been seen by the Genetics Clinic, although useful in terms of information assimilated, allows no comparison of satisfaction with service measures. Practically speaking, access to this group is arduous and problematic. Comparisons with other groups suffering from different genetic disorders also raise impediments as inheritance patterns, risk factors and outcome cannot easily be controlled for. If it were feasible, however, cross group discriminations would allow distinction between responses that reflect attitudes to the disease and responses that reflect attitudes to the service. How helpful clients found the service served as one way of attempting to pick up this discrepancy if it arose. Women who found the service unhelpful could be seen to be expressing an opinion that was actually related to the disease itself.

Conclusion

Despite some words of caution, several recommendations can be outlined.

Recommendations

1. A long risk register should be compiled in addition to a high risk register since many of the low risk carriers do not feel at low risk and would like further contact with the clinic.

2. When presenting risk figures, terms such as low, moderate and high might be more usefully employed as many women were unable to give accurate responses.

3. To avoid confusion, families should, where appropriate, be given the risk of having an affected son rather than given the risk of carrier status.

4. Families would like written information which could be achieved in the form of a leaflet. As it is unlikely that one leaflet would be sufficient for the needs of all the clients, a number of leaflets may be required. These could range from simple information relating to the genetic counselling service through to more sophisticated and comprehensive literature encompassing modes of inheritance, how to estimate risk and aspects of decision making in connection with the options available. Literature from the clinic should provide space in which to record an individual family's risk of DMD.

5. Content of counselling sessions should include support for decision making and acknowledgement of emotional reactions to the disorder, counselling and information. Many women would like to discuss a range of options during counselling even if they are not immediatly relevant to their life situation.

6. A newsletter would be useful to provide information about new research and new available procedures. This also allows impressions obtained from television programmes to be substantiated or disconfirmed.

7. The Genetic Counselling Service should aim to keep fuller records of each counselling session so more objective assessments can be carried out and clients' assumptions can then be tested.

8. Involvement of fathers should be included in any genetic counselling. Men should be invited to attend when the field worker makes a domiciliary visit.

8

Psychological Services for the Elderly

There is an increase in the impact of an ageing population on most developed countries. There has been a dramatic rise in the numbers of those surviving to over seventy-five years of age in the last fifty years. Current projections envisage some 20 per cent of the population in the late twentieth century being over sixty-five with an increasing build-up of the very old (over eighty). This group of clients will provide a continuing challenge for the helping professions as the emphasis changes from keeping people alive to ensuring that the quality of life is maintained into old age. Psychology has much to offer in this area.

As we explore the impact of the needs of the elderly it is interesting to note the attitudes of potential clinical psychologists to work in this area. In a survey of applicants for training in clinical psychology (Liddell and Boyle, 1980), the prospect of work with the elderly did not seem at all appealing, indeed, it was among the lowest rated areas. Obviously, there is a need for some effective communication of the potential for significant change which the involvement of modern psychology can bring.

We will explore the scope of the work of psychologists in relation to the older client and attempt to evaluate current approaches. It is relevant that the past few years have seen the emergence of interest groupings of psychologists concerned with the care of the elderly in the United Kingdom. Such a development gives an indication that the involvement of psychologists has moved from the work of a few pioneers into a more stable phase of evolution. This should greatly assist in the dissemination of knowledge of the potential of psychology for this group and in an improvement of impact and image.

Despite the inevitability of ageing and of its impact upon society there was little evidence of much systematic study of the psychological processes involved in the early part of the century. However, the economic recession of the 1930s provoked interest in problems associated with the ageing process. Many workers in middle or old age were thrown out of employment and in their subsequent retraining and adjustment it was realized that far too little was known about the underlying psychological process of ageing. The work of Miles at Stanford in the first major research unit on the psychology of ageing in this era provided a foundation for much later work. The importance of a multi-disciplinary approach was soon recognized and continues to date. A re-examination of the work of the psychologists of this period is enlightening as we today face similar problems of economic recession and technological change.

The years since 1945 have seen an upsurge of interest in the study of the ageing and aged. The Nuffield Unit at Cambridge, set up by Bartlett and associated with the books by Welford (1951, 1958) on *Skill and Age*, carried out work on the ageing process which had a significant impact and is still highly relevant. On the clinical side the work of Martin Roth and his associates at Newcastle provided from 1955 an increasing awareness of the incidence of mental disorder in old age and its psychological consequences. In the USA long-term studies at the University of Chicago under Havinghurst and the Duke University project under Buss have made a significant contribution. These projects have provided longitudinal data on both general measures and trends in ageing and on very specific processes.

In recent years research has been considerably assisted by advances in knowledge of the methodology relevant to age-related change. The work of Schaie (1965 *et seq.*) deserves particular mention in drawing attention to the necessity for appropriate methodology to avoid the many traps of inference which exist in this area.

As psychology and in particular clinical psychology has expanded from an interest in the definition of behaviour to intervention, a similar trend has been seen in relation to ageing research. The 1970s have seen a move into the application to the elderly of a wide variety of psychological treatment techniques which have been found to be as relevant to this age group as to many others. Perhaps, the fundamental change has been from an acceptance of the common myth of seemingly inevitable deterioration, towards an approach which seeks out and reinforces the positive and adaptive aspects of behaviour.

The remainder of this chapter will attempt to explore some aspects of the current situation. We will first concentrate on the contribution of the psychologist to late middle age and the retirement phase, and look then at stable old age with a final examination of some problems which are liable to occur in the aged.

Preparation For Ageing and Old Age

Despite the inevitability of ageing there has been a marked reluctance actively to prepare people for the changes which may occur in the later phases of working life, through retirement to old age. In the past ten years economic changes have consistently eroded the previously clear distinction between 'working life' and 'retirement'. A combination of economic and technological factors has produced an indistinct phase of adjustment which may occur at any point in the 40 to 60 age range. Retirement has taken on a new and broader meaning (Council of Europe, 1977).

Education of those involved in this period of adjustment is clearly essential. There are many myths and misconceptions about the older worker. A typical example is that of an excessive behavioural rigidity, a resistance to change or inability to compensate. However, the studies of the older worker carried out by a variety of psychologists over the years suggest a more positive approach. Provided that retraining is appropriate, with attention paid to factors such as subdivision of skills to basic components, initial overlearning and appropriate reinforcement, the older worker can adapt. Indeed, if one takes motivation into account the determination to succeed can be far higher than in those who are younger.

Some problems remain, particularly for the worker who finds a rapidly changing job situation as his adaptive ability lessens. On the one hand compensation may occur, for example the automatic lathe capitalizes on the skill and experience of the older worker to set it up, then performs the repetitive work itself. On the other hand change may be hard to accept in other skilled tasks such as those of the compositor in a printing works who faces a non-repetitive task with severe memory load and requiring perceptual motor-skills of a high level. However, even in this case technology is again providing new methods such as computer typesetting which can make the impact of ageing less acute.

Life satisfaction for the individual moving into retirement involves much more than the work situation. The influences of family and home environment must be taken into account. As the age of retirement reduces it is likely that it will increasingly concentrate the psychological impact of other significant life events, such as the movement of children from the nuclear family on marriage, and the death of parents into a smaller age span. This is likely to have cumulative stress effects which may require specialized counselling.

As we have previously stated, preparation for the changes in this phase to encourage positive adaptation seems crucial. The topic has been approached in a variety of ways ranging from formal 'Preparation for Retirement Courses' such as those mounted by the Glasgow Retirement Council to informal education provided by interest groups. Such help is currently available only to a very small proportion of those in need. Only rarely do individuals at this stage actively seek help from psychologists or social workers.

Such courses may include information on the medical, psychiatric, financial, and social aspects of age change and within the psychological and behavioural area cover a broad range of topics. These may include ideas of expected changes in intellect, personality, and adjustment and advice on coping with continuing demands for such diverse skills as social and sexual behaviour.

The necessity for adequate preparation for the retirement process and the broader changes associated with adjustment from middle to old age seems well proven. There is an obvious need for more specific psychological research and resource provision in this area. An attempt should be made to evaluate the relation between the provision of information and later adjustment.

Stable Old Age

Once the problems of a change in role at retirement have been overcome the ageing person can reasonably expect a period of relatively active and productive life. There are obvious consequences of the varied but inevitable changes in physical ability with increasing age. Changes in the locomotor, cardio-vascular, and respiratory systems are likely to impose increasing restrictions on activity. However, unless these occur in combination, maintenance of a level of activity conducive to reasonable adjustment is usually possible.

On the psychological side there are some interesting ideas to explore. An unfortunate and fairly general misconception is that general intellectual abilities suffer a significant and inevitable decline after the age of sixty. Psychological research in the past decade has shown that this is not a reasonable assumption. Attitudes to personality and adjustment often reflect negative images of increased and overwhelming introversion, of rigidity and 'bloody mindedness'. Again this common image is far from the reality.

The involvement of the clinical psychologist with intervention and treatment, support and guidance has actively increased with elderly groups as it has with other age groups. The techniques for handling, for example, normal adjustment problems, depression, anxiety and stress related difficulties and sexual disharmony, pioneered for use with a younger population, have been adapted for use with the elderly and found to be effective. Taken together these psychological approaches have much potential for adding to the quality of life for the elderly.

Intellectual Functioning

Clinical psychologists have had a traditional role in the assessment of intellectual functioning and the interpretation of changes in aspects of this functioning. The effects of age on intellectual performance have been a matter for discussion since the earliest collections of 'behaviour samples' into intelligence tests. Whilst much earlier consideratiion concentrated on the developments of intellect in children the widespread use of intelligence tests in the First World War produced results which, for the first time, extended these discussions throughout the life-span.

The fifty-year period from 1916 to 1965 produced many studies on whole life intellectual development of which a typical summary would be that in the earlier editions of the classic textbook by Wechsler *The Measurement and Appraisal of Adult Intelligence*. A view of intellectual development emerged which placed strong emphasis on the apparent decline in abilities from a peak in the twenty to thirty age range. The 1972 edition of Wechsler's book (Matarazzo, 1972) suggests that this decline may be of the order of one-third of peak capacity.

This view of inevitable overall decline seems to accord with the expectancies of the man-in-the-street who has strong negative views of the elderly and an expectancy of intellectual decline. This inevitable decline model continues to be presented in texts for many professions including social work, nursing, and medicine.

The past fifteen years have seen a re-examination of these hypotheses. This has been assisted by an increasing awareness of the methodological factors influencing studies of age related change. This whole topic is too extensive to cover in detail here; the reader might consult a review such as appears in *The Handbook of the Psychology of Aging* (Botwinick, 1977). The main problem is that most of the traditional conclusions on decline were derived from cross-sectional studies which confound the age variable with other influences. Groups of different ages will have had different socio-cultural backgrounds with a potential influence on their intellectual development. In the United Kingdom a useful illustrative variable is length of normal school education. This can vary with a school leaving age ranging from twelve to sixteen in today's population. Indeed our studies at Newcastle (Savage *et al.*, 1973) have shown that many of the older individuals were only intermittently in school after the age of ten.

Longitudinal studies, following the individual over a period of time are a possible alternative, although cultural changes may still prove something of a problem. These are particular difficulties when rapid changes, perhaps within a generation, affect the population studied. Longitudinal studies also raise practical problems such as continuity of finance and the danger that the tests or measures used may seem inappropriate to investigators in later years.

Various alternatiive models have been suggested which combine features of cross-sectional and longitudinal methodology. These enable inference to be made relating to age changes with a greater awareness of confounding issues, even if there is no 'perfect' experimental model. A few significant studies have emerged using either longitudinal or mixed model which greatly influenced psychologists in the attitudes to intellectual changes with advancing age.

Schaie and Strother (1968) provided early evidence in a comparison of a cross-sectional and a mixed model which suggested strongly that overall decline was not a reasonable expectancy. The Newcastle-upon-Tyne group (Savage *et al.*, 1973) using simple longitudinal data did not find substantial decline in their studies. Recently results from a methodologically sophisticated study by Siegler and Botwinick (1979) which took features such as selective attrition of subjects into account, provided further evidence of a lack of overall decline in intellect. They say 'there is a sizable proportion of old people who decline very little as old age advances or decline not at all, except perhaps in extreme old age'.

This would appear to be the current position and needs to be brought forcibly to the attention of those caring for the elderly. An expectation of decline as a matter of course in all old people is not justified by the evidence.

Two other features on interest relate to sub-groups within the aged population. The Newcastle studies suggest that there is an exceptionally well preserved group of the aged, who seem to carry into old age their intellectual quality of life. There is also a suggestion that there may be a pre-death change in intellectual ability which is identifiable. The latter will be discussed later, the former is of interest in that this group could be used as a resource to provide care for their fellows.

Personality and Adjustment

Changes in personality with age have interested psychologists and their links with adjustment and life-satisfaction have been investigated. The 1960s saw a considerable interest in this topic and investigations attempting to produce models of age related change. Unfortunately, many of the methodological problems which we have considered in relation to changes in intellectual performance relate to this area as well. Similar difficulties occur in isolating age-related changes from cultural and environmental factors.

If one can produce a caricataure of the personality and adjustment changes which our man-in-the-street expects in old age we find increased withdrawal, increased emotionality, anxiety, and other negatively evaluated features. This expectancy is likely to be general and cover all the aged.

The extensive review of personality and psychological adjustment studies of the 1960s and early 1970s carried out by Savage *et al.* (1977) suggests that the changes found tended to support the general picture above. Introversion appears to increase, anxiety and depressive behaviour likewise appear more frequently. However, the overwhelming characteristic of these studies is the variability of their findings. Compared with the intellectual behaviour there are far fewer clear-cut conclusion. It would appear that the research methodology has tended to obscure change and confuse interpretation.

Gaber (reported in Savage, 1977) evaluated a group of the aged on a variety of personality and life-satisfaction measures and produced interesting results. These were summarized in four basic groups.

Group I: Contained 54 per cent of the aged and were found to be comparable to younger groups in their personality. There were small and insignificant changes in introversion and anxiety, certainly no changes major enough seriously to affect adjustment.

Group II: Almost 20 per cent were noticeably more introverted and withdrawn.

Group III: Ten per cent of the sample were noticeably perturbed, suspicious, and emotionally unstable.

Group IV: Sixteen percent of the sample were exceptionally well adjusted and reflected very little personality change.

This study is of interest in that it clearly suggests that it would be unreasonable to expect all the aged to reflect the negative changes in personality and adjustment which seem to be expcted with advancing age. If we combine groups I and IV 70 per cent of the sample were well adjusted reflecting little personality change and reasonable life satisfaction. Again, as with some studies on intellectual change it is important to note the emergence of a noticeably well-preserved group of the aged.

The abnormal adjustment found in this study seems to separate into two distinct groups. The introverted tend to stick to themselves, retreat to their homes and internalize conflicts. They may well be a diffiicult group to identify as they will keep away from helping agencies. The perturbed, on the other hand, may well be constantly and actively seeking help, often to the stage of being over-demanding of relatives and care agencies.

Similar findings which appear in other recent studies confirm that it would be unfortunate to assume overall negative personality change with all old age. A substantial group of the aged show little prsonality change and adjust remarkably well to the demands of later life.

Psychological Intervention

The past few years have seen a rapidly expanding interest in supporting the aged in their natural environment. Clinical psychologists can play a significant role in this exercise by applying their knowledge of the psychological changes to be expected and capitalizing on their increasing skills in behavioural intervention. The economics of the situation will increasingly dictate that expensive care of a whole-time nature be avoided if at all possible.

The changes in memory which may occur with ageing place increasing demands on the individual. Particular problems may be a reduction in memory capacity at input and recall. This area is readily open to prophylactic treatment based on our rapidly improving psychological knowledge of memory processes.

A good example is the potential for using cues to assist recall. The older person may well have markedly deficient free recall for important factors supporting day-to-day life, but be dramatically assisted by even the smallest cue. An illustration would be a cue board containing something like a daily timetable, for example:

In the bedroom	--	put on slippers
Wake up time	--	put on drssing gown
	--	go to kitchen
	--	put on kettle
In the kitchen	--	set out teapot, cup, etc.
Early morning	--	put out pills
		etc. etc.

Lists of this type, which can concentrate on the deficient areas, should be easily adaptable to individual circumstances, and are remarkably effective in assisting adjustment. The possibilities are wide and once the idea has been grasped the psychologist does not need intensive involvement, the family or often the client will build on the basic concept.

A recent client was helped in her baking by a simple ingredient cue list which reminded her of basic constituents. This seemingly small change encouraged her husband and herself to apply the same technique to other problem areas they both had, and a dramatic change in their personal relationship and general life satisfaction ensued.

At a more complicated level attempts have been made to apply microprocessors and microcomputers to these problems (Lyle, 1980). They can provide an interactive cue pattern with features such as relationship of cueing to time of the day built in. Thus many activities of daily living may be cued on a sophisticated alarm clock basis.

The vast range of behavioural techniques used in the community by psychologists are equally applicable to the aged. Among these are the techniques which assist independence and reduce stress. A wide range of problems can affect the elderly below the threshold of psychiatric referral and reduce the quality of life. There can be the pressing problems of anxiety or depression related behaviour. Minor intervention can avoid this sort of problem developing into acute and disabling illness. All too often such features which would be identified and corrected in adulthood are ignored and untreated in the aged, leading to eventual maladjustment or even hospitalization.

Other areas of possible assistance include counselling and advice on family relationships and personal problems including sexual difficulties. Recent work by Stirling (1980) has suggested that many aspects of family therapy, developed in relation to children's problems, may be quite relevant to the family which incorporates an aged relative. All too often aged individuals are considered as separate units, and the overall dynamic of the family and environment ignored. A comprehensive approach can greatly assist positive adjustment.

Sexual difficulties and adjustment problems are by no means absent in the aged. Recent years have seen powerful techniques of marital and sexual therapy successfully applied to a wide range of adult problems. Only recently have active efforts been made to support the quality of marital and sexual functioning into old age. The psychological techniques are well established. Attitudinal change is more difficult, attempts to persuade doctors and care agents that sex after seventy is possible, fruitful and fulfilling, can at times verge on the hilarious.

An important factor in stable old age is the inevitable involvement with death, dying, and bereavement. This can rank alongside sex as a taboo topic in our society. Psychologists now are much more aware of the behavioural aspects of these topics and it is possible to facilitate adjustment by appropriate counselling. Bereavement counselling can greatly assist the return to positive adaptation by encouraging adaptive behaviour.

Pain is often a persistent feature of otherwise stable old age. Advances in pain control and an awareness of the psychological components is leading to increasing attempts to support those affected, particularly by chronic pain. This again is an area where techniques developed in relation to other age groups can be of obvious use to the aged.

This selection of possible areas for psychological intervention represents a few of the many possibilities. The main point to be emphasized is that it is essential to explore the possibility of using the whole range of psychological intervention and support techniques to assist the adjustment of the normal, stable aged person. In this way one can, hopefully maintain the quality of life for as long as possible. It is also necessary that these techniques are as widely publicized as possible so that the whole range of helping professions interacting with the aged are aware of their potential.

Problems in the Aged

In the earlier sections we have explored aspects of stable old age and now must pass to a consideration of some of the specific problems and abnormal changes which may occur. These incorporate both qualitative and quantitative differences from stable ageing and pose specific problems for the caring professions and clinical psychology.

Traditionally, clinical psychology first encountered the aged in relation to these problems and abnormalities. Most large hospitals have their quota of wards full of demented, depressed, or otherwise highly problematical aged. The nature of these wards has been such as to deter even the most determined psychologist. However, in the 1960s the balance of care began to change with a considerable increase in local authority and NHS provision. This structured care was based on adequate assessment of both medical and behavioural difficulties.

The range of care available now varies from support in the home, through day hospitals, to sheltered housing. The elderly mentally infirm have their separate provision and the psychiatric hospital ward is very much a last resort. At all of these levels some psychologists have been playing an increasing part in assessment and care for many years. There is still a vast untapped area of greater psychologist involvement with much potential for an increase in the quality of life.

Intellectual Deterioration

We have referred to the psychological finding that deterioration in intellectual processes is by no means a universal expectancy in the aged. However, in some individuals, deterioration does occur and has a marked influence on their lives. Deterioration may be the result of a wide range of processes, some general, some specific which affect brain function. A thorough review of this area is available in Miller's now classic book. *Abnormal Ageing: The Psychology of Senile and Presenile Dementia* (1977).

The nature and extent of intellectual change and its effect on behaviour have been extensively studied in recent times. Some of the findings are worthy of examination since they raise interesting possibilities. In an earlier part of this chapter when considering intellectual development we found that there was a small group of people with overt deterioration. The nature and extent of deterioration in this group of the aged has proved a useful area of study.

The Concept of Terminal Decline

When the aged with overt intellectual deterioration are examined (Kay *et al.*, 1977) it is evident that they have a markedly reduce life expectancy. This raises the possibility of some process related to terminal decline, an idea which first appeared in the early 1960s. Our Newcastle studies on intellectual change (Savage *et al.*, 1973) examined this suggestion by following our aged group through to death. We then used time of death as the baseline and analysed our data with assessments arranged in months before deaths.

An interesting picture emerged of marked pre-death deterioration in intellectual processes with both the experimental, long-term, aspects of intellectual functioning and the immediate adaptive behaviour aspects deteriorating. This is a significant finding. Its practical implications are wide ranging, and include possible prediction of a terminal state. These findings related closely to the experiences of care agents which suggest that the normally accessible and stable aspects of intellect such as vocabulary and long term-memory deteriorate markedly before death. It would appear that when an old person *stops* being able to reminisce is the time to get really worried about survival.

Support for these findings has come from American studies by Botwinick *et al.* (1978). They reviewed the area finding evidence supporting the concept of terminal decline and conducted a study which found that a group of some thirteen psychological tests could predict early death. Important predictors included such items as maze tracing, digit-symbol substitution and vigilance tests, as well as self-ratings of health and depression rating scales. This concept of detection of terminal decline with psychological tests remains an active research issue. Should further studies produce stable evidence of patterns of change we will be faced with interesting practical and ethical issues in the application of the findings.

Intellectual and Behavioural Assessment

The search for appropriate tests to distinguish aspects of intellectual change which are predictive has led from general intelligence measures to very specific tests derived from Experimental Psychology. Deterioration may manifest as a global problem but there is likely to be more benefit in distinguishing differential changes in long-term experiential abilities from changes in immediate adaptive abilities.

Unfortunately, the psychological tests available in the early 1970s were not at all optimal as discriminators of specific psychological processes. Such discrimination is essential for directed treatment.

The past few years have seen a renewed interest in the construction of more appropriate psychological tests for the aged. These have drawn on vastly increased knowledge in such areas as information processing and neuropsychology. The availability of microcomputers to store, present, and analyse test material is a possibility currently being actively explored in many research units. This coming together of sound psychological theory and technology of presentation is likely to have much to offer for the future.

Two important new batteries of psychological tests for the aged have emerged in the United Kingdom in the past few years. They both attempt to assist in the identification and monitoring of change and are likely to have extensive practical application. They are the Kendrick Battery for the Detection of Dementia (Gibson and Kendrick 1979) and the Clifton Assessment Procedure for the Elderly (Pattie and Gilliard, 1979).

The Kendrick Battery incorporates tests said to be those 'most sensitive to age changes: immediate recall of briefly perceived data; and speed processing and recording information'. The Clifton Procedures assess the client's current grasp of the intellectual process such as information/orientation and have further sections assessing adaptive behaviour and dependency. It is likely that specific scales such as these will have an increasing use in the future in the hands not only of psychologists but of a wide variety of care agents to assess and monitor change.

The concept of measurement of adaptive behaviour, exemplified in the Adaptive Behaviour Scales (Nihira, 1969), developed for use with the mentally handicapped has a considerable potential in the care of the elderly.

Once deterioration has occurred and dependency builds up one of the most important facets of assessment is the degree of independent functioning which remains for the individual. Assessment of remaining abilities in this area can be of crucial relevance to practical care and placement.

As yet there is no global scale which has been specifically devised for the elderly and widely accepted. However, there are many prototype scales of which an adaptation of the Crichton Geriatric Rating Scale by Woods (1979) is typical. It covers competence in these areas:

1. Orientation
2. Mobility
3. Feeding
4. Dressing
5. Continence
6. Interest in environment
7. Interest in others
8. Social behaviour
9. Restlessness
10. Co-operation
11. Sleep
12. Communication
13. Complaints

Scales of this type are essential if one is to initiate and monitor attempts at behavioural intervention. It is likely that much effort will be expended to produce more effective scales in the coming years.

A decline in the 1970s with attacks on the concept of intelligence tests which had changed little since 1930. The 1980s are seeing a new assessment concept. This is closely related to the planning and monitoring of effective intervention and is founded on the vast knowledge of behaviour possessed by contemporary psychology integrated with new assessment technology.

Aspects of Treatment

Active psychological treatment of the behavioural problems encountered in abnormal ageing has increased markedly in the past few years. Some general journal articles in the late 1970s (Miller, 1977; Woods and Britton, 1977) reflected growing interest, as did a significant and substantive review article by Patterson and Jackson (1980). This article illustrated progress in the application of behavioural techniques across a broad range of difficulties encountered by the aged and evaluated the use of a wide variety of procedures.

Intervention and treatment with the aged necessarily involves the same problems as exist with any population. For example, facile attempts to induce behaviour change in alien environments, such as day centres, are likely to face identical problems of generalization and maintenance to those evident in younger people when the client returns home. Similarly, the attributes of family, nurses, and other care staff must be taken into consideration and their ability to facilitate or destroy any programme evaluated. The efficacy of intellectual processes must be taken into account; it is unlikely that the client will be able to learn as quickly, or be quite as compliant as when younger.

Many attempts at improving the quality of life of elderly clients have been based on an assumption that care environments, sensory deficits, or ongoing dementing processes may result in some form of sensory deprivation which leads to maladjustment. The answer to these problems is seen in stimulation and activity programmes or attempts actively to promote engagement. Sensory stimulation programmes seem to produce some stabilization and may halt decline in institutionalized clients. However, it has been suggested that there are considerable difficulties in pursuing these or any types of treatment without specific psychological models which take into account the psychological context of the elderly.

The problem is illustrated by a study of Simpson *et al.* (1981) which examined the relationship between engagement and depression in a residential home for the elderly. Depression is a significant problem in the elderly in both community and residential settings. It might be expected that an absence of stimulation related to overt disengagement from the activities of the home might be closely related to depressive symptomatology. The study did not find any link between overt disengagement and depression.

A more detailed examination of their conclusions suggests that there may be much to gain from considering covert as well as overt behaviour. The authors state 'the quiet individual who is apparently staring into space . . . may report recall of happy memories . . . which . . . may have considerable functional importance'. This suggests that the techniques of cognitive therapy may be as important with the elderly as they are with younger people. Cognitive therapy stresses the integration of modification of overt behaviours with modification of underlying thoughts or cognitions. As yet there has been very little direct application of such approaches to the treatment of the aged.

A psychological treatment approach which has dramatically caught the attention of those involved with the aged in the UK is Reality Orientation (RO). The past five years have seen many hospital and residential settings using RO programmes and attempting to evaluate them. RO is based on a rationale outlined by Folsom (1968) and is essentially an active attempt to re-orientate clients to their current environment. The programme may continue throughout the whole day or may be 'classroom based' in specific sessions. The client is continually reminded of orientation today, time, and place; identity is reinforced and the environment external to the unit is emphasized (it is raining, look at the daffodils outside).

The full implementation of RO implies a massive change in ward or unit environment and uses considerable staff resources. Yet the procedures only deal with part of total adjustment, the area of orientation. Attempts to evaluate RO face the considerable difficulties which await those attempting to evaluate any behavioural treatment regime. Recent controlled studies (Woods, 1979; Hanley *et al.*, 1981) in the UK seem to suggest that RO may reduce deterioration in confused patients, but at the cost of massive resource input. It would seem that those who regard RO as the cornerstone of a treatment revolution for the confused elderly are perhaps a trifle premature. The real need is for some better theoretical rationale for intervention of this type.

In addition to specific techniques developed for the elderly a wide range of standard behaviour modification techniques have been applied to the elderly. Phobic symptoms can effect the aged and be as crippling as with younger patients. The effective techniques devised and proven with younger patients have been used with considerable success. Attempts to re-establish basic skills such as toilet training can be successful even in extreme old age and after considerable brain damage. Social skills and communication can be re-established. There is no scope in this chapter to add to these illustrations with detailed discussion and evidence. Examples have been given and the very firm point made that behavioural problems and disorders in the elderly can and must be approached with the same positive attitude, skills, and techniques as would be used with younger clients.

Overview and Prospect

Those topics which have been considered should indicate that clients covered by narrow concept of 'psychogeriatrics' are among those who can be greatly assisted by the application of the clinical psychologist of his knowledge and skills. However, there is much more to be gained from a more general application of psychological techniques and awareness to a wider range of possibilities from retirement throughout all aspects of care of the aged.

It has been shown that retirement is not the simple concept it might have been a few years ago. Economic change has producd a life event which may occur from middle age onwards and which must be positively approached to obtain optimal adjustment for the future. Stable old age is not a time of inevitable intellectual deterioration and personality disintegration with little life satisfactiion. On the contrary, most individuals can expect a fruitful period of years building on the foundation of adulthood.

Real problems do exist, mental illness can attack the aged, behavioural disorders may occur, dementia and strokes may intervene. However, as we become more aware of the psychological processes involved we are devising ever more potent treatment techniques which prolong the quality of life for as long as possible. Psychologist in the UK have been and will continue to be active in such development and as active in making others aware of the potential contribution of psychological knowledge to their own interactions with the aged.

9

Child Health

It is a moot point whether the practice of clinical psychology in child health settings should be regarded as part of the development of specialist groupings'. Indeed, as clinical psychology services develop into the 1980s, the tension between the generic nature of training in clinical psychology and the rapid development of specialist areas of application presents a major challenge to the profession. How this and other tensions to be examined in this chapter are resolved will have a major bearing on the delivery of child health services well into the twenty-first century.

It is the aim of this chapter to examine the need for clinical child psychology services within the National Health Service and to examine how these needs are currently being or might best be met. Inevitably this leads to a critical examination of the training of clinical child psychologists and their career structures. It will be argued that clinical child psychology is an integral part of clinical psychology and, because of its breadth of application, it is not just a 'specialism'. In working towards integrated psychology services for children, it must be recognized that clinical child psychologists differ in orientation and skills from educational psychologists. The existence of two parallel groups of professional psychologists each providing partial psychological services for children cannot be ignored and some of the problems of collaboration will be discussed.

Precisely how any changes will affect services remains unclear. What is relatively clear is the size of the problem facing us and that is a useful place to begin.

The Implications of the Court Report

Traditionally, child psychology services within the NHS have developed alongside child psychiatry services. As the number of psychologists increased and as their skills became more readily available to medical specialities other than psychiatry, so the range of problems presented to psychologists increased dramatically. It is probably true to say that the bulk of referrals still involve the investigation and treatment of problems, and that psychologists are still not heavily involved in preventive work and health education. Accepting this as a starting point, what sort of problems exist in a typical community and how should psychology services be organized to meet such problems?

Britain has a tradition of undertaking epidemiological studies to help answer such questions. It has long been recognized that waiting lists and other administrative measures give misleading estimates of the need for services. Epidemiological studies of total populations provide much more reliable estimates of the prevalence of different defects, diabilities, and handicaps within a community.

The Court Report (1976) on the Child Health Services summarized the results of a number of reliable surveys, and came to the following conclusions. If one considers the average health district, then it will have approximately 60,000 children under the age of 16 years living within its boundaries. There will be approximately 3,750 children in each yearly age group. Applying the prevelence rates obtained from studies such as the Newcastle-upon-Tyne survey (Miller *et al.*, 1974), the Isle of Wight surveys (Rutter *et al.*, 1970), and the National Child Development Study (Sheridan and Peckham, 1973), the following calculations were made:

The estimates suggest that about 1.125 children aged 0-4 years will be moderately or severely handicapped by either physical (somatic), motor visual, hearing and communication, or learning disorders which require special health care; 140 of them might need to attend a special school, full-time or part-time according to their age. About 4,125 children of compulsory school age will be similarly handicapped. Of these 700 might need to attend special schools.

The report emphasizes that these are only approximate numbers and that there will, of course, be considerable variations between districts. Moreover, these figures *do not* include estimates of the numbers of children with behavioural and/or emotional disorders. The report recognizes that minor difficulties are often made worse by adverse social factors, again emphasizing that these figures should only be used as rough guidelines for planning.

Even so, let us consider these figures so far; 5,250 children in the average health district will have some sort of physical handicap and about 850 will need to have some form of special education. This, then, is the level of need in those areas where, in the past, child psychologists have been less active. Of course, not all these children present simultaneously for help. Assuming that problems are identified equally throughout the years, then approximately 225 new pre-school cases will be identified in every year. However, more children with suspected handicap will be seen and this begins to mount up. It could easily mean that 10 new cases should be investigated every week — and what time does that leave for intervention and follow-up?

The Court Committee noted that the diagnosis of handicap is not an exclusively medical responsibility, it may require the help of psychological, educational, social work and nursing personnel. The assessment of handicap is a prescription for action — which may be medical, educational or social.

Even so, they recommended that '... the primary health care

team should provide the main health service contribution in quantitative terms to the diagnosis, assessment and treatment of handicapped children' , and psychologists are not often members of the primary health care team.

The committee recommended that a District Handicap Team be established in each health district and they viewed the setting up of such teams as 'central to our proposals for the comprehensive care of handicapped children'. Such teams would have both clinical and operational functions. The clinical functions would include the investigation of complex disorders, the provision of advice and support to parents and other professionals within the district, and to liaise with schools. The operational function were to include the surveying of district needs and the monitoring of services as well as the education of professionals.

The basic staff of this team should comprise a consultant community paediatrician, a nursing officer for handicapped children, a specialist social worker, a principal psychologist and a teacher, together with supporting administrative staff.

The committee deliberately called for a 'Principal Psychologist' to be a core team member as they wanted to emphasize the importance they show in having a senior and experienced psychologist to provide psychological input. Equally deliberately they did not specify whether that psychologist should be clinical or educational as they felt that they should not get drawn into the disputes between the two professions. The point to note here is that the Court Committee clearly recognized the value of a high level of psychological services for physically handicapped children. What have they to say about psychological services for children with behavioural and emotional problems?

The committee recognized that in discussing psychiatric disorders, they were not dealing with 'illnesses' or 'diseases', but rather with quantitative differences from normality. Emotional disorders and disorder of conduct form the bulk of the problems requiring investigation and treatment, with disorders of development, such as speech delay, enuresis, and learning disorders forming a noticeable proportion of the work load. Epidemiological studies such as those on the Isle of Wight and in Inner London (Rutter *et al.*, 1970; Rutter *et al.*, 1975) indicate that in any one year some 5 to 10 per cent of children have disorders which handicap them in daily life. This level of disorder is considerably greater than can be dealt with by services presently available and organized along traditional child guidance clinic lines.

A partial solution to improving services was seen as an increase in the numbers and an improvement in the training of a variety of professionals, including psychologists.

Psychologists are particularly needed when emotional or behavioural problems are associated with educational difficulties or developmental delay and when disorders are most likely to benefit from the special treatment techniques developed by psychologists.

One of the reasons for the emphasis on educational difficulties and developmental delay is that children with such problems are known to have a considerably increased risk of also having a behavioural or emotional disorder (Rutter *et al.*, 1970). It is important to bear this overlap in mind. Children are no respectors of inter-professional disputes and in planning services to meet the needs of children, then skills in assessing behaviour and emotion are as essential as are skills in assessing cognition and attainment.

The Court Committee urged that there should be further moves towards integrated child psychology services, but rightly, did not see it as their function to suggest how this could be achieved. They commented on the training of child psychologists, and this will be returned to later in this chapter. They gave the following advice on the role and location of child psychologists:

Although their role in inter-disciplinary clinic teams will

remain crucial, psychologists also have much to offer in helping children and advising other professional (such as teachers) outside the clinic setting; we believe that this aspect of their work should be increased. More psychologists should be involved in the assessment and treatment of young children as well as those of school age. It is also necessary that there be a closer liaison between psychological (and indeed all other) services for children and those for school leavers and young adults. The services for older adolescents are particularly weak and need strengthening.

It seems to me that the Court Committee's views on the future of the child Health Services and of the role of child psychology within these services are valuable in guiding any discussion on child psychology services. Not only does the Court Report indicate the extent and the nature of need for services within any community but it also indicates an awareness of some of the problems facing psychology -- the divison of services between clinical and educational psychologists, the imperfections in training of both groups, the overall lack of trained child psychologists, the need to continue working within multidisciplinary teams while extending independent contributions to other areas. Before examining these problems in turn, what else has DHSS had to say regarding the development and organization of psychology services for children? To discover that, we need to turn to the Trethowan Report on *The Role of Psychologists in the Health Services* (1977).

Implications of The Trethowan Report

The Trethowan Committee was established in 1972 'To consider the role of psychologists in the health services'. Their report was drafted by 1974, at a time when the NHS was newly reorganized into 218 Health Districts and there were only 585 whole-time equivalent psychologists. This clearly affected the view the committee took on possible patterns of organization of psychological services.

For the majority of the health services with which psychology is associated the focus will be in the District and there would be obvious advantage if psychology could fit into this general pattern ... for the foreseeable future it is on an Area basis that psychology services will need to be organised.

The Trethowan Committee saw that the first priority of any Area department of clinical psychology should be to continue the development of services in the traditional fields of mental illness and mental handicap. Thereafter, in response to representation from many quarters, ther shall be expansion into physical handicap, child and adolescent health problems, neurology and neuro-surgery, general medicine, geriatris, community medicine, and general practice. In order to develop these services, it was rcommended that each Area department woul have a number of Principal Psychologists each with rsponsibility for the development of psychological services in particular areas. Obviously, this was a long term aim, but senior grade psychologists should be appointed as soon as possible. One possible way of subdividing services was seen as:

1. Physical handicap
2. Mental handicap
3. Child health
4. Neurological science
5. Mental illness
6. Geriatrics
7. Adolescent services
8. Primary health care

It can be inferred from the description given of each of these eight areas that clinical child psychology would be exclusively involved in two of them (child health and adolescent services), make a major contribution to two others (physical handicap and mental handicap), and some contribution to yet two other areas (neurological science and primary health care). In round terms, clinical child psychology could be seen as contributing to about 50 per cent of the work of psychologists in the health services. Hence one reason for being wary of regarding child psychology as a 'specialism'.

Services for children were singled out for special comment by the Trethowan Committee. They recognized that 'the need for psychological help among children and their families far exceeds what could be provided from the resources of the National Health Service'. Teacahers, social workers and others need access to psychologists for advice and this has usually come previously from educational psychologists. They saw that, following the Summerfield Report (1968) there would be an increase in the number of educational psychologists who would be more readily accessible to schools and to working with pre-school children. They did not think a convincing case has been made out to bring the two professional groups together and establish a new discipline of child psychology. Instead, they exhorted the two groups to collaborate more closely. Thus, an opportunity was lost for examining in greater detail how such collaboation should be encouraged so as to develop better integrated psychological services for children.

Nevertheless, the Trethowan Report makes the role of psychology services for children central to its overall plan for the organization of psychology services within the NHS. By encouraging the development of co-operation with paediatricians in general hospitals and general practitioners at primary care level, the report recognized many of the initiatives made in these areas. Thus, the stage has been set for clinical child psychologists to work with children and their families in a variety of NHS settings in order to meet a wide range of needs. Before returning to a consideration of how clinical child psychology services might be organized, let us now examine what clinical child psychologists can and might do in the modern NHS.

Some Psychological Contributions to Child Health

Throughout childhood, there are many points at which good psychological advice can be helpful in alleviating distress and preventing further difficulties. It is no part of my thesis to suggest that all such advice needs to be given directly by qualified psychologists, but it is desirable both that other health service personnel can turn to psychologists for the advice and that the psychologists are properly trained to give it. Thus, a fully developed District Psychological Service should eventually be able to help with all the problems listed below. No one is suggesting that all probationers should receive experience in all areas.

The earliest point of intervention is during pregnancy. Some women can be identified as being at high risk of having a handicapped child. Increasingly sophisticated obsteric techniques involving ultra-sound scanning, amnio-centesis, and various blood tests all contribute to screening for handicaps such as Down's syndrome, spina bifida, or anencephaly. Where a disability is detected, the mother can be offered a therapeutic termination. The danger is that mothers may not be sufficiently psychologically prepared to deal with all the conflicts around these issues. The availability of psychological advice should greatly enhance the quality of the service being offered. Wherever a couple have had a handicapped child, there is a need for genetic counselling and advice on appropriate contraception. Psychological input to such clinics is needed.

Parents appear to benefit from good preparation for labour and delivery. Hospitals have run ante-natal classes for years, as has the National Childbirth Trust. In addition to educating prospective parents on what happens during labour, most classes teach some form of relaxation as an aid to delivery. There is evidence to support the view that good preparation during pregnancy is associated with easier deliveries, the use of fewer drugs in labour and with fewer complications (Doering and

Entwisle, 1975; Hennenborn and Cogan, 1975; McNeil and Kaij, 1977). More particularly, there are suggestions that systematic desensitization may be even more effective than general psycho-prophylaxis methods in shortening labour and lowering the intensity of pain (Kondas and Scentricka, 1972). Since the usual alternataive is to use pain-killing drugs which both cloud the mother's consciousness and affect the newborn's level of alertness, it is clearly desirable that psychologists get more involved in this important area.

From a variety of sources, professionals have recently shown more interest in preparing couples for parenthood as a means of preventing later difficulties brought about by faulty child management. Hawkins (1972) has argued that all parents should receive systematic training in child management along behavioural lines. Pugh (1980) summarizes a wider variety of initiations already under way in Britain. Even if only broad goals can be agreed at present, there is still a major problem in determining at what stage in the life cycle such preparation should be given. Of course it should not be a once-and-for-all event, and undoubtedly it would help if all school-children (not just early leavers) were given broader introduction to family life and child care. But teaching parenting skills at a point in time remote from their application may not be effective (Yule, 1980). Introduction to more than feeding and nappy-changing at ante-natal classes would be helpful, and more use of informal groups at child welfare clinics would allow advice to be made available at the point problems were being first manifested. Psychologists now have considerable experience in using behavioural techniques, in particular in training parents to manage a wide variety of children's behaviour problems. Whilst the origins of much of this work is in America, recent studies in Britain show the value of such approaches here (Herbert, 1981; Herbert and Iwaniec, 1981; McAuley and McAuley, 1977; Yuke, 1975; Sibisi and Yule, 1982). Closer links between psychologists on the one hand and general practitioners, health visitors, and social workers on the other would ensure that advice on parenting becomes more readily available.

To return to the birth, should the baby be recognized as handicapped there is a need for someone to break the news to both parents as soon as possible. This must not be done hurriedly or on a one-off basis. Parents need to be given information about the nature and extent of their child's disability and must be given time to assimilate it. Personnel in the District Handicap Team have a role in educating other professionals in how best to ensure that parents really get the help and support they need at this time.

As envisaged by the Court Committee, the District Handicap Team could also have the responsibility for ensuring that appropriate intervention was arranged as early as practicable. In this context, at least for severely developmentally delayed children, the detailed materials developed in the Portage Project (Shearer and Shearer, 1972) have proven to be extremely valuable (Revill and Blunden, 1979; Clements *et al.*, 1979). The availability of such materials has proven a great boon, but, as psychologists, we must be careful that the needs of individuals are not overlooked simply because such materials are so readily accessible.

The more psychologists are involved in paediatric assessment clinics, general practice, and well baby clinics, the more they will encounter a wide variety of developmental problems which may not be seen so frequently in child guidance clinics or departments of child psychiatry. Particularly in the early pre-school years, young children present their parents with a bewildering array of difficulties in sleeping, eating, and elimination. Delays in speech and language are more likely to be brought to the notice of family doctors, or at least they are currently more likely to be referred on for specialist help. By their very nature, such developmental difficulties disappear over time, but they can cause untold mislery in the interim. Hopefully, psychologists will get much more involved in the investigation and treatment of such problems and it will not be too long until the advice 'Just ignore it, it'll go away' or 'He'll grow out of it' will be seen in its proper perspective.

Many children have special educational needs. As noted earlier, the Court Committee recognized that very young children with severe handicaps will be identified by healtah service personnel and it is important that representatives of the Local Education Authority are involved at an early stage in planning to meet the children's educational needs. Hence the reason for having a teacher as a full member of the District Handicap Team and for involving psychologists. The younger the child at the time his handicap is identified, the broader the sense in which 'education' has to be interpreted. The need to work along with parents and to provide them with support and advice has already been noted.

With regard to education in schools, the Warnock Report (1978) had a great deal to say about meeting children's special educational needs both in ordinary and in special schools. The main thrust of the Warnock Report was to argue that the existing system of categorizing child handicap was insufficiently flexible to meet their special needs. In response to this, the Education Act (1981) will greatly alter the way in which children's special educational needs are assessed and the role of psychologists in this process. At the time of writing, it has not been announced just what this will entail, but hopefully any legislation will give full recognition to the part which clinical psychologists can play.

Since Circular 2/75 was issued by the Department of Education and Science, educational psychologists have played a greater role in ascertaining children's educational needs. In many parts of England and Wales, it has become customary for whichever psychologist is first involved with the child to complete Form SE3, the psychologist's report on the child. This saves time and unnecessary duplication. Normally, it is rightly an educational psychologist or other responsible officer of the Local Education Authority who completes Form SE4, the summary of recommendation to the Education Officer, Hopefully, even though the forms and procedures will alter, this same spirit of co-operation will continue whatever directives emerge from the Department of Education and Science. Obviously a good deal will depend on good relations at local levels, but clear leads can be given by government departments.

Many children have to go into hospitals, often for painful procedures. Repeated hospital admissions are associated with behaviour problems and learning difficulties later on (Douglas, 1975), but the admissions are probably an index of a variety of social disadvantages rather than being directly casually related to the later sequelae (Quinton and Rutter, 19976). In general, adverse effects of separation can probably be reduced by prior experiences of separation from parents under planned and pleasant circumstances. In particular, adverse effects of hospitalization can be mitigated by the proper preparation of both children and adults for planned admissions. Psychologists have already contributed greatly to novel ways of preparing children for hospitalization (Melamed, 1977). Once in hospital, there are many ways in which hospital routines can be set up to accommodate the needs of children (Lansdown, 1980).

In hospital, most children will be under the care of a paediatrician. As Lansdown (1980) shows, many of the conditions which bring children into hospital have associated psychological aspects which psychologists can best deal with. Psychologists can help with diagnosis and investigations as well as continue basic research into the nature of childhood disorders. However, psychologists are probably best able to help nursing staff over the general managment of difficult behaviour, irrespective of the particular medical problem. Whether it be in devising a treatment programme to help a child needing transfusion to overcome his needle-phobia or advising a ward sister on the management of separation anxiety, psychologists have a great deal to offer.

And of course psychologists continue to offer advice to parents when their children are in hospital. Where the child is suffering a life-threatening complaint, work with parents is even more essential. How much should be a child be told? How best should parents be supported? Is there a place for group support? The more psychologists get involved in wards, the more such psychologically important questions are raised. The whole area of death and bereavement and the sorts of services required to deal with the problems presented is at long last being considered seriously.

Children also leave home when for one reason or another, their parents cannot adequately care for them. Usually, they are taken into the care of the Local Authority Social Services Departments. In England and Wales, over 50,000 children are received into care each year (the figure for Scotland being 12,000) (CCETSW, 1978). The largest single reason for children being received into care is short-term illness in the family, although nearly 7 per cent are in care for no other reasons than lack of adequate housing. Nearly 50 per cent of children in care are rated by their teachers or houseparents as having significant emotional or behavioural problems (Yule and Raynes, 1972), houseparents need advice on complex problems of child management and social work managers need consultation on wider organizational aspects of child care.

Increasingly, social services departments are realizing the value of good psychological services. Although there remains a need for psychologists to participate in the assessment of juvenile delinquents, it is increasingly recognized that this traditional fucntion, largely carried out by educational psychologistgs seconded from Local Education Authorities on a sessional basis, is a poor use of scarce psychological services. Particularly with the advent of techniques of assessment and interaction based on social learning theory, social service departments look to psychologists for more active advice on management. (Brown, 1981; Brown and Christie, 1981). As the Trethowan Report (1977) pointed out, social service departments can indeed ask for help from NHS clinical psychologists. 'Section 11 of the National Health Service Reorganization Act 1973 provides for the services of health services profession to be made available to local authorities .... Hopefully, more will avail themselves of this as more clinical child psychologists are appointed.

Finally, children will continue throughout childhood to present to a variety of services with those problems of emotion and conduct which have been the mainstay of psychological services for children these past sixty years. I have examined in detail elsewhere (Yuke, 1981) the nature and extent of childhood disorders. It is clear that the time is overdue for psychologists to re-examine these problems and recategorize them from a psychological point of view. Meanwhile, psychologists have made large advances in the treatment of child psychiatric disorders, as is attested to by an examination of a number of recent texts (e.g. Lahey and Kazdin, 1977 onwards; Mash and Terdal,1981; Ross, 1981; Yuke, 1977; Herbert, 1981). Clinical child psychologists require training and experience both in dealing with the wide variety of disorders and in working with co-therapists of different disciplines in a variety of settings.

This leads on to a consideration of how best psychologists should be trained to work with children and their families from within a NHS setting in order best to meet the range of problems detailed above.

The Training of a Clinical Child Psychologist

This problem has concerned my colleagues and me for many years. It has long been recognized that initial two-year postgraduate degree training or three-year in-service training are both insufficient fully to equip clinical psychologists to fulfil all the functions required jof a psychologist working with children. But, then, initial training is only an introduction to the profession and basic grade is still essentially a training grade. By careful selection of options and placements, a number of trainees can gain considerable supervised expereicne with a variety of child clients, whilst at the same time having experience of adult patients within the NHS. The generic aspects of training are highly valued and allow a clinical child psychologist to work with adult patients as well as to understand the neurophysiological basis of many cognitive problems. Moreover, virtually all clinical psychologists are taught in multidisciplinary settings and this is invaluable in participating in multidisciplinary teams later. Even so, the basic disciplines of child psychology have expanded at such a rate that it is difficult to do the subject justice in the confines of present training (Berger, 1975).

Some years ago, Dr. Berger and I argued that there was an urgent need to improve the standard of applied child psychology available in the NHS (Berger and Yule, 1975). Regarding child psychologists as applied scientists, we argued that in addition to having a detailed knowledge of child and adolescent psychology and the phenomenology of children's problems, what was required was a good grasp of appropriate research methodology, assessment, treatment, and the understanding of the structure and organization of services. We put forward detailed proposals for the syllabus of a one-year course which could be taken as a post-qualifying course after at least one year on basic grade. We made the 'mistake' of suggesting that such a course would be open to educational and research psychologists, and the repercussions of that suggestion are still reverberating through the British Psychological Society's sub-systems. Despite this, I stand by the basic premise which is that currently neither clinical nor educational psychologists are sufficiently trained by their initial training to provide a comprehensive psychological service for children.

The outline syllabus proposed by Berger and myself is given in the Appendix. I believe that this can still form the basis for post-qualification courses, the need for which is now widely recognized within the profession.

Strategically, however, it is clear from the number of advertisements which appear that there is still a large need for well-qualified basic grade psychologists towork with children. All the courses need to ensure that they are able to provide sufficient and sufficiently varied supervised experience of working with children and adolescents. Whilst some of this should continue to be within a child psychiatry setting, this is not mandatory under current British Psychological Society regulations. Greater advantage should be taken of the increasing opportunities to work in paediatric settings.

Returning to post-qualification training, not only is there an urgent need for a variety of short and long term courses, but there is also a need to examine how funding for such training can best be obtained. The 'medical model' of disease is rightly reviled by many psychologists, but the 'medical model' of continuing education has been largely ignored. Our profession needs to have provisions for paying for short courses, for paying for secondments of up to a year, and for the establishment of post-qualification training places. Until this is fully worked out, we will be unable to develop our skills to the full advantage of the country's children. This need has been recognized by the recent British Psychological Society Working Party on 'Psychological Service for Children' (1981).

Some Current and Recurring Problems

Earlier in this chapter I have touched on a number of professional issues which apply particularly to those of us working with children within the NHS. Let me now examine each of them briefly.

A 'Specialism'

At the outset, I said that I was not too happy with clinical child psychology being regarded as a 'specialism'. That is not to say that psychologists working with children do not require a great deal of special knowledge. The critical thing is the extent to which their core professional skills are shared with other clinical psychologists. Of course, clinical child psychologists are 'marked off' by working with one identified group of clients -- who form a very large proportion of the total population. Their needs and problems differ in content from those of adult patients but they are not in any way fewer or more 'specialized'. Thus if 'specialism' is intended to denote 'less general', then I repute the usage.

As I noted earlier, child psychologists have contributions to make to six of the eight areas of practice differentiated in the Trethowan Report. Again, if 'specialism' means 'minority application', child psychologists are not specialists. If 'specialist' means well-trained, fully professional and able to deal with the majority of the problems described in earlier sections, then I will admit of clinical child psychologists having aspirations to being regarded as specialists.

My concern here is not merely a semantic one. Our profession has recently reasserted its belief in the value of the initial generic training shared by clinical psychologists. As I noted, I believe that our exposure to adult patients, to neurophysiology, to other professions in training, all of these contribute to our ability to deal with the varied challenges to be met in the NHS. There is a danger that if child psychology is seen as a specialism, then there may be attempts in some quarters to teach it separately from other aspects of clinical psychology, and I think that would not be in the interests of NHS clients.

I have another worry and that concerns promotional prospects for people who specialize in working with children. The number of Principal posts in this area is growing at a gratifying rate. However, in recent years I have seen too many Area Principal or Top grade posts where the administrative promotion is tied to clinical work with adult patients -- thereby effectively blocking psychologists who work with children from promotion. I sometimes get the feeling that 'adult psychologists' are seen as able to supervise 'child psychologists' but not vice versa. In so far as a specialist label contributes to this false perception, it should be avoided.

Relations with Educational Psychology

From the age of 5 to 16, all children are required to attend school (or receive satisfactory education otherwise). All Local Education Authorities now employ educational psychologists and provide schools psychological services. Despite the amazing growth in the number of educational psychologists throughout the 1970s, there are still too few psychologists -- either clinical or educational -- working with children.

According to the BPS working party (BPS, 1981) 311 educational psychologists are employed in Scotland and 1037 in England and Wales. Within the NHS, out of a total of 1,100 clinical psychologists, approximately 300 work with children, including handicapped children. About half of these only work part-time with children. Thus, clinical child psychologists are already providing a sizeable amount of service to children. We know from epidemiological studies that if all child psychiatric services were to rely on school referrals by teachers, then 50 per cent of the children requiring help would not be identified (Rutter *et al.*, 1970). Many parents discuss their difficulties with their GPs and access the rest of the NHS that way. Thus, it is obvious that the need for child psychology services within the NHS will continue.

A recent court case involving an educational psychologist in dispute with his employers, has been interpreted by Sutton (1981) as demonstrating that educational psychologists must conform to their employers' instructions. In other words, their degree of professional independence is not as wide as was believed. This has serious implications when one realizes that parents often wish to turn to psychologists for advice on school problems -- advice they hope will be independent of local authority policies. Doubtless clinical psychologists are also constrained by their terms of employment, but perhaps it is a blessing in disguise for the families of our clients that they can turn to the other group when they want a second, truly independent opinion.

Be that as it may, it is likely that the two professions will grow in parallel and that services to children will improve. There are clear needs for formal and informal liaison between the psychologists providing services within a district -- the exact form of collaboration will depend on local circumstances. The BPS working party's (1981) recommendation that Area Groups of Psychological Services for Children be set up has much merit and hopefully will succeed in promoting even greater co-operation between the disciplines.

Multidisciplinary Team

Child psychologists are used to working in multidisciplinary teams, largely taking over the role structures from early child guidance days (Sampson, 1980). There is a great deal to be said for bringing together in the views of different disciplines when trying to understand the complex problems of children presented from within complex social networks. Most of us who have worked in such a way can appreciate its strengths. But there are also weaknesses.

The different team members all too frequently are accorded different status (and salaries) which bear no relation to their experiences or expertise. Too often the medical member espouses the hollow doctrine of *primium inter pares.* The system has been vigorously criticized by sociological analysts and equally vigorously attacked on pragamatic grounds (Tizard, 1973). Structural changes in the provision of services have dealt heavy blows against the notion of permanent teams and substituted the concept of shifting networks of services (DES, 1974).

In my view, whilst it is important that the independent professional contribution of clinical child psychologists is properly recognized, it would be foolish to deny the value of interdisciplinary collaboration. Psychologists are, and should remain, accountable through other psychologists to their employers, but that is not to say that they should not work closely with other disciplines. Hopefully we will see the emergence of proper child psychology clinics to which other disciplines provide consultation as requested, in the same way as psychological consultation is currently provided to medical and social work clinics.

The British Psychological Society Working Party on Psychological Services for Children (BPS, 1981) put forward the unusual concept of the need to define Independent Professional Status with respect to psychological work with children. Not surprisingly this has alraeady been disavowed by the Division of Clinical Psychology who prefer to keep the profession generic. All clinical psychologists exercise independent professional judgement once they reach senior grade. The need for the concept was introduced after complex discussion with child psychiatrists and psychiatric social workers on the future of training for work in child guidance clinics. No need to guess which profession attained 'Independent Professional Status' earliest! I suggest, rather than waste precious professional time debating such status issues, psychologists should continue to improve their skills and allows sapiential authority to develop where status may lay behind.

Organization of Services

Even allowing for an estimated 150 full-time equivalent child psychologists being in posts in about 200 district health authorities, not only are many of these working in mental handicap but many of the others work in and around London. In other words, there are too few people inequably distributed to begin to decide an optional organization for services. Now that services are to be reorganized at District Level, the role of Regional Speciality or organizing committees will be increased. It will be essential for clinical child psychologists to co-operate throughout regions on plans to develop adequate services at a time when little growth is to be expected.

Taking this gloomy, but realistic, view, the advice of the Trethowan Report remains valid. Priority has to be given to developing services in child psychology and mental handicap before branching into newer areas. That does not mean that all sessions in an understaffed service have to be committed to those areas only that relatively speaking it is advisable to give those areas some priority. Simultaneously, any good Senior or Principal will be providing occasional sessions in other services to broaden experience and gain a feel for the likely level of future demand.

It is vital that as many trainees as possible are given excellent child health experience as early as possible so that more can elect to take extra placements with children during preliminary training. That way district services can build up a pool of experienced basic grades on whom future expansion will depend.

A Final Word

This chapter has concentrated on the organizational and policy aspects of providing psychological services for children. Since it could not have done justice to the vast new literature on applications of child psychology to children's problems it has not attempted even a superficial coverage. It has assumed that clinical psychologists do not need to be convinced of the potential value of improving child psychology services within the NHS. Instead, it has tried to discuss the broad nature of problems presenting within the child health services. It has recognized that there are many organizational problems ahead, not the least being the improvement of collaboration with educational psychology colleagues.

Children *are* different from adults. Working with children is more demanding in many ways. Not only are they developing rapidly, they are also inextricably involved in a variety of social networks. Therein lies one of the challenges for an applied child psychologist. With the burgeoning interest in child development, the nature of the work will change dramatically in the next decade. It is up to all of us to ensure that, built on those developments, the services to our clients really improve.

The Content of Focused Training

The content outlined below is intended to provide a basis for the development of practical applications of psychological research. Indeed, it is the constant emphasis on such applications which will provide one of the major justifications for focused training.

The following outline indicates specific topics to be covered in a training programme. While it may appear to be over inclusive candidates will already have covered a substantial proportion of the topics in their previous training. Hence, courses will have to be flexible enough to cope with individual experience, cater for the development of individual interests and needs, yet ensure that they leave the course with a core of common knowledge and practical experience.

Section A: Child Development and Adolescent Psychology

1. The Psychology of Development

   To include an introduction to:

   Genetics, particularly behaviour genetics

   Neuroanatomy, neurophysiology, and psychophysiology

   Physical growth and change

   Neuropsychology

2. Individual Development

   To include:

   Sensory processes

   Motor development

   Conditioning and learning

   Perception

   Cognition

   Attention

   Motivation and emotion

   Personality and individual differences

   Speech and language

3. Socialization

Interaction and attachment

Family influences

Peer group

School

Cultural differences and their implications

4. Theories and Models of Child and Adolescent Development

Approaches to the study of child development

Mechanistic and organismic theories

Stage and phase theories

Specific theories -- including Piaget, social learning, etc.

5. Integration of Topics covered in Sections 1 to 4

This section is intended as an integration of the material covered above. Its goal is to describe the interrelationships among various mechanisms and processes at different phases of the life-span.

Pre-natal development

Post-natal (neonate and infant)

The first two years

Pre-school

Middle childhood

Adolescence

Section B1: Clinical Orientation and Phenomenology

To include:

Paediatrics

Adult, adolescent and child psychiatry

Neurology, including paediatric neurology

Orthopaedics

Ophthalmology

E.N.T.

Dentistry

The purpose of introducing these medical aspects is to alert child psychologists to the major medical conditions which afflict children and adolescents with special reference to their associated psychological difficulties. Some of these topics should be given more weight than others (for example, child and adolescent psychiatry), and some should be complemented by psychological approaches where these are available (for example, neurology complemented by neuropsychology).

Aetiological aspects

Genetic and constitutional

Endocrine

Metabolic

Infectious

Traumatic injury

Malnutrition, neglect, and child abuse

Familial and social factors

Temperament

Phenomenology

To include:

Sensory and motor defects

Cognitive (intellectual/educational; reading, writing, spelling, number, etc.)

Emotional

Social

Language

Single and multiple handicap (the overlap and interaction of handicaps) Giftedness and special abilities

Section B2: Associated Problems

To include:

Psychopharmacology

Hospitalization, physical and psychological aspects

Preparation for surgery and aftercare

Institutionalization, physical and psychological aspects

Doctor - patient - parent communication

Treatment and the problems associated with failure to follow advice / utilize professional help / services

Health education and propaganda

Section C: Statistics and Research Methods

To include:

Methodology

Research design and statistics

Introduction to multivariate analysis and Bayesian statistics

Single case researach and 'statistics'

The evaluation of intervention and services

Translating research problems into actual studies with special emphasis on applied research

The determination of service needs

The use of computers

Section D: Assessment Procedures

To include:

Test design, construction and evaluation

Test procedures: (a) conventional -- baby tests, intelligence attainments, language, motor functioning.

(b) an extension of the concept of 'test', involving the use of:

direct observation procedures

interviewing

neuropsychological procedures

psychophysiological measurement, biofeedback

conditioning techniques as tests, habituation procedures

techniques for the evaluation of quality of care

the utilization of research techniques as 'tests', for example the measurement of attention, impulsivity, reaction time using techniques and findings of published studies

Testing and assessment and their relationship to treatment

Section E: Treatment

Behavioural approaches

Counselling

Psychodynamic approaches

Educational approaches -- including remedial techniques

Working with families

Ethical problems in treatment

Parents and other non-psychologists as therapists

Rehabilitation, and the integration of individuals with special needs into the general community

Coping with the transition between various forms of special care

Where possible teaching should include demonstrations in the form of video and audio recordings, role playing and mini-workshops.

Section F: Legislation, Services, and Institutions

1. Legislation concerning children and regional variations (Scotland, Ireland and Wales), Education, Adoption, Fostering, Care.

2. National organization

   DHSS, DES, Home Office, Structure in Scotland, Ireland and Wales.

3. Regional structure and organization

   NHS Areas, etc.

   DES Structures (e.g. School Health)

   Local Authority (Education, Social Services, Health Structures, Child Minding, Fostering, Playgroups, Nursery Schools etc.)

4. 'Charitable' organizations concerned with children, for example NSPCC, Spastics Society, NAMH, IRMH, Autistic Society, etc.

5. Research units (e.g. MRC), Sponsoring organizations (SSRC)

6. Professions associated with child health and care GP, Midwives, Health Visitors, Nurses, Speech Therapists, Physiotherapists, Occupational Therapists, Child Care Staff, Social Workers, Probation Officers, School Counsellors.

7. The social psychology of management, administration and institutional change.

8. The 'Politics of Services'; for example using the Autistic Society as a case study.

9. Co-operation with governmental and other agencies aimed at effecting policy changes.

Section G: Practical Experience

The practical work should be planned so as to avoid spectator placements: it is essential to ensure that candidates are actively involved in the on-going work. Given that they already have had some practical experience, candidates will be able to contribute to the on-going work in their placements.

1. Assessment

   To include the following, preferably as part of 'clinical' work:

   The administration of conventional tests

   The administration of other procedures as 'tests', such as GSR, direct observation procedures, qualaity of care measures.

   Development and use of specially designed tests

2. Treatment and intervention: individual, group and institutional

   To include:

   The planning and implementation of a variety of treatment regimes, for example behavioural with individual/parent training: counselling with adolescent; 'remedial' reading, maths, etc.

3. Detailed case studies of instances of institutional change, for example Brooklands experiment; Southampton Services.

4. Placements

   There should be a minimum of three months in a number of supervised settings, determined in part by the individual's previous experience.

   Essential:

   Paediatric

   Social Services

   Optional (Choice of two, depending on initial training/ experience)

Subnormality

Psychiatric

LEA Clinic

Community/Group General Practice

Section H: Area of Special Interest

The course should provide the opportunity for individual members to work intensively in an area that is of special interest to them, both at an academic and a practical/research level.

Many of the candidates will have had the opportunity during their initial professional or other courses to complete a small research project. While on the proposed course, they should undertake a research project which has practical implications. It will be necessary to provide certain back-up resources, such as technical help, funding for equipment, etc.

10

Routine Clinical Psychology Service

Introduction

This study assessed two recurring and alternative explanations for clinical recovery, transient life stress and improved psychological coping. The study took place in two 'primary care' settings, a General Practitioner's (GP) surgery and a general purpose health clinnic. Unlike the existing studies of clinical psychology in primary care, the present study considered three variables that appear to be logically required in an analysis of clinical improvement in primary care. They are stressful life events, personal coping strategies and strain (Cohen & Lazarus, 1979). These terms are defined by these authors as follows: 'stress' refers to problematic life experiences that require action; 'coping' refers to the patient's problem solving responses when faced with stress; while 'strain' refers to unpleasant thoughts, feelings or behaviours (as in anxiety of depression). The operational definitions provided by the measures elaborates the meaning of these variables.

These three factors need to be considered in order to draw valid inferences about therapy outcome. This kind of analysis has not yet taken place in primary care because researchers have been content to infer changes in personal coping from changes in outcome. One illustration has been the frequent reliance on medication levels or GP attendances as an index of 'improvement'. However, research designs have failed to exclude alternative explanations for changes in these indices, such as altered trends in GP's general prescribing habits (Freeman & Button,1984).

There is, therefore, a need to investigate whether the therapy provided by clinical psychologists affects the patients' coping and thereby their strain; or whether the alternative hypothesis of transient life stress can account for improvements.

Method

Measures and Research Design

The patients' stress, coping and strain were measured by means of published self-report questionnaires. Stress was assessed with the 'Schedule of Recent Events', a comprehensive inventory of stressful life events (SRE; Tennant & Andrews, 1976). The 'Coping Responses Questionnaire' of Billings and Moos (CRQ, 1981) gauged three relevant dimensions of coping, namely 'active cognitive', 'active behavioural' and 'avoidance' strategies. Strain was measured by the short form of the 'General Health Questionnaire' (GHQ, Banks *et al.* 1980).

In addition, patients and referring agents completed outcome ratings based on questions derived from Robson *et al* (1984). Finally, patients provided 'consumer satisfaction' ratings on a 20 item ad hoc measure.

These measures were administered in a 'waiting list' control group design, with two baseline measurements prior to therapy and two following therapy. The first set of questionnaires was completed at the time of receiving the referral, the second after the first appointment. On average, the interval between these two baseline assessments was 3.4 months. The immediate effects of therapy were assessed after a further 3 months of appointments by a third administration of the stress, coping and strain measures. The fourth and final assessment, a follow-up, occurred one year after the first appointment when the questionnaires were re-administered and the referring agents were asked to rate the therapy outcome.

This research design, therefore, provided a comparison between equivalent baseline and therapy intervals, allowing an estimate to be made of the relative effects of the two conditions upon the patient's stress, coping and strain. It was predicted that therapy would result in a significant improvement in the patient's coping, leading in turn to reduced strain. This effect would be expected to be absent during the baseline period. As a corollary, stress was not expected to vary with strain.

Subjects

All patients were recruited from a one-year series of consecutive referrals from General Practitioners and Psychiatrists. A total of 47 patients were treated from the 65 who were offered initial appointments. The 18 who did not participate in the study were excluded because they did not attend the first or subsequent appointment (7), because they did not commence therapy (7), or because they were regarded as unsuitable for therapy (4). The mean age of the 47 treated patients was 36.9 years. They reported having had the referral problem for an average of 7.4 years, with professional help for the last 4.3 years preceding this study, mostly from their GPs and psychiatrists. Half of the patients were on psychotropic medication and as a group they consulted their GP on average 7.3 times per year. The problems identified in referral letters were anxiety (40%), depression (24%), specific phobias (24%), obsessional compulsive disorders (8%) and sexual dysfunction (4%).

Therapy Procedure

Each patient was seen individually by the author, a clinical psychologist employed by the National Health Service.

The first appointment was occupied largely with an explanation of the therapy and evaluation procedure, a clarification of the problem and the collection of demographic data. Clients were then seen weekly or fortnightly in order to establish a behavioural analysis of their problems, leading to appropriate behaviour therapy. On average, patients were seen for 11.6 appointments lasting 31.8 minutes over a period of 5.3 months.

The range of techniques employed included progressive muscular relaxation, response prevention, sex therapy, cognitive restructuring methods and anti-depressive activities. Written material and audio-tapes were provided to aid the development of understanding and self-control (e.g Milne & Linford, 1984).

More detailed objective specifications of the therapy provided in this study have been reported elsewhere (Milne, 1986a). In short, it was found that the type of therapy corresponded most closely with 'behaviour therapy' that the therapist's proficiency was 'satisfactory' and that the patients perceived the therapist as high on interpersonal effectiveness.

Results

The main hypothesis of improved personal coping consequent upon behaviour therapy was supported by the data. Table 10.1 shows the trend for the three scores derived from the coping responses questionnaire (CRQ) to remain stable during the baseline phase, but to increase both immediately following therapy and between then and the follow-up assessment. This statement is true for the two strategies regarded as adaptive by Billings and Moos (1981), 'active cognitive' and 'active behavioural' coping; and untrue, as would be expected, for the maladaptive strategy of 'avoidance'. Statistical analyses, employing the t-test, indicated that the only significant changes occurred in the two 'adaptive' coping strategies, which increased significantly following three months of therapy ($p<0.05$). These improved scores were maintained at levels significantly higher than baseline figures at the one year follow-up assessment.

In addition to demonstrataing the successful impact of behaviour therapy upon personal coping strategies, the data in

Table 10.1 also seem to rule out the alternative hypothesis; no significant change in the patient's stressful life events was obtained during the study. Taken together, these stress and coping data suggest that reductions in strain are mediated by improved coping, rather than by reduced stress. This relationship is indicated by the significant reduction in the General Health Questionnaire (GHQ) score at the same point in time as the CRQ changes.

Expressed in terms of clinical rather than statistical significance, the reduction in strain represented a decline in the proportion of psychiatric 'cases' from 49% and 38% during the initial baseline assessments, to 13% following three months of therapy, and to 2% at the one year follow-up assessment.

The independent ratings made by the referring agents and patients' self-ratings corroborated the impression of real clinical progress apparent from the GHQ and CRQ data. At the one year follow-up assessment 74% of the patients were regarded by the referring agents as requiring no further psychological treatment (with a further 12% stating 'don't know'). Similarly, in the case of 72% of the patients they thought that a 'satisfactory outcome' had been achieved through the patient seeing the psychologist (12% 'don't know'). These figures are very comparable with the '70% improved' short-term findings of most outcome studies.

Overall, the patients also felt that the therapy had been successful. Their replies to the two questions above were similar to those of the referring agents. Also, on an ad hoc anonymous 'consumer satisfaction' measure, administered after three months of therapy, they highly endorsed the clinical 'outcomes', 'process', 'content' and 'goals' of therapy. These were the four logically derived dimensions of the scale. Mean scores were, respectively, 4.3, 5.3, 4.4 and 5.3, on a bi-polar Likert scale where 0 equalled strong dissatisfaction and 6 represented strong satisfaction. These figures compared very favourably with those achieved on the same measure by a popular local GP, dealing with routine surgery attenders.

Table 10.1

Mean scores obtained for the patients' (N=47) stress (SRE), coping (CRQ) and strain (GHQ) during each assessment phase.

MEASURES		*ASSESSMENT PHASES*							
		First Baseline		*Second Baseline*		*After 3 Months of Therapy*		*One Year Follow-up*	
		Mean	*Standard Deviation*	*Mean*	*Standard Deviation*	*Mean*	*Standard Deviation*	*Mean*	*Standard Deviation*
Schedule of Recent Events (SRE)		3.4	2.2	4.0	3.8	4.1	4.3	-	-
Coping	(a) Active Cognitive	1.7	0.8	1.7	0.8	2.1	0.8	2.5	1.0
Responses	(b) Active Behavioural	1.6	0.8	1.5	0.7	1.9	0.6	2.1	1.0
Questionnaire (CRQ)	(c) Avoidance	1.6	0.9	1.5	0.7	1.4	0.7	1.5	0.7
General Health Questionnaire (GHQ) (Likert scoring)		21.5	9.5	17	9.1	10.3	7.9	8.9	6.8

Discussion

The principal finding of this study was that behaviour therapy led to significantly improved personal coping and that this, rather than transient life stress, appears to have been the explanation for the reduced strain reported by these patients. This conclusion is a reassuring one for therapists who have always inferred improved coping from reduced strain. However, such inferences can prove invalid, as we know from the use of medication as an outcome measure. This suggests that future studies should investigate the effect of their interventions upon specific and immediate targets, as well as upon the more traditional outcome measures. A failure to do so appears to lead to at least two difficulties. One of these lies in developing our understanding of the precise mediators of therapeutic change from coarse outcome measures. It would seem that in order to produce more efficient interventions we need also to consider mediating variables, such as personal coping strategies, in much greater detail.

The second difficulty lies in the premature abandonment of the 'primary care' approach, on the basis of the inferences drawn from existing studies. These have tended to provide pessimistic conclusions regarding the incremental value of a clinical psychology service and to bolster the view that GPs are dealing adequately with a transient 'worst year' phenomenon (Robson *et al*, 1984; Freeman & Button, 1984).

The present data dispute these conclusions: baseline data do not suggest a transient period of stress or strain, nor do they indicate the development of better coping strategies. The reason for the unaltered strain in this sample may well be due to the chronic nature of the presenting complaints. In contrast, we found that a randomly selected sample of 40 patients attending the same surgery for the usual range of complaints did fluctuate quite considerably in their level of strain over the same period. These findings suggest that the transient 'worst year' explanation may be adequate for minor, acute episodes of psychological distress, but may be quite inadequate to explain changes in the more chronic sample, as typically referred to psychologists in routine practice.

The implication of the present coping analysis for the role of clinical psychologists working in primary care seems to hold whether or not we accept the above arguments regarding transient episodes or the effectiveness of GPs. This implication is that we need to develop our understanding of personal change if we are to prove optimally successful, either as direct or indirect therapists.

A clear parallel exists in the area of staff training in behaviour therapy, where such an indirect approach to patient care was regarded as unsuccessful by the mid 1970s. However, more systematic investigations subsequently indicated not only that these interventions could prove effective, but that by studying the immediate target of the training more closely (i.e. skills acquisition) we could learn a lot more about the psychology of change at the organisational level, so developing our analysis and effectiveness (Milne, 1986b). As a consequence of this kind of precedent and the present findings, we may wish to re-appraise our role in primary care. There may yet be benefits in pursuing traditional approaches, provided that these are allied to a more thorough analysis of the effects of our work. In turn, the findings should guide the nature of our future contribution to primary care.

Acknowledgements

I am indebted to Eileen Greaves, Trish Harrison, Keith Henshall, Fiona Castle, Julie Sowerby, Sue Candy, Janet Rowntree and Judy Milne for their help in administering, scoring and analysing the measures. My former colleague, Rosemary Jones, participated in the project initially, providing support and encouragement. I am grateful to the referring agents for their ratings, particularly Drs. K.M. Souter, G.D. Slater, P.F. Slater and D.O. Oughtibridge of Southgate Surgery. This study was undertaken in Wakefield while I was employed by the District Health Authority. The manuscript was typed by Stella Dickinson.

11

Study of Stress in Psychiatric Nursing

This paper is a critique of traditional models of organisational stress and outlines an alternative analysis of stress in psychiatric nursing which is illustrated with data from an ongoing empirical study.

Transactional models of organisational stress have been criticised for failing to develop satisfactory accounts of the causes of stress within particular occupational groups. Middle-range theories which are more closely tied to the empirical data, more complex and more limited in scope, are often proposed as a practically useful alternative (Argyris, 1982). Qualitative methods are advocated for similar reasons as they provide more depth and flexibility than positivist methodologies.

The middle range theory of stress in psychiatric nursing is derived from the critical psychiatry literature. The fundamental premise of this literature is that the functions and structures of psychiatry are contradictory. Thus whilst the manifest function of psychiatry is to cure the mentally ill, its latent function may well be to control social deviance and deny its social significance by individualising and medicalising it. Similarly, whilst the organisational structure of psychiatric hospitals is superficially aimed at helping patients, closer inspection often reveals a structure geared to routine care and control.

One implication of this model is that a fundamental cause of stress in psychiatric nursing may be that nurses internalise the official ideology of psychiatry and identify themselves professionally as helpers whereas the organisational structure means that in practice they usually operate as a cross between room-service and jailers. Since the nurses are unable to articulate the discrepancy between ideology and practice they are unable to take rational action to change the organisation and may therefore become cynical towards patients whilst developing feelings of guilt because they no longer care. In other words, stress in psychiatric nursing may arise because nurses are repeatedly faced with problematic situations brought about by the contradictory nature of the psychiatric system. They then interpret and act upon these situations using a contradictory knowledge base derived from their socialisation within the system and by doing so perpetuate the cycle.

The analysis is illustrated with qualitative data from the empirical research. The raw data from a diary kept by a pupil nurse is presented in Figure 11.1 to show how the inappropriate and inconsistent use of a medical framework generates dysfunctional inter-personal dynamics which help maintain the very acts which the hospital system purports to alleviate. The nurses' comments suggest that the cost in staff stress may be high.

Cognitive Therapy: Is It Always Cognitive, Is It Always Therapy?

Cognitive Therapy, particularly that described in detail by Beck *et al* (1979), has become widely accepted in clinical research and practice. A number of well conducted controlled trials have demonstrated that cognitive therapy of depression is as effective as tricyclic antidepresant medication (e.g. Blackburn *et al*, 1981). We are awaiting the completion of further longer term follow up studies, but there is already some evidence that cognitive therapy may be more effective in preventing relapse than

Figure 11.1

Diary Extracts from Second Year Pupil Nurse

Extract one

Nurse's Description of Events	*Nurse's Comments*
Admitted an over-active patient. A lady who had delusions of grandeur-Christ reborn. Little insight into her condition. Prior to her admission had been seen over-acting and walking around the streets naked. Admitted as an emergency DV by Dr.	Tried to remain calm throughout admission, took several questions to get this lady to participate with admission forms etc. Frustrated with her as present day happenings are always affecting her — has everybody elses worries on her mind.

Extract Two

Nurse's Descriptions of Events	*Nurse's Comments*
Admitted another lady, an old patient who I've known in the past. Hypomanic—also suffers from mood swings. Believes in San Yasin (Orange people). Neglecting hygiene, stopped eating. Varying emotions — crying to laughing, screaming.	Mad at the thought of admitting this lady again as it has only been six weeks since her discharge. Always admitted after her bi-sexual boyfriend has found another girlfriend. X cannont cope with this — always plays the psychiatric sick role and always warrants admission. Since her arrival has been kissing walls, lifting clothes up in the lounge. Counselled her re this but to little effect. Maintains it is through (boyfriend) she has ended up coming in. Given prescribed injection to calm her.

pharmacotherapy (Blackburn *et al*, 1986). Until recently, cognitive therapy has proved most useful in areas such as depression where the impact of psychological treatment had previously been minimal. However, the last few years have seen the increasing application of cognitive techniques in a variety of disorders where *limitations* in psychological treatments have become apparent, particularly in those areas where behaviour therapy has been generally successful. Notable examples of this trend are anxiety (Beck, Emery & Greenberg, 1985; Clark, 1986), panic (Clark, 1986; Salkovskis & Clark, 1986) and obsessions (Salkovskis & Westbrook, this volume).

As research into cognitive treatment has progressed two important conceptual and methodological issues have come to the force: (i) What is the nature of the link between experimental cognitive psychology and cognitive therapy? (ii) What are the necessary and sufficient criteria for an intervention to be acceptable as properly conducted cognitive therapy?

There are some interesting parallels between these issues now being debated in cognitive psychopathology and the situation which arose in behaviour therapy in the late 1960s.

12

Primary Health Care

The expansion of community involvement in the treatment and management of psychiatric patients, particularly as exemplified by the 1974 and 1982 reorganizations of the NHS, gradually changed the traditional psychiatric settings which had originally nurtured and supported clinical psychologists. Initially clinical psychologists had found themselves in psychiatric hospitals built in the nineteenth century away from centres of population. After the inauguration of the NHS, new psychiatric units were sited in general hospitals and local networks of support services were developed. As clinical psychologists became more involved in general hospitals and out-patient clinics as opposed to being used as an ancillary hospital provision of a department of psychiatry, the range of problems they were asked to deal with increased with consequent greater utilization of the many skills they possess to assist with various aspects of health care. Trethowan (1977) envisaged psychological services which would include commitment to primary health care and the development of preventive services.

Lamberts (1979) viewed primary health care as the boundary between the medical system and society. For most people, primary care means the first level of contact when seeking help from the NHS. In practice, the point of entry is usually through the GP who occupies a key position among the professional staff involved in primary health care. The other professionals most involved in primary health care are the health visitors, community nurses, treatment-room sisters, district midwives, and social workers. Pritchard (1978) in his *Manual of Primary Health Care* regarded health visitors, community nurses, treatment-room sisters, and district midwives as the main primary care team. Social workers were considered to be in a special relationship as their main concern is not health and clinical psychologists were listed among other professional staff, such as physiotherapist and occupational therapist, who may be included in a primary health care team under certain circumstances to offer specialist help. Psychological skills were deemed useful by Pritchard in the following conditions: agoraphobia and other phobic states, excessive dependence on psychotropic drugs, marital and sexual problems, excessive smoking and obesity, and intellectual deterioration after strokes and head injuries. In addition, the psychologist's training in group work was thought to be useful to help the primary care team to make group work effective. Rehabilitation work, particularly after injuries and strokes and the long-term care of the elderly, mentally handicapped, or other chronically ill in their homes, community or day hospitals have changed greatly with the involvement of clinical psychologists.

General Practice and Community Clinical Psychology

The movement of clinical psychologists from a hospital base into the community had undoubtedly been an important factor in redefining the profession. A great many discussions took place as to its feasibility, advisability, and morality. Kincey (1974), anticipating the first major reorganization of the NHS, made a cogently argued case for a closer liaison between GP and clinical psychologists. He suggested that clinical psychologists could be usefully employed on a 'peripatetic basis serving several practices or by attachment to health-centre teams'. The most compelling reasons given for this proposed change of location regarded the advantages of treating patients outside hospital, in the environment where problems had arisen (and were maintained), and the prophylactic value of psychological treatment at an early stage before hospital treatment had become necessary. His challenge was widely taken up, at least by clinical psychologists in the first instance.

Broadhurst (1977) published the results of a postal survey addressed to all clinical psychologists practising in the UK in 1975 and enquiring into their community involvement, particularly through general practitioners. Some 33 per cent or 216 completed questionnaires were received at the close of the survey. Among the respondents, the great majority were employed in psychiatric hospitals with a small number employed in general hospitals. There were also four clinical psychologists employed primarily to work with GPs, 30 worked both in a hospital and a community setting and 78 described their work as community orientated. Furthermore, the majority of respondents acknowledged that they were working with general practitioners, with medical specialists other than psychiatrists and/or with other workers in the community.

The type of referrals received from GPs included 56.9 per cent for individual treatment of behaviour problems, 14.4 per cent for group treatment, and 38.4 per cent for individual assessment. Other requests were received for involvement in research (27.3 per cent), teaching (56.9 per cent), and consultation (34.3 per cent) on various related clinical matters. It was evident from the above survey that clinical psychologists had been largely responsible for initiating their community contact and, through these, had made a substantial contribution to the community. The community involved psychologists found many advantages in their contacts with GPs such as early treatment, treatment in the natural environment without stigma of mental illness, increasing acceptance of psychological models for behaviour disorders and ease of communication with GPs. Another survey carried out a year later and addressing itself directly to GPs of the Croydon Area Health Authority showed that there was considerable support among the GPs surveyed for having direct access to psychological services (Davidson, 1977).

In a study investigating GP and clinical psychologist agreement in their respective evaluation of the degree of psychological involvement seen in problems presented in two group medical practices, it was estimated that 8.4 per cent of the total population which consulted the GPs could benefit from referral to a clinical psychologist (McPherson and Feldman, 1977). Although the GPs were more likely to see a greater need for the psychologist's intervention than the clinical psychologist, there was a high level of agreement between them regarding the relevance of psychological factors in the cases they examined. The majority of problems which were encountered during the study as likely to be helped by a clinical psychologist were those involving anxiety and depression, insomnia, obesity, excessive use of alcohol, marital and sexual problems, and child and elderly person management. McPherson and Feldman concluded from their experience, that if their findings were extrapolated nationally, this would necessitate a threefold increase in the number of clinical psychologists to meet the potential primary care demand. In view of this, they made a number of suggestions designed to maximize effectiveness such as careful selection of patients, teaching other professionals or the families of certain client groups, as well as treating similar clients in groups. Other pleas for restraint and for the careful monitoring and evaluation of GP-clinical psychologist relationships in the wider context of NHS psychological services ensued (Hood, 1979; McPherson, 1981; Eastman and McPherson, 1982).

Evaluation

Evaluation of such a complex set of relationships, as is involved when assessments of clinical psychologists working in primary health care are made, is not an easy task and benefits are unlikely to be spread evenly among all participants. McPherson (1981) reviewed assessments made of the contribution of clinical psychologists to primary care by attempting to identify the advantages which had accrued for the various parties involved such as patients, the NHS, GPs, and for clinical psychologists themselves. Various conclusions can be drawn from the tentative data available and, until there is more concrete evidence of quantifiable benefits, there is no doubt that the evidence will be used to back up different positions regarding the main issue of whether or not psychologists should be seen to work in primary health care. As things stand, it would also be wrong to underestimate the strong feelings among certain clinical psychologists, GPs, and patients that the enterprise had been successful and valued. While it is too early to be able to give definitive answers on all aspects of the contribution of clinical psychologists to primary care (or otherwise), at least it can be said that a salutary climate in favour of such evaluations has permeated this area of psychological practice from the start. It is hoped that cost/benefit issues will be pursued with equal vigour in other areas where clinical psychologists have involved themselves. As long as clinical psychologists remain a numerically small group, one service or other will be undermanned. Who is to say that one client group is more deserving than another?

Siting of Primary Health Care Services

The most suitable location for clinical psychologists in primary care has been a matter for concern and has depended largely on the local conditions individual psychologists found themselves in. It would seem at first glance that a mental hospital sited some distance away from its nearest town is unlikely to attract referrals from any other source than psychiatrists. However, Broadhurst (1977) found that psychologists working from mental illness hospitals had been able to contribute to primary care as well as their colleagues in general hospitals. For a number of clinical psychologists who wished to hasten the process of direct and close collaboration with GPs, as well as with other members of primary health care teams, the solution was to follow the model suggested by Kincey (1974) and to attach themselves to one or a small number of related GP group practices on a sessional basis (Johnston, 1977, 1978; Kat, 1978; Ives, 1979; Koch,

1979; Earill and Kincey, 1980; Spector, 1980). There is no doubt that, through their pioneering efforts, the above (and many others who followed similar leads) have been instrumental in demonstrating the capability of clinical psychologists to make valid and sustained contributions in primary health care settings.

Another group of clinical psychologists who had developed a service in a health centre without GPs and wished to attract referrals from them fared less well initially (Hallam and Liddell, 1978; Liddell *et al.*, 1981). It was not until after they had contacted their District GPs individually to describe their service that they started to receive the referrals they had hoped to stimulate. One reason for their initial lack of success seemed to be that the GPs of the District had not been in the habit of dealing with clinical psychologists in the past and consequently appeared hesitant to entrust their patients to people whose qualifications, training, and skills were something of an enigma to them. On the other hand, the GPs in question were found to be very approachable and interested once contacted and 69 per cent of the total number of GPs in that District made time available to speak with the clinical psychologist who had contacted them. As a result of these contacts, a substantial and steady flow of GP referrals was subsequently received at that particular clinic. In addition other members of local primary health care teams such as community nurses, health visitors, and social workers also sent referrals and, on a number of occasions, phoned for advice in regard to particular patients they were responsible for.

From the above experience, it was evident that GPs varied a great deal in the degree of psychological involvement they perceived in their surgeries and/or willingness to refer their patients. In a follow-up study conducted some two and a half years after individual GP contacts were made, it was found that 38 per cent of the contacted GPs (scattered over 21 practices) had referred between one and ten of their patients and that over 50 per cent of the total referrals came from *three* of these practices (Liddell *et al.*, 1982). Eastman and McPherson (1982) also found great variation when they interviewed a sample of 30 GPs in the West Midlands regarding their perception of psychological problems. Kat (1981), having taken as a theme the processes of Primary Health Care in the NHS, pointed to the vagaries in general utilization of health services and the complex explanations given for this phenomenon which included the involvement of social and psychological factors in addition to epidemiological ones. He observed that 'activities of general practice -- consultations, visits, etc. cannot be used as a measure of morbidity because it cannot be presumed that referral and illness are perfectly correlated. In view of these known variations, it would seem that clinical psychologists who are concerned with the provision of district services should think of locating themselves in a place which is accessible to all GPs and other primary health care professionals of their particular district rather than just a few practices. On the other hand, it is also hoped that salaried posts will be developed in some large GP practices or among smaller group practices who may like to join forces to employ such persons to complement their existing services. Such posts would certainly be welcomed by psychologists who wish to specialize in this type of setting and continue in its development and evaluation.

Clinical Psychologists on Primary Health Care Teams

Pritchard (1978) saw psychologists in a rather peripheral position in relation to primary health care teams but welcomed further considerations in the light of contributions made by them on some teams. The BPS was asked to provide evidence to the DHSS Joint Working Party on the Primary Health Care Team. In its report (BPS, 1979), it commented that, in practice, primary health care teams operated under different models and that such diverse and flexible organizations should be retained to meet local needs. It was also pointed out in the report that a variety of activities were included under the heading of primary health care, making the concept ill-defined and amorphous. For instance, under this generic term, activities with widely differing time perspectives and requiring different priorities in the workload of the different professions involved were included. At the time of the report, primary health care applied equally to acute and crisis oriented services, prevention oriented services, and services for those with long-term chronic problems. One of the most basic confusions was seen as the lack of distinction made between primary health care which is characterized as a generalist service and specialist care in the community. It was concluded that clinical psychologists were able to work in the generalist manner required in primary health care as well as the specialist manner they had adopted in the past, but that the potential demand for psychologists in the genralist role could not be realized without profound changes in the size and structure of the profession.

Psychological Problems Seen in Primary Health Care Settings

In practice, there is fairly close agreement between clinical psychologists and their other professional colleagues regarding the type of problems, both acute and chronic, which are likely to benefit from a psychological approach. This agreement may be due in part to the increasing involvement of psychologists in the large number of areas of health care provided by the NHS. District based clinical psychologists were better able to demonstrate their skills, under such an arrangement, than they had been able to do under the constraints which necessarily operated when they were solely attached to departments of psychiatry. The increasing visibility psychologists gained through district appointments made them better understood and valued by more people than had been the case in the early days of their establishment in the NHS.

The classification of individual clinical problems offered by Kincey (1974) appeared just as relevant after almost 10 years of its publication. At the time, he offered the following framework for clinical problems with which psychologists could help in primary care settings: (1) problems of anxiety and stress, (2) habit disorders, (3) educational-occupational difficulties or decisions, (4) interpersonal-social-marital problems, (5) psychological adjustment to problems stemming from physical illness or other significant life events involving medical care. The above framework accommodated a wide range of clients, many of whom cannot be appropriately labelled mentally ill, therefore likely to be the province of psychologists more than psychiatrists, although they have been referred to both in the past. In view of this, the expansion of psychological services is likely to relieve some degree of pressure from psychiatrists whose numbers are acknowledged to be too small to supply the demand made on their expertise. Some of the concepts of mental illness were discussed earlier It should also be pointed out that mental illness classifications have gone into several systematic revisions and that psychiatrists have been well aware of the deficiencies inherent in a system which classifies diseases rather than people. In the Ninth Revision of the International Classification of Diseases (WHO, 1978) several welcomed changes were made, one of which was the addition of adjustment and stress reactions to the existing categories. It had become increasingly evident that the classical descriptions of neurosis and psychosis did not apply to a large number of individuals who presented with abnormal but transient states of emotional disturbance. Adjustment and stress reactions were described thus: (1) acute reaction to stress to apply to a transient state induced by several mental or physical stress, and (2) adjustment reactions denote more prolonged reactions usually in response to stress of a less spectacular nature but of longer duration. Individuals suffering from these adjustment and stress reactions are less likely to be seen by their GPs in the first instance who are in turn often unwilling to refer these patients as 'psychiatric cases'.

Behavioural Medicine

Stress regarding physical illness is increasingly acknowledged as an important factor within medicine itself which is encouraged to adopt a biopsychosocial approach to replace the more rigid biophysical approach of previous generations (Engel, 1977; Lipowski, 1977). Rachman and Philips (1975), in a now classic book, took the initiative in Britain in demonstrating the contribution of psychology to medicine; other relevant books by British clinical psychologists followed (Vingoe, 1981; Griffiths, 1982) as well as publications of interventions in specific medical settings (Broome, 1980; Nichols, 1981). There is a growing feeling of optimism among clinical psychologists that the behavioural techniques which had been successful in the treatment of mental illness will be equally if not more successful in the field of general health care. Lang (1980) justified this optimism in the following way:

> Experimental behavioral psychology is primarily a psychology of the intact central nervous system and the neurochemically normal brain. The tradition of experimental psychology is the study of normal human beings and animals, in search of general principles which can explain and systematize all behaviour. Thus, most of our information concerns how people in general learn, perceive, are motivated, and so forth. Instances of serious psychopathology represent deviations from the norm, which are by definition less readily predicted from our knowledge of human action and, indeed, represent inconsistencies with the principles of behaviour in which psychologists have confidence. Thus it is reasonable to expect that behaviour modification methods will be more effective with the psychologically normal individual (who happens to be suffering from illness) than with people afflicted by a fundamental disturbance of behaviour. The application of behavioural engineering to such tasks as psychological preparation for surgery, encouraging behaviour consistent with disease prevention, or maintaining a drug regime is more straightforward, more within the bounds of present knowledge, than the cure of a serious psychological defect.

Reading (1982), addressing himself to clinical psychologists in medical specialities other than psychiatry, advocated the development of group interventions, the use of ancillary staff, and the development and refinement of research methodologies including new measures of psychological states to meet the growing demand.

Matarazzo (1980) followed the development of behavioural health and health psychology from behavioural medicine. He offered the following definitions of behavioural health and health psychology:

> *Behavioural health* is an interdisciplinary field dedicated to promoting a philosophy of health that stresses *individual responsibility* in the application of behavioural and biomedical science knowledge and techniques to the *maintenance* of health and the *prevention* or illness and dysfunction by a variety of self-initiated individual or shared activities.
>
> *Health psychology* is the aggregate of the specific educational, scientific, and professional contributions of the discipline of psychology to the promotion and maintenance of health, the prevention and treatment of illness, and the identification of etiologic and diagnostic correlates of health, illness, and related dysfunction.

Clinical Psychologists in the Social Services

During the 1970s posts for clinical psychologists were developed in social services departments. Brown (1981) examined the differences between social services departments and the other two state agencies which had employed professional psychologists in the past, namely the health service and the local education authorities. In his view, social services departments differ from the other two in that they employ less trained professionals of any description, they foster a generic training and mode of operation for social work, and the scope of their responsibilities is more extensive than either health or education since these responsibilities extend to the welfare of every individual from birth to death. In addition, the department of social services has not yet created a dominant professional group and most departments have still to find a satisfactory mode of operation.

Bender (1979) proposed a multi-level approach as a model of operation for psychologists in social services departments. The three main levels suggested by his model were:

1. Working with clients, either individually or in groups,
2. Working with staff in helping larger groups of clients,
3. Working with managers in monitoring, policy, and planning.

Examples of activities carried out at each of the above levels were given from the activities of a group of psychologists who have developed services in the same social services department during a period of over ten years. Other clinical psychologists have been in evidence in assisting social services departments with their services for children, the mentally ill, and the mentally handicapped (Brown, 1981).

Regarding care in the community, a recent DHSS document stated:

Most people who need long term care can and should be looked after in the community. This is what most of them want for themselves and what those responsible for their care believe to be the best (DHSS, 1981, p.1).

The above document, although mainly concerned with the needs of elderly, mentally ill, and mentally handicapped people, also considered the physically disabled and the chronically sick for transfer to the care of social services departments. In view of this, one can only agree with Bender (1979) who concluded that -- 'social services departments, with their very wide range of provisions, offer great opportunity for the development of *community psychology*' (p. 9).

There has been a great deal of confusion regarding the nature of primary health care which has encompassed a variety of diversified activities carried out in the community.

Clinical psychologists have amply demonstrated their ability to contribute to acute or crisis intervention services as well as to those which cater for individuals who need long-term care and support in the community. Hopefully more prevention services will be developed including them in the future. In the view of their small numbers, it seems that they need to increase their effectiveness by using a combination of approaches and by being less case oriented than they have been in the past.

REFERENCES

Bender, M.P. (1979). Community psychology: When? *Bulletin of The British Psychological Soociety*, 32, 6-9.

British Psychological Society (1979). *Evidence to the DHSS Joint Working Group on the Primary Health Care Team.* Leicester: BPS.

Broadhurst, A. (1977). What part does general practice play in community clinical psychology? *Bulletin of The British Psychological Society*, 30, 305-309.

Broome, A.K. (1980). Clinical Psychology within obstetrics and gynaecology. *Bulletin of The British Psychological Society,* 33 357-359.

Brown, B. (1981). Constructing psychological services in social services. In 1. McPherson and A. Sutton (eds), *Reconstructuring Psychological Practice,* London: Croom Helm.

Davidson, A.F. (1977). Clinical psychological and general practice: A preliminary inquiry *Bulletin of the British Psychological Society*, 30, 337-338.

Department of Health and Social Security (1981). *Care in the Community: A Consultative Document on Moving Resources for Care in England.* London: DHSS.

Earill, L., and Kincey, J. (1980). Evaluation of psychological intervention at primary care level — a controlled trial. Paper presented at The British Psychological Society Conference, Aberdeen.

Eastman, C., and McPherson, I. (1982). As others see us: General practitioners' perceptions of psychological problems and the relevance of clinical psychology. *British Journal of Clinical Psychology*, 21, 85-92.

Engel, G.L. (1977). The need for a new medical model: A challenge for biomedicine. *Science,* 196, 129-136.

Griffiths, D. (ed.) (1982). *Psychology and Medicine.* London: BPS/ MacMillan.

Hallam, R.S., and Liddell, A. (1978). A community clinic for teaching psychotherapy. *Bulletin of The British Psychological Society,* 31, 145-146.

Hood, J.E. (1979). Clinical psychology and primary care: A plea for restraint. *Bulletin of The British Psychological Society,* 32, 422-423.

Ives, G. (1979). Psychological treatment in general practice. *Journal of The Royal College of General Practitioners,* 29, 343-351.

Johnston, M. (1977). The treatment of agoraphobia in general practice. *Behavioural Psychotherapy,* 5, 103-109.

Johnson, M. (1978). The work of clinical psychologist in primary care. *Journal of The Royal College of General Practitioners,* 28, 661-667.

Kat, B. (1978). Primary Health Care: On finding one's place in the team. *Bulletin of The British Psychological Society,* 31, 154-156.

Kat, B. (1981). The processes of primary health care. Paper presented at the West Midlands Branch of the DCP Symposium. 'The Why, What and How of Psychology and Primary Care', Worcester.

Kincey, J. (1974). General practice and clinical psychology — some arguments for a closer liaison. *Journal of The Royal College of General Practitioners,* 24, 882-888.

Koch, H. C.H. (1979). Evaluation of behaviour therapy intervention in general practice. *Journal of The Royal College of General Practitioners,* 29, 337-340.

Lamberts, H. (1979). Problem behaviour in primary health care. *Journal of The Royal College of General Practitioners,* 29, 331-335.

Lange, P.J. (1980). Foreword. In B. Melamed and L.J. Siegel (eds), *Behavioral Medicine: Practical Applications in Health Care.* New York: Springer.

Liddell, A., May, B., Boyle, M., and Baker, M. (1981). How to stimulate GP referrals to a clinical psychology unit. *Bulletin of The British Psychological Society,* 34, 164-165.

Liddell, A., May, B., Boyle, M., Baker, M., and Hughes, M. (1982). GP satisfaction with a clinical psychology unit service. *DCP Newsletter,* No. 37, 21-24.

Lipowski, Z. J. (1977). Psychosomatic medicine in the seventies: An overview, *American Journal of Psychiatry*, 134, 233-234.

McPherson, I., and Feldman, M.P. (1977). A preliminary investigation of the role of the clinical psychologist in the primary care setting. *Bulletin of The British Psychological Society*, 30, 342-346.

McPherson, I. (1981). Clinical psychology in primary health care: Development or diversion? In I. McPherson and A. Sutton (eds), *Reconstructing Psychological Practice*, London: Croom Helm.

Matarazzo, J.D. (1980). Behaviour health and behavioural medicine: Frontiers for a new health psychology. *American Psychologist*, 35, 807-817.

Nichols, K. (1981). Psychological care in general hospitals. *Bulletin of The British Psychological Society*, 34, 90-94.

Pritchard, P. (1978). *Manual of Primary Health Care: Its Nature and Organization*. Oxford: Oxford University Press.

Rachman, S.J., and Philips, C. (1975). *Psychology and Medicine*. London: Maurice Temple Smith. (2nd ed. 1978, Harmondsworth: Pelican).

Reading, A.E. (1982). Strategic and methodological aspects of behavioural medicine. *British Journal of Clinical Psychology*, 21, 79-84.

Spector, J. (1980). An evaluation of clinical psychologists' involvement in primary care. Unpublished M.Sc. thesis, North East London Polytechnic.

Trethowan, W.H. (1977). *The Role of Psychologists in the Health Services*, London: HMSO.

Vingoo, F.J. (1981). Clinical Psychology and Medicine: *An Interdisciplinary Approach* Oxford: Oxford University Press.

World Health Organization (1978). Glossary of mental disorders and guide to their classification. *In Manual of the International Statistical Classification of Diseases, Injuries and Causes of Death*, 9th ed. Geneva: WHO.

13

Psychological Factors for Spontaneous Regression of Cancer

Introduction

The phenomenon of spontaneous regression of cancer (SRC) has attracted the attention of medical-biological researchers as well as of psychologists and psychiatrists, the first being interested in the understanding of the biological mechanisms involved, the latter in the role of psychological factors. For both, the importance of this research is that the understanding of this phenomenon will eventually be of significance to the therapy of the cancer process.

Researchers of psychotherapy are familiar with the phenomenon of spontaneous remission of psychoneurotic disorders: in research on the effects of psychotherapy the spontaneous remission group represents the control group for the estimation of the degree of natural recovery from these disorders, independent of the formal psychotherapeutic treatment. This type of research is directed exclusively however to the calculation of the quantity of natural recovery and not, of course, at the exploration of the psychological change processes involved in it. There is, on the other hand, very interesting research on the phenomenon of spontaneous remission which is directed exclusively at the process of spontaneous remission itself. An excellent example is the research on spontaneous remission in alcoholics (Tuchfeld, 1981). In this paper we consider the possibility that psychological change processes are also involved in the phenomenon of SRC. It is clear however that, in comparison to psychoneurotic disorders and addictions, SRC poses a special problem, because the role of psychological factors in cancer remains controversial (Cassileth *et al*, 1985). Research on SRC is therefore also directed at the question of whether and how psychological processes influence the course of the somatic cancer process.

We start our paper by discussing some problems of definition. Then follows a review of the medical and psychological research on SRC and some theoretical explanations are discussed. Next, our own experience with psychological research on SRC is described and we conclude by discussing briefly the practical and theoretical relevance of this type of research.

Definition

In popular literataure and alternative thinking SRC is considered an example of a so-called "miracle cure". This indicates that the phenomenon is widely known in medical and lay experience. We need not follow, however, the popular (often occult or religious) thinking about it, but can approach the phenomenon in a strictly scientific way (van Kalmthout, 1985). This means that it should be defined in clear operational terms, and that explanations should be given by natural psychological and/or medical-biological theories. In this paper we will try to approach the phenomenon of SRC in this manner.

Everson and Cole (1966, p.4) give the following definition of SRC:

> "..... the partial or complete disappearance of a malignant tumor in the absence of all treatment or in the presence of therapy which is considered inadequate to exert a significant influence on neoplastic disease. It is not implied that

> spontaneous regression need progress to complete disappearance of tumor *nor that spontaneous regression is synonymous with cure;*...It is our feeling that the factors responsible for temporary regression of cancer in some patients may be the same factors which are responsible for permanent regression of cancer in other patients."

This definition implies not only that partial regression of the cancer-process is included, but also prolonged arrest and delay of metastasis or recurrence of cancer-growth. The latter assumes that reliable knowledge is available as to normal expected survival time, which is not always the case. The more extreme the arrest or delay the more reason there is to consider it a case of SRC according to the above definition.

In the reliable assessment of SRC it is important that no medical misdiagnosis is present. For that reason histologic confirmation of the primary tumour and/or metastasis is a prerequisite. Besides that, strong decay in general health (a manifest in loss of gut and weight) is an important indication of the seriousness of the illness, as is the opposite of SRC.

It should be noted also that the presence of medical or other therapies does not necessarily mean that SRC is excluded. If it can be reasonably assumed that the regression is not due to these therapies, SRC can be a possible explanation.

Although there are many pitfails here (even histologic misdiagnosis is possible), careful examination of each case certainly makes the material trustworthy regarding the question of the real existence of SRC. For our own research purposes we use the following criteria for including the case in our SRC group:

1. There should be no doubt about the diagnosis of cancer. Most of the time this means that histologic confirmation is necessary.

2. In the cancer process there must be a remarkable turning point, which is unlikely to be the result of a recognised adequate medical therapy. This turning point must manifest itself as a clear improvement of the somatic condition of the patient and in regression of tumour and/or metastasis.

3. Remarkable cases of arrest of the cancer-process are also included as possible cases of SRC. The longer the duration of the arrest (as manifest in prolonged survival-time, arrest of tumor-growth and delay of metastasis and/or recurrence of cancer growth) the greater the probability of SRC.

Review of Research

The most extensive medical documentation of SRC has been given by two surgeons, Everson and Cole, in their 1966 book (Everson & Cole, 1966). They collected 176 cases of SRC (according to their own definition as cited in this paper) from the published world medical literature during the period 1900 to 1965. In fact they studied many more cases, but a large number of cases were rejected by them because of about, inaccurate, or controversial histological diagnoses. The same scientific rigour was present in a conference on SRC, organised in 1976 by the National Cancer Institute of America (National Cancer Institute, 1976). Most notable from the present authors' perspective is the complete absence in these studies of any reference to the role of psychological factors. The medical explanations mentioned are, amongst others, misdiagnosis, false estimation of the effectiveness of medical treatment used, endocrine influences, and allergic or immune reaction. The latter two factors are certainly not incompatible with psychological explanations, since it is generally accepted that if psychological factors influence the cancer process this will be via the immune system (The Lancet, 1985).

Psychosomatic studies of SRC are much rarer than medical studies. As far as we know only three groups have published data on this topic, the psychosomatic cancer study group in New York, headed by psychiatrist Weinstock (1977), a Japanese group of the department of Psychosomatic Medicine of Kyushu University (Ikemi et al, 1975) and a Dutch group headed by the pathologist De Vries (Vries, 1986). Weinstock (1977) mentions twelve cases of SRC. On psychosocial aspects he stresses a favourable change in the situation just preceding the cancer shrinkage, the supportive role of the family, the placebo effect, and ".. the favourable inner change that occurs upon facing death (and deciding to live differently and more constructively)".

The 1975 Japanese study (Ikemi et al, 1975) is a carefully documented psychosomatic study of five cases of SRC. Besides the clinical history and course of illness a well documented life history is presented for each case. Among the psychosocial factors mentioned by these researchers are: accepting the responsibility for resolving an existential crisis in their life, the absence of anxious and depressive reacations and a dramatic change of outlook on life.

De Vries (1986) reports seven cases of SRC, selected from fifteen cases referred to his team. All seven cases could be demonstrated to obey the strict criteria of SRC. This study used semi-structured interviews to elicit psychosocial correlates of SRC and concluded that a relatively sudden increase in autonomous behaviour and/or a sudden change in attitude towards the illness, treatment or environment, are among the most important psychological correlates of SRC.

The studies certainly represent interesting pioneering efforts on the eventual role of psychological factors in SRC which deserve more extensive research in the future.

One Year of Research on SRC

Research in this field is directed at exceptional cases rather than at statistically determined group means. Therefore research methodology must be adapted to this end. As far as the medical diagnosis is concerned the most rigorous approach is necessary. In our research project we have ensured this by collecting the written documents from the medical specialists. After studying them carefully we make a precise summary of the crucial elements and ask the opinion of one external pathologist and one external oncologist. The search for psychological factors is conducted in an exploratory manner using semi-structured interviews. The specific questions asked concern medical history, reaction to diagnosis, changes during SRC and life history. The more data we collect the more specific our questions become. The same is true for our theorising. We consider it premature to make use of one limited theory, but little by little, our insight into this complex phenomenon is increasing, making it possible to formulate useful explanatory concepts. In the first year of our project we studied eight cases. In addition, two cases were referred that could not be interviewed because they did not know their diagnosis and their family physician, quite rightly, did not want to cause them worry. One other patient refused to cooperate because she denied her diagnosis. After extensive study two further cases had to be eliminated because medical intervention could not be excluded as the reason for the cure. One other case had to be excluded because of the lack of a histologically confirmed diagnosis, although the patient was known in her town as being a "miracle cure". So, five cases were left. One of these five cases could not be interviewed because the patient had died many years before (not because of cancer). We included this case is our project however, because the medical evidence was very convincing and the interview with the family physician gave us some information on the psychological factors.

All interviews were audiotaped and later transcribed. We are currently analysing this material and as more patients are interviewed we hope to find some general characteristics of this group of "survivors of expected death".

Discussion

Here we have briefly discussed the phenomenon of SRC, reviewed the relevant literatures and summarised our own one year experience with research on SRC. In concluding we would like to emphasise that this research seems to us of great importance both for psychosomatic medicine and psychotherapy in general. In cases of SRC a fundamental change process seems at work which may be crucial and common in all forms of psychotherapy and mental healing (Kalmthout et al, 1985).

REFERENCES

Cassileth, B.R., Lusk, E.J., Miller, D.S., Brown, L.L. & Miller, C. (1985). Psychosocial correlates of survival in advanced malignant disease. *The New England Journal of Medicine,* 312, 1551-1555.

Everson, T.C. & Cole, W.H. (1966). *Spontaneous Regression of Cancer.* W.B. Saunders: Philadelphia.

Ikemi, Y., Nakagawa, S., Nakagawa, T., & Mineyasu, S. (1975). Psychosomatic consideration on cancer patients who have made a narrow escape from death. *Dynamische Psychiatrie, 2, 77-92.*

Kalmthout, M.A. Van (1985). The scientific study of so-called miracle cures. Paper presented at the Second European Conference on Psychotherapy Research, Louvain-la-Neuve, Belgium, September 3-7.

Kalmthout, M.A. Van, Schaap, C.P. & Wojciechowski, F. (eds) (1985). Common Factors in Psychotherapy. Swets & Zeitlinger: Lisse.

The Lancet Editorial (1985). Emotion and immunity. *The Lancet,* July 20.

National Cancer Institute (1976). *National Cancer Institute Monograph,* 44.

Tuchfeld, B.S. (1981). Spontaneous remission in alcoholics. Empirical observations and theoretical implications. *Journal of Studies on Alcohol, 42,* 626-641.

Vries, M.J. de (1986).Crisis on transformatie: Lessen van wonderbaarlijke patienten. *Medisch Contact, 24,* 751-756.

Weinstock, Ch. (1977). Notes on spontaneous regression of cancer. *Journal of the American Society of Psychosomatic Dentistry and Medicine,* Vol. 24 (4), 106-110.

14

Psychosomatic Disorders

This chapter focuses on critical review of studies on cross-cultural epidemiology of some so-called psychosomatic disorders and of their over-hasty conclusions. There is a widely held view that migraine, essential hypertension, coronary heart disease (CHD), asthma, peptic ulcer and ulcerative colitis are rare and do not occur at all in many non-European countries or in "untouched" societies. Furthermore, this is often regarded as proof that such disorders are caused by western civilisation and emerge from industrial stress and the decay of families or other intact communities.

This is only true to some extent. Differences in prevalence of the disorders listed above certainly do exist, but they are mostly overestimated. Some of the differing prevalence rates can easily be explained by less subtle diagnostic means in non-European countries, for example by the lack of sophisticated X-ray examination, colonoscopy or electrocardiography. In addition it is a well established fact that even in European cities many people with migraine, essential hypertension and CHD will not seek a doctor's help, because they do not suffer from pain or decide secretly to endure it. For instance, a large epidemiological study on migraine in Wales yielded the results that approximately 50% of the persons suffering from migraine have never been seenby a doctor (Waters and O'Connor, 1975). A psychological investigation at the University of Hamburg found that even among students the percentage of migraine sufferers who never seek a doctor's help was nearly 45% (Koehler, to be published). On screening more than one million Americans it was detected that 27.7% of persons with high blood pressure (diastolic of 95mm Hg or above) were not previously diagnosed as hypertensives; the percentage of undiagnosed hypertensives was 49.2% for persons under 40 years of age (Stamler *et al*, 1976). In West Germany six million people have been diagnosed as hypertensive by medical examination; it is estimated that another three million hypertensives go unnoticed (for references see Koehler, 1985). Thus prevalence figures as assessed by clinical statistics are greatly underestimated which suggests that this effect is even more pronounced in rural societies, especially in isolated communities of the Third World. This general remark should be kept in mind since it applies to the remainder of this paper.

As for migraine, to my knowledge, no large-scale epidemiological investigations have yet been carried out in countries outside Europe or North America. Nevertheless it is a well established fact that attacks of typical migraine headache were observed in Mesopotamia 3000 years ago and Roman, Byzantine and Arabian physicians have tried to describe, explain and treat migraine attacks (for references see Koehler, 1985). In a very undisturbed part of Madagascar, I have diagnosed a case of severe classical migraine in a young man and in Bali I observed a young woman suffering from an acute attack of common migraine. These arguments are not very convincing of course, and they don't tell us anything about the real rate of prevalence. However, they should refute the widely held view that migraine is strictly limited to countries of western civilisation and emerged only some decades decades ago.

According to Groen (1970,p. 202) "ulcerative colitis is a disease of western culture, it is very rare in underdeveloped countries of Asia and Africa". No exact figures were communicated in Groen's acticle; however, cases of ulcerative colitis have been observed in India, Thailand, Turkey and some African countries (for references see Koehler, 1985). Furthermore one should bear in mind that diarrhoea is very common in underdeveloped countries, and that most of these patients are not examined properly to establish the cause of their disease. This I think we should not jump to the conclusion too early that western civilisation is the major cause of ulcerative colitis.

As for peptic ulcer, the assumption can definitely be refuted that prevalence rates are notably higher in western countries (for a thoroguh overview of empirical data see Pflanz, 1971). In spite of some difficulties in comparing data about prevalence rates we still have sufficient information that the incidence of peptic ulcer is not remarkably lower in at least some African or Asian countries. For example, in post-mortem examinations, peptic ulcers and scare were found more often in Uganda (14.5% in 1958) than Germany (11.4% on average between 1953 and 1962). Furthermore some studies yielded the result that the percentage of patients with duodenal ulcers amongst patients in hospitals was greater in India, Peru, Uganda and Sengeal than Italy, Greece or the Netherlands (see Pflanz, 1971, p. 127 f.). I shall not go further into details, but I quite agree with Pflanz who states: "nor can the psychosomatic claim be supported that duodenal ulcer is a 'disease of civilisation', in other words that 'civilisation' is conductive to certain kinds of psychological conflicts not found in persons who live in 'underdeveloped' countries" (p. 123).

To my knowledge, no large-scale epidemiological investigations on prevalence of asthma have been carried out in any part of the world (cf. Clark & Godfrey, 1977). Thus all figures communicated so far are based on clinical estimations, therefore not many conclusions can be drawn from these statistics. There are some interesting hints, however, that prevalences of asthmatic symptoms grows with the degree of industrialisation and adaption to western civilisation. For instance, it has been shown that asthma is very uncommon in the inhabitants of the Tokeleau Islands in Polynesia, whereas people from these islands who shift to New Zealand are much more likely to develop the disorader. The relative risk of asthma was found to be about 19 times greater in Tokeleau males and about 4.5 times greater in Tokeleau females in New Zealand compared with those in the Tokeleau Islands (Prior, 1977). It is questionable, however, what accounts for this. It must be left open for discussion whether the absence of industrial pollutants and chemicals in the home islands or the limited availability of daily products (the consumption of which can lead to allergic reacations) may be sufficient to explain the difference in prevalence rates. Similar data were communicated by Japanese authors (Ikemi *et al*, 1974). The incidence of child asthma, for instance, has increased twice as much in Japan since the war. It was discovered that incidence is considerably greater in industrial areas with a high degree of air pollution: furthermore the percentage of adult asthmatics has been shown to be higher in smokers than non-smokers. So one should be careful in drawing the conclusion that the psychological impacts of sociocultural changes account mainly for the growing prevalence of asthma in some countries.

There is ample evidence that hypertension is much less frequent in untouched isolated societies and rural populations of the Third World (for reviews see Prior, 1977; Ostfeld & D'Atri, 1977; Murphy, 1982, Koehler', 1985). Though, to my knowledge no epidemiological studies have been carried out in underdeveloped countries, it is fairly obvious that the prevalence of coronary heart disease (CHD) is much lower in less industrialised parts of the world. This statement should still be valid even if we take into account the fact that, due to less subtle diagnostic means figures concerning prevalence of CHD are certainly underestimated. In post-mortem examinations in Nigeria, for instance, myocardial infarctions were seldom found (Williams, 1971). It seems at first sight that lower prevalence rates of hypertension and CHD can be attributed to fewer stress factors in untouched societies, but this conclusion is certainly drawn too rapidly.

First, it should be kept in mind that essential hypertension and CHD develop on a larger scale only in individuals over 40-50 years of age. In the above mentioned screening study it was found that, based on the 95mm Hg cutoff, the rate per 1000 people with elevated diastolic blood pressure rose from 39.9 for the age group under 20 years (and 112.2 in the age group between 20 and 29) to 348.8 for those 60 to 64 years old (Stamler *et al*, 1976). Thus in populations where life expectancy is reduced, prevalence of these disorders is necessarily lower. In addition, nutritional factors play an eminent role in the pathogenesis of essential hypertension and CHD. It is a well established fact that excessive salt intake raises blood pressure, and that heightened fat intake and obesity increase the risk of hypertension and CHD. After a thorough review of data concerning epidemiology of high blood pressure, Ostfeld & D'Atri (1977, p. 31) come to the conclusion: "Our view is that rapid sociocultural change does, indeed, lead to a higher prevalence of high blood pressure and a greater rise in pressures with age. The intermediary mechanism is a change in diet that causes gain in weight. There is no need to assume that breakdown of traditional social roles and conflict about them directly affect blood pressure."

Finally it should be kept in mind that smoking habits also play an important part in the pathogenesis of arteriosclerosis. The influence of these variables must be eliminated before assumptions are made about different prevalence rates in European industrial countries and non-European rural societies and about the potential casual role of psychological factors.

Taking all this into account we cannot rule out that there are still differences in prevalence rates which cannot be attributed to statistical or biological factors, but they are certainly much smaller than figures published so far seem to suggest.

There is no doubt that the onset and course of somatic illnesses can be influenced by psychological variables, and that cross-cultural epidemiology can reflect their influence. This paper does not intend to demonstrate that cross-cultural epidemiological studies in psychosomatic medicine have yielded no or at best trivial results, and should thus be given up entirely. On the contrary, cross-cultural epidemiological research is a very sophisticated way of deriving hypotheses about psychological variables that may have some bearing on the development or maintenance of somatic diseases. Therefore, these should be carried out on a much larger scale than at present, but we should endeavour to keep the errors previously mentioned to a minimum. We must be sure that what we attribute to hypothetical psychological factors cannot simply be explained by organic variables we did not think of.

REFERENCES

Aoki, H., Ikemi, V. & Ikemi, A. (1982). Some psychosomatic disorders in the Japan from a cultural perspective. Psychosomatics, 23, 1171-1184.

Clark, T.J.H. & Godfrey, S. (Eds) (1977). *Asthma* Chapman & Hall: London.

Groen, J.J. (1970). Influence of social and cultural patterns on psychosomatic diseases. *Psychother., Psychosom., 18,* 189-215.

Ikemi, Y., Ago, Y., Nakagawa, Sh., Mori, Sh., Takahashi, N., Suematsu, H., Sugita, M. & Matasubara. H. (1974). Psychosomatic mechanism under social changes in Japan. *J. Psychosom, Res.* 18, 15-24.

Koehler, Th. (1985). *Psychosomatische Krankheiten.* Kohlhammer: Stuttgart.

Murphy, H.B.M. (1982). Blood pressure and culture. The contribution of cross-cultural comparisons to psychosomatics. *Psychother. Psychosom., 38* 244-255.

Ostfeld, A.M. & D'Atri, D.A. (1977). Rapid sociocultural change and high blood pressure. In Kasl, S. & Reichsman, F. (Eds), Epidemiogical studies in psychosomatic medicine. Advanced Psychosomatic Medicine, 9, 20-47.

Pflanz, M. (1971). Epidemiological and sociocultural factors in the aetiology of duodenal ulcer. *Advanced Psychosomatic Medicine, 6,* 121-151.

Prior, J. (1977). Migration and physical illness. In S. Kasl & F. Reichman (Eds). Epidemiological studies in psychosomatic medicine. *Advanced Psychosomatic Medicine, 9,* 105-131.

Stamler, J., Stamler, R., Riedlinger, W.F., Algera, G. & Roberts, R.H. (1976). Hypertension screeing of 1 million Americans. *Journal of Americal Medicine Association, 235,* 2299-2306.

Waters, W.E. & O'Connor, P.J. (1975). Prevalence of Migraine. *Journal of Neurology, Neurosurgery and Psychiatry, 38,* 613-615.

Williams, A.O. (1971). Coronary arteriosclerosis in Nigeria. *Br. Heart J.* 33, 95-100.

15

Changing Health Behaviour Outcomes in Asthmatic Patients

Together, asthma, chronic bronchitis and lung-emphysema constitute a group of lung diseases called Chronic Obstructive Pulmonary Diseases or COPD. Asthma is less destructive to the lung tissue than both the other diseases, for, between attacks, the asthmatic's respiration is normal and the patient has a normal life expectancy. Bronchial hyper-reactivity and immunological over-sensitivity play an important role in the pathogenesis of asthma, and attacks can be variably elicited by exogenous and psychological factors. In addition to the fact that COPD is still responsible for a considerable part of the mortality in western countries, a notable degree of morbidity exists, as these diseases are essentially incurable. According to the Dutch Asthma Fund, twenty per cent of the total absence from work and thirteen per cent of the total invalidity can be ascribed to COPD.

The true cause of asthma is unknown. On the one hand we find authors who claim that asthma is only an allergy: and on the other are those who believe that psychological disturbances are at the base of the illness. What is established, however; is that the way patients deal with their chronic illness influences both the course of the illness and the medical outcome. It is this which provides the focus for the present paper.

In a first study we investigated the relationship between coping with asthma and health behaviour outcomes. In order to do this, we developed a research model for coping with asthma on the basis of the stress appraisal theory of Lazarus and his colleagues (Lazarus & Folkman, 1984). The central idea of the model is that coping fulfils a mediating role in the relationship between anxiety and health behaviour outcomes, and that both disease characteristics and cognitions stored in long-term memory play a crucial role in the experience of emotions, in coping, and in health behaviour outcome in asthmatic patients (Maes & Schlosser, 1987a). The main research question derived from the model was "What is the influence of objective aspects of asthma (such as number of attacks and lung function), cognitive attitudes (such as optimism, locus of control and shame), anxiety and coping on: (a) well-being, (b) use of medical resources (such as the amount of medication taken daily and the number of hospital admissions during the last year), and (c) absence from work?" The results showed that coping variable such as reacting emotionally during attacks, focusing on asthma in everyday life, and maintaining a restrictive life-style explained considerable parts of the variance in the well-being of asthmatic patients, in the number of hospital admissions, and in the number of days absent from work because of asthma (Maes & Schlosser, 1987a). These findings were considered a solid starting-point for an intervention study, which aimed at altering coping behaviour in asthmatic patients in order to influence emotional distress and use of medical resources. The nature of the intervention and a pilot study to test it are described below.

Method

In order to change cognitions and coping in asthmatic patients, we chose Ellis's Rational Emotive Therapy as the basis for our intervention (Ellis, 1962: Ellis & Grieger, 1977). The programme itself consisted of eight two to three hour group sessions, in which ten asthmatic patients and their partners took part. During the first session, Ellis's scheme was introduced to the patients by a health psychoogist. The following sessions were devoted to a specific topic related to asthma. The topics were selected on the basis of prior need assessment, and concerned medical issues, physiotherapy and breathing exercises, use and consequences of medication, working situation and social security, sanitation, emotional distress, and professional and leisure activities. With the exception of the initial meeting, the standard course for each session was that, first, a health professional (depending on the topic, a lung specialist, physiotherapist, pharmacist, social worker, nurse or health psychologist) gave relevant information about the topic. The format was less a lecture than answers to questions which had emerged from the prior need assessment. Next, patients and their partners divided into three small groups and tried (under the supervision of a health psychologist and with the help of a list of specific questions) to discover irrational beliefs and inadequate coping strategies related to the topic. Finally, using the Ellis scheme, the results of the small group work were discussed in the larger group with a health psychologist. At the end of each meeting, the session was evaluated and homework was given. The effects of the intervention on cognitive attitudes towards asthma, emotional distress (anxiety, anger and depression), and medication consumption were determined by means of a pre-test post-test control group design which is described below.

Nineteen patients (9 females and 10 males) were referred to us by two lung specialists. They had a confirmed medical diagnosis of bronchial asthma and a forced expiratory volume in one second (FEV) of at least 80% of the predicted value either with or without use of a brochodilator, to exclude patients with emphysema. All patients were characterised by a high consumption of medication in proportion to more objective measurements of severity, but were not in hospital at the time of the study. The patients were matched for sex and age in order to obtain a comparable experimental (n=10) and control group (n=9). The experimental group received our programme in addition to standard medical care, whereas the control group received standard medical care only.

In order to measure the effects of the programme, the following instruments were administered to both groups of subjects before and immediately after the completion of the programme: the Respiratory Illness Opinion Survey of Kinsman et al (1976); the Asthma Coping Questionnaire of Maes et al (1986); the Dutch version of Spielberger's State-Trait Anxiety Inventory (Ploeg et al, 1980); the Dutch version of Spielberger's State-Trait Anger Scale (Ploeg et al, 1982); the Depression Scale of van Rooijen (Rooijen, 1977); and the General Questionnaire for Asthmatic Patients, developed by the present authors (Maes et al, 1986).

Results

Table 15.1 shows the results of analyses of covariance, using the pre-test scores as covariates. For the medication variables, the number of attacks was used as a second covariate. The table shows that there were significant effects for the coping variable "focusing on asthma in daily life" and for state depression, state and trait anger, and trait anxiety. In addition, there was a significant decrease in the number of cortiscosteroids taken in daily life.

Discussion

The results show that there was no significant effect of our intervention on cognitive attitude variables, perhaps because they are relatively stable personality characteristics, which cannot be changed in eight three-hour sessions. There were also no effects for the way patients coped with attacks. This time the explanation may well be that our programme focused on coping with *asthma* in everyday life rather than coping with *attacks.* In addition, it may be difficult to induce changes in the way patients cope with attacks by means of a cognitive intervention for the anxiety during attacks is so overwhelming that patients can hardly gain rational control over their behaviour. The programme did, however, have a significant reducing effect on "focusing on asthma in everyday life". In other words, when

Table 15.1

Results of analyses of Covariance with Pre-test Scores as Covariate on Post-test Scores in the Experimental Group Compared to the Control Group

Variables	*Experimental Group Means*		*Control Group Means*		*F Value*
	pre	*post*	*pre*	*post*	
Optimism	16.10	16.50	17.33	18.56	3.25
Locus of control	13.50	13.40	9.66	10.89	0.70
Shame	11.00	11.00	8.44	10.22	0.39
Minimising seriousness of attack	41.56	39.67	39.13	35.22	2.07
Rational action	22.60	21.70	21.57	20.89	0.35
Reacting emotionally	13.10	13.33	11.63	12.50	0.28
Maintaining a restrictive life-style	18.60	17.50	16.13	17.89	1.72
Focusing on asthma	16.50	15.78	15.13	16.67	3.25*
Hiding Asthma	10.10	10.50	11.00	9.22	2.99
State depression	10.00	8.33	7.33	10.33	3.13*
Trait depression	10.80	10.00	7.22	9.56	0.41*
State anger	15.00	14.70	12.78	18.22	3.58*
Trait anger	19.10	17.30	19.22	21.44	6.24*
State anxiety	54.50	52.80	50.89	50.00	0.38
Trait anxiety	47.80	40.50	41.22	52.13	44.52*
Oral corticosteroids	0.9	0.7	0.6	1.3	5.27*
Inhaled corticosteroids	0.9	0.5	0.8	0.8	1.58

* p<0.05

compared to the control group, patients who had received the programme were less preoccupied with their asthma in everyday life afterwards than before. Thus, the programme appears effective in altering one of the variables which may mediate reduction of emotional distress and use of medical resources.

As for emotional distress, the programme seems to be effective in reducing attack-related depression and anger but not attack-related anxiety. The intervention also had a significant effect on the experience of anxiety and anger in everyday life, but not the experience of depression. Although depression is a known form of emotional distress in asthmatic patients, anxiety may be considered a more important variable, since it predicts the use of medical resources (Fix et al., 1981; Creer, 1982, Steptoe, 1984; Maes & Schlosser, 1987b). The reduction of trait anxiety must, therefore, be considered an impressive result, especially since the effect is paralleled by the already mentioned change in coping with asthma in everyday life. Trait anger too was significantly reduced by the programme, perhaps suggesting that anger is another important measure, which the programme taught patients to control.

The intervention also led to a decrease in the number of oral corticosteroids taken in daily life - an important achievement, since the patients referred to us were generally taking large amounts of medication, which were disproportionate to their objective measures of severity. One possible explanation comes from Kinsman et al (1977), who demonstrated in a large group of asthmatic patients that people reporting high panic and fear were likely to be prescribed more intense doses of corticosteroids and to be maintained on steroid treatment for longer than similar patients who reported lower levels of anxiety. As there seems to be a linear relationship between anxiety and the prescription and use of cortiscosteroids, it is most likely that a decrease in *anxiety* is what brings about changes in the number of corticosteroids taken in daily life.

Finally there was no significant effect on the number or inhaled corticosteroids during attacks which was only to be expected since the intervention was not designed to change the way patients coped with attacks. In future interventions, more attention should be paid to attack related behaviour, and at least part of the programme should deal directly with attack-related coping patterns. In a second post-test one year after the intervention, we shall also be measuring the number of attacks, hospital re-admissions, visits to the physician and days absent from work because of asthma. The post-test will also inform us about the stability of the effects.

In summary, our programme has been found to have impressive effects. Patients who received the intervention were less preoccupied with their asthma in daily life; they experienced less emotional distress, both in attacks and in daily life; and they needed less maintenance medication. There is still, however, a long way to go; the effects must be demonstrated in a larger group of patients; and they must prove to be stable over time.

16

Psychological Problems and Support in a Burns Unit

Introduction

Advances in medical care since the Second World War have enabled previously unsaveable patients with serious burns to be saved, but there has been relatively little study of the quality of life for these survivors, nor developments in professional services geared to improving the psychosocial outcomes for these survivors.

The present study was initiated in collaboration with Professor Norman Bernstein whose work at the Shriner's Burns Institute of Boston has stimulated interest in the immediate and long term psychological impact of burns. This study investigates the psychological disturbance of patients inan English turns unit as the first step in planning a comprehsnive professional and self-help support service.

Design

As the study was conducted by a psychology student Jackie Lees, on placement with the Principal Clinical Psychologist (Physical Health), Louise Wallace, standard screening questionnaires were employed to measure mood state, adjustment to illness and self esteem. The questionnaires selected were approximate to the age range of patients from a few months to the very elderly.

The Mood and Adjustment scales were: Hospital Anxiety and Depression Scale (Zigmond and Snaith, 1983); Psychosocial Adjustment to Illness Scale (Derogatis and Loopez, 1983) and the Burn Specific Health Scale (Blades et al. 1982), for adults aged 16 years of over. Parents were interviewed for children and aged 3½-16 years usingthe Child Behaviour Checklist (Achenbach and Edelbrock, 1983) and the Behaviour Checklist of Richman and Graham (1971) for toddlers aged 2½-3½ years. Self-esteem measures were completed by the patient. These were the scales developed by Rosenberg (1965) for adults, Piers (1972) for those aged 8-16 years and an adapted version of the Coopersmith Self-Esteem Inventory (Coopersmith, 1967).

It must be recognised that these methods may only produce minimum estimates of disturbance since more skilled questioning is often needed to elicit problems such as alcoholism.

Procedure

Every effort was made to obtain a complete sample of patients discharged from the unit within a six week period. However, patients with little English (3) or major communication problems such as senile dementia (2) were excluded, although where possible information was obtained from relatives. Patients were seen in the clinic or at home, but a significant number (7) refused to be interviewed, and a small proportion (6) were untraceable, leaving 85 out of 99 patients who were interviewed at least once, 45 inthe first sample and 40 in the two year follow-up sample.

Results

It was expected that the sample would reflect the high degree of psychosocial problems typical of major burns injury. Table 16.1 shows the levels of psychological disturbance of patients in comparison to the norms available for the measure. As the sample contained patients across the whole age range, inevitably there are relatively small numbers represented in some of the age groups. For the adult patients at discharge from hospital, 31% showed clinically significant levels of anxiety, and

12.5% showed clinically significant levels of depression. The rates of depression were similar to those of a mixed medical sample, but the rates of anxiety were twice as great (Zigmond and Snaith, 1983). There was evidence of a slight decrease by six months follow-up, but the sample at two years showed no overall reduction in symptomatology. It is also interesting to note that 47% of patients at six months were experiencing significant problems of psychosocial adjustment on the Burns Specific Health Scale, that is, they were showing 22% or above levels of disability. Also in the two year sample, 33.3% of patients were showing above the 38% mean level of the normative sample. Using the Pasychological Adjustment to Illness Scale, which is standardised on healthy people, psychiatric and burn patients, the estimates of "psychiatric caseness" were 40% at 6 months and 35.7% at 2 years. The small samples of child and adolescent patients made interpretation difficult, but there was evidence that, while few patients showed behavioural problems at discharage, 1 out of 8 and 2 out of 12 patients at six months and two years were showing behavioural problems typical of a clinical population. Approximately two thirds of patients at discharge and six months, and a quarter of patients at two years were showing problems of social competence. Children less than 2½ years were not assessed for behavioural disturbance. Of the eligible children assessed at two years after injury, 75% were showing problems of significant behavioural disturbance.

The responses to specific questions asked of parents of children at six months and at two years revealed that they believed that all 24 children were significantly more withdrawn as a result of their burn injury at six months but only 1 out of 26 (4%) of the sample at two years believed their child was significantly withdrawn. Problems of sleep, toileting, aggression, overactivity, eatingand bedwetting were reported by not less than two and not more than seven out of 24 parents at six months and between one and five out of 26 at two years. Parents reported they had received no special professional help for these problems at either time period.

Table 16.1

No. of burn patients with "abnormal adjustment" in comparison to norms for the measure

Age/Measure	Discharge Total N	Discharge % of age sample	6 Months Total N	6 Months % of age sample	2 Years Total N	2 Years % of age sample
ADULT						
Mood:						
Anxiety	5/16	31.25	3/16	18.7	4/15	26.6
Depression	2/16	12.5	3/16	18.7	3/15	20.0
Psychosocial Adjustment:						
B.S.H.S.	-	-	8/17	47.1	5/15	33.0
P.A.I.S.	-	-	6/15	40.0	5/14	35.7
Self Esteem:						
Rosenberg	2/199	10.5	4/16	25.0	2/15	13.3
ADOLESCENTS						
Behavioural Adjustment:						
Achenbach* C.B.C.L.						
1. Behaviour	0/3	0	1/8	12.5	2/12	16.7
2. Social Competence	2/3	66.7	5/8	62.5	3/12	25.0
Self-Esteem						
Coopersmith	0/1	0	0/2	0	2/6	33.0
CHILDREN 3½ yrs						
Behavioural Adjustment:						
Achenbach* C.B.C.L.						
Self-Esteem:						
Coopersmith	1/1	100	1/2	50.0	3/6	50.0
CHILDREN 2½-3½ yrs						
Behavioural Adjustment:						
Richman Graham B.C.L.	2/2	100	0/1	0	9/12	75.0

*Data combined for adolescents and children.

T-test comparisons were made between scores at six months and two years on all measures with sufficient data, and there were no significant differences. This may indicate pre-existing differences between the two samples, or alternatively it may disprove the commonsense hypothesis that psychological problems diminish once the major medical treatment has been completed.

Conclusions

As discussed, the methods are only likely to produce minimum estimates of psychological disturbance. The psychological adjustment results confirm that clinically significant levels of mood disturbance are manifest in between 20% and 40% of adults and, although a number of the children were showing levels of behavioural disturbance equivalent to those of clinic populations, none of the patients were receiving professional help for their problems. Although the samples at discharge and six months and the sample at two years were different, there was no evidence that the majority of problems diminish by two years post injury. There is therefore evidence of a continuing need for psychosocial care for extended periods after a major burn injury for at least 20%-40% of patients. Further analyses are required to delineate those patients most at risk for adverse effects; likely factors include specific age groups, the visibility of injury and the availability of familial support.

Evidence from a survey of U.K. burn units to be reported shows that the problems of this particular unit are by no means unique, and that the psychosocial problems of burn injured patients are typically neglected. There are, however, models of some forms of both professional and self-help initiated supports which may go some way to ameliorate the psychological problems experienced by burn injured patients and their families which persist well beyond the time that the physical aspect of the burn injuries are healed, reconstructed and rehabilitated. Future studies will compare the samples with American samples studied by Professor Bernstein. In particular, in depth studies will be made of survivors who have completed all physical treatment in order to determine how well people cope with the residual permanent physical disability and disfigurement, and how they can best be helped.

17

Bulimia: Research and Treatment in France

Interest in Bulimia (repeated binges followed by self-induced vomiting or some other stringent strategy to avoid weight gain) has only received the serious attention of the French medical and scientific community since 1983. The aim of this paper is to report briefly on research already carried out or under way.

First Study: Epidemiology

The first research study carried out was a replica of the Fairburn and Cooper (1982) pilot study. The aim of the study was to ascertain the presence of Bulimia in France.

Results

An analysis of 500 questionnaires returned by women corresponding to DSMIII criteria yielded the following characteristics. The mean age of the sample was 29 (s.d. 8) and average duration of the eating disorder was 10 years (s.d. 7). Two thirds of the population were normal weight (measured by a body mass index W/h2). Half of the 500 women (49.3%) binged once a day or more. Among the strategies to avoid weight gain, self-induced vomiting was used by 51.2%(N=256 cases). Laxative abuse and medical complications (amenorthoea, spasmophilia, dizzy spells) were also commonly found.

The difference between the main body index of the vomiters and that of the non-vomiters was significant at the threshold $p<0.01$, which tends to indicate a relative efficacity of the method.

This study of confirms the presence of Bulimia in France, obtaining comparable characteristics of the population to those obtained by Fairburn and Cooper in their pilot study. The main differences [a higher mean age of the sample, 29 (s.d. 8) versus 23.8 (s.d. 5.5) and greater laxative abuse (38.5% vs 18.8%)] could be due to the different readership of the magazines involved or a real difference between the two populations.

Second Study: A Preliminary Report

In November, 1985, a two-page questionnaire on eating habits was published in another woman's magazine (younger readership, accent on health, exercise and beauty).

One of the aims of the survey was to ascèrtain how many women considering themselves Bulimic actually correspond to the DSM criteria.

Results

The number of women who reported binge-eating and who could not currently be diagnosed as anorexic was 1227.

When the questionnaires were analysed as to conformity with the other four diagnostic criteria required to qualify as bulimic, only 494 subjects (40.3%) could be considered as fulfilling all the DSMIII criteria. Of these, 23.1% were vomiters (N=114) and 76.9% non-vomiters (N=380). Approximately the same percentage of subjects reported three out of the four criteria (40.42%, N=496), but not always the same ones. Finally a group of 247 subjects. (20.1%) corresponded to only one or two of the criteria (binge-eating episodes, either alone, or else with one other criterion). These figures confirm that the DSMIII excludes a certain number of cases (in our study 60%) of women who manifestly suffer from binge-eating behaviour and need treatment for this disorder.

The preliminary results of the second study also bring to light a significant difference in the percentage of vomiters among women meeting the DSMIII criteria: in the first study, 51% in the second 23%. The discrepancy between the vomiting figures obtained is possibly due to the younger, health-orientated readership of the second magazine.

Outcome Research

A controlled treatment programme was set up in three medical centres in 1984-85. Clinical and psychological testing was carried out at the beginning and end of each six month period. Two groups of patients started treatment, one in March, 1984, the other six months later.

Of the 34 patients who returned for evaluation after treatment, most had been treated by cognitive behavioural methods, one third individually and two thirds in groups.

Results

Acting as their own controls, the bulimic patients showed definite improvement in bingeing behaviour and in all the personally characteristics assessed at the end of six months of treatment. The difference in the mean scores of the various tests before and after treatment was significant for all measures, with $p<.01$ for the scales of Depression and Extraversion (E.P.I.) and $p<.001$ for Self Esteem, Self Assertion, Body Image and Interpersonal Sensitivity.

These results correspond to an increase in Self Esteem, Assertiveness and positive Body Image and a decrease in the factors measured by Eysenck's E.P.I. (Extraversion and Interpersonal Sensitivity)as well as a decrease in Depression.

Discussion

Surprisingly, the mean score obtained on the Extraversion scale of the E.P.I. is significantly less after treatment than before (8.76 vs 11.47). However, this scale includes a certain number of

Psychological Assessment of Bulimics before and after Treatment **Comparison of mean scores**					
	Pretest	*s.d.*	*Posttest*	*s.d.*	*Sig.*
E.P.I. Neurot	14.15	4.95	7.85	5.28	.001
E.P.I. Extrav.	11.47	3.93	8.76	3.90	.01
Depression	30.24	14.3	18.24	12.09	.01
Self Esteem	33.26	12.59	42.18	13.89	.001
Assertiveness	101.35	23.26	117.35	16.59	.001
Body Image	21.97	9.71	30.97	10.44	.001

items related to impulsivity, and most bulimics consider their bingeing to be impulsive and due to lack of control. An improvement in bingeing behaviour is therefore most likely to modify any measure of impulsivity.

It does seem that such variables as poor Self Esteem, lack of Assertiveness, Hypersensitivity, Impulsiveness, poor Body Image and Depression are closely linked to the presence of Bulimia and improve when this condition itself improves.

REFERENCES

Aimez, P. & Michaut, S. (1986). Bulimia Nervosa in France. *In Proceedings of the 15th Conference on Psychosomatic Research,* London, Chapter 37, John Libby & Co.

Fairburn, C.G. & Cooper, P.J. (1982). Self-induced vomiting and bulimia nervosa: an undetected problem.

British Medical Journal, 284, 1153-1155.

18

The Mental Health of Ethnic Minorities

Britain has always been a centre for migration. Many people have left this country to settle elsewhere in the world and fewer, but still substantial numbers of people, have come from elsewhere to live here. Since the second world war, however, there have been some changes in the patterns of immigration to Britain which have affected the way in which immigration is regarded. First, an increased proportion of immigrants are non-white and therefore more visible than the previous waves of Irish, Jewish and European immigrants which occurred earlier in this century. Second, some of the immigrants came from very different religio-cultural backgrounds to those of the host society and, what is more, some groups have shown no desire to abandon their culture of origin and to become homogenized into the dominant Anglo culture. Third, perhaps as a result of the fact that many post world war II immigrants came from societies which had previously been subjected to British imperialism, prejudice, racism and discrimination against them has become widespread.

In the 1970s the liberal establishment became concerned about a number of aspects of this migration, one of which was the mental health of those involved (others were, for example, the progress of children of immigrants in schools, equality of opportunity in employment and housing, "race" relations etc.).

Perhaps the most extreme, and in many ways misleading and distorted expression appeared in a booklet published by the Commission for Racial Equality entitled: "Aspects of Mental Health in a Multi-Cultural Society". Based on a few early studies of mental illness rates among West Indian and Asian immigrants which were methodologically weak and which have been discredited (Cochrane, 1983), the CRE perpetuated the myth that ethnic minorities, and immigrants in particular, pay a heavy psychological price in terms of mental illness for living in Britain. This booklet listed the following as being groups at special risk of mental illness: immigrant adolescents, second generation immigrants, Muslim women, Sikh women, Hindu women, West Indian women, West Indian men, Asian men, the elderly - in other words almost everyone who was not native born white British.

The fact of the matter is that rates of mental illness, however these are indexed, are very variable between different ethnic groups, some being higher than those of natives but more often they are lower than those of natives (Cochrane, 1977; 1983).

Take, for example, the most recent figures available from the DHSS. The considerable difficulties involved in defining and analysing these data have been described elsewhere (Cochrane & Bal, in press) but they do provide the most accurate picture of mental hospitalisation rates broken down by country of birth (not ethnic origin) available anywhere.

These data are broadly in line with those resulting from an analysis of 1971 admissions data (Cochrne, 1977). The most obvious differences between the two studies are the lower rates of admission in 1981 compared to 1971 found for those born in India and for Pakistani born females. What is clear however is that the rates of admission for Asian born groups are actually substantially lower than those of the native born. The rates of admission for the Caribbean born are basically similar to those of the English born - the males being slightly higher, the females slightly lower. The rates of admission for the Irish born are particularly high.

Table 18.1

Age Adjusted Rates of Admission to Mental Hospitals in England, 1981, per 100,000 Population aged 16 Years and over by Country of Birth

Country of birth	*No. in population (1000s)*	*No. of admissions*	*Rates per 100,000 Males*	*Females*
England	41,084	157,763	419	583
Scotland	731	5,451	740	847
N. Ireland	202	1,601	793	877
Ireland	567	6,192	1,051	1,102
Caribbean	292	1,590	565	532
India	379	1,210	317	326
Pakistan	227	500	259	233

1. Includes "Ireland - part not stated".
2. Includes Bangladesh.
3. Includes those for whom country of birth was not stated, redistributed as described in Cochrane, 1977.

The admission data in Table 18.1 are for all diagnoses combined and this, of course, conceals many interesting variations in diagnostic patterns between the various groups. The most significant of these are the extraordinarily high rates of schizophrenia found among the Irish born and the Caribbean born populations of England. The figures for men (expressed as rates per 100,000) are English born - 81, Irish born - 191, and Caribbean born - 278. Thus, Caribbean born males have a schizophrenia rate approximately three and a half times that of English born males. The rates for those born in India and Pakistan are also higher than the native born rate (with the exception of Pakistani born females). Interestingly, although the Scottish born residents of England have high overall admission rates (Table 18.1), their rates for schizophrenia are not so exceptional, being 99 per 100,000 for men and 112 per 100,000 for women. These findings for schizophrenia are difficult to explain but a number of hypotheses have been put forward (Cochrane and Bal, in press), and the possibility of misdiagnosis, especially of black patients, cannot be ruled out.

The data in Table 18.1 raise several other important questions, some of which are addressed in subsequent papers:

1. Mental hospital admission figures refer only to actual migrants, i.e. those born abroad but now living in England - what of the "second generation"? If the patterns of mental illness found in the different groups is associated with the stresses of migration and relocation into a different culture, should we expect the children of immigrants and subsequent generations to show a pattern more similar to that of the native born white English? Dermot McGovern will consider one aspect of this question with regard to schizophrenia among the Caribbean born and their descendants.

2. The repeated finding that those migrating from India and Pakistan have relatively low rates of mental hospital admissions inevitably raises the question of whether this particular index of mental illness is equally appropriate for all ethnic groups. It has been suggested, for example, that Asian born residents of Britain are likely to take advice from traditional healers and thus possibly avoid coming into contact with formal psychiatric services. It is also possible that some psychologically disturbed immigrants return to their native land rather than seek help here and so again do not appear as a statistic in the mental hospital admission data, even though they may be severely disturbed. Even if Asian people do seek medical help for their problems is it not possible that misunderstandings between doctor and patient are more likely to occur than in the case of an English person consulting a doctor? There are good reasons for thinking that the way in which psychological problems are

conceptualised, developed, described and presented, differ considerably between cultures (Marsella and White, 1982; Rack, 1982).

Sukhwant Bal takes up one of these themes when he discusses the hypothesis that Asian patients are more likely to "somaticise" psychiatric problems than are English patients and therefore run the risk that the true nature of their disorder will go undetected by their doctors.

3. Some particularly striking data contained in Table 18.1 are those showing the exceptionally low rate of admission of Pakistani born females, which is considerably less than half that of their English born equivalents. Again, while this is not a new observation, it has never been satisfactorily explained. One possible reason for their very low rate of in-patient treatment is that Pakistani women shun contact with the medical and psychiatric services, but the evidence to hand indicates that this is unlikely to be the whole story (Cochrane, 1983; Brewin, 1980). It could also be that Pakistani women have more successful ways of dealing with the stresses they encounter in everyday life than do English women and this is one of the questions addressed by Shamim Mahmud in her paper which reports on a comparison of life stresses and symptoms in Pakistani and English women.

4. So far this paper has dealt exclusively with the mental health of migrants to Britain with no reference to the great deal of work that has been done in other countries. Indeed, there are good reasons for suspecting that the situation of newcomers in those countries which have traditionally received a lot of immigration (such as Canada, Australia and the USA) will be different from those pertaining here. In the USA for example most immigrants typically come to a society used to large scale migrations from many sources and arrive with

every intention of settling for good, and of adapting, to some extent at least, to the dominant culture. Neither of these conditions necessarily exist in Britain. Neither is it the case that immigrants to the USA came from societies which have previously experienced colonial subjugation by the society to which they are migrating, as is the case for many migrants to Britain.

If extrapolations from the American (and the white Dominion) situation to Britain are unwise, what about the rest of Europe? Are there more continuities of experience of migration (from both sides) in countries which have a greater geo-political similarity? Elina Haavio-Mannila presents a detailed analysis of the mental health and social adjustment of Finns and Yugoslavs living in Sweden. It shows that there are some similarities between the way Finns respond to their new environment (and the way in which they are perceived by native Sweedes) and the patterns of adaptation of the Irish in England.

There are now sufficient data on the relative mental health statuses of different ethnic groups within societies. It is time to focus more explicitly on explanations for these patterns of differences in adjustment. The four papers which follow are examples of such studies. They take off from what is well established and attempt to show how survey research, epidemiology and statistical studies can be used to provide valuable insights and practical implications for clinical psychology.

19

Life Stress and Symptoms: A Comparative Study

Introduction

Comparisons of the psychological health of immigrant ethnic groups with that of the native population in Britain, have yielded ambiguous results. The rates differ depending on whether treated morbidity or untreated morbidity figures are examined. For instance, Pakistani immigrants had low admission rates to mental hospitals in comparison to the natives but reported similar symptom levels in a community study (Cochrane and Stopes-Roe, 1977).

Two explanatory hypotheses have been put forward to account for the differential rates found. It has been suggested that low rates of treated morbidity could be attributed to differential selection. That is where migration is difficult and failure to achieve acceptable living standards is not due to personal failure, it would be the most stable and enterprising individuals who succeeded in migrating. Higher rates of psychological ill-health have been explained in terms of negative selection. However, equivalent rates of untreated morbidity have been attributed to under utilisation of psychiatric services and the use of lay health networks. Furthermore, there has been no published research validation to indicate whether immigrants are a negatively or positively selected group in comparison to the non-migrants remaining in their country of origin.

The other major hypothesis put forward to explain differential rates of illness between migrants and natives is that of stress. Although a number of studies have linked higher rates of illness among migrants with stress, this has been a post hoc explanation. With two exceptions most investigations in the field of migration and mental health have largely ignored the findings of the increasing literature on stress and psychological disorder.

It was against this background that the present work was done. There were two aims: to investigate whether the earlier findings of equivalent rates in a community survey could be repeated, and to determine whether there was a link between stress and illness in a group of Pakistani women.

Women were specifically selected to minimise the effect of self selection. Usually the decision to migrate is made by Pakistani men, with women migrating to join their families later. It is unlikely that mate selection would be operating either, with enterprising men choosing similar spouses, as Pakistani marriages tend to be arranged by families who favour traditionalism rather than enterprise in a prospective wife.

Selection of Sample and Instruments Used

Two groups of women, 39 Pakistani and 40 English, were randomly selected from the general practice records of a Health Centre in Central Birmingham. Details of the criteria for inclusion in the study and specific procedures for selection have been reported previously (Mahmud, 1983).

Initially, potential respondents were contacted by a letter in either Urdu or English, as appropriate, and this was usually followed by a telephone call or visit. The response rate was 87% for the English sample and 82% for the Pakistanis. All women were interviewed in their own homes, in the appropriate language, on at least three occasions. Information was collected about stressful life events and long term difficulties in the year prior to the interview; the presence or absence of symptoms as well as degree of severity; and finally the appropriate general practitioner was contacted for information on the frequency and type of consultation in the previous year for each woman.

Information on stressful life events was collected using a translated and adapted version of the Life Events Interview (LEI) developed by Brown and Harris (1978). This interview had been adapted to include events which would be relevant to the immigrants experiences in Britain. The adapted and translated interview was piloted in a reliability study in Edinburgh (Mahmud, 1983). The results had indicated a satisfactory degree of reliability for use with Pakistani immigrants. Obviously when the English women were interviewed, the English version of the adapted instrument was used, with the exception of items which were only relevant to immigrants.

A scoring system developed by the original authors was used to determine the differences between events and difficulties as well as the degree of threat these held, for the women concerned. The level of threat corresponded to scores for major or minor events and difficulties. Previous work based on the life events interview has indicated that it is the occurrence of major (or severely threatening) events and diffculties which have consequences for the psychological health of the individual.

Symptom level and symptom severity were established using the comprehensive Psychopathological Rating Scale (CPRS). However as the correlation between reported and observed symptoms for both the Pakistani sample ($r=0.64$, $p<.001$) and the English sample ($r=0.83$, $p<.001$) was high, the decision was made to base later analyses on the dependent variables of reported symptoms and consultation rates only.

Finally information about GP consultations was collected by requesting the G.P. concerned to complete a form giving date of consultation, nature of the problem, whether it was a first or subsequent episode of the problem and, finally, the action taken.

Results

The results will be discussed in two sections. The first section will focus on the difference and similarities between the two groups (Table 19.1) while the second will focus on the relationship between the independent and dependent variables for both samples.

The expectation that Pakistani women would have equivalent levels of psychological symptoms to the English women was not substantiated. Pakistani women reported significantly fewer symptoms in comparison to the English sample. Similarly Pakistani women had significantly fewer consultations with their GP compared to the English women. The mean annual consultation rate was 1.92 for the Pakistani women in comparison to 3.75 for the English women. However no differences were found between the two groups when symptom severity was examined.

Table 19.1

Differences in scores on measures of stress, symptoms and consultation rates in two samples of women

Variable	*Ethnic Group*				*t value*
	Pakistani N=39		*English N=40*		
	$\bar{x}$	s.d.	$\bar{x}$	s.d.	
Reported symptoms	8.18	5.45	11.20	5.21	2.52*
Observed symptoms	3.38	2.99	4.03	3.25	0.91
GP visits in year	1.92	1.94	3.75	1.94	3.02*
Total LTD	4.69	1.82	5.78	2.55	2.18*
Major LTD	1.77	1.37	2.23	1.75	1.29
All events	2.64	1.66	6.03	3.38	5.67**
Major events	0.18	0.39	0.35	0.92	1.08

*=p<0.05; **=p<0.01

Significant differences were found between the two groups for two measures of stress. English women reported significantly more of both total Long Term Difficulties (LTD)and total number of events, while Pakistani women reported fewer LTDS as well as a smaller total number of events. However, when stress was broken down into separate categories of severe and non-severe stress for both LTDs and events, no differences were found.

Stress was directly related to the dependent variables of psychological symptoms for both samples. For the Pakistanis, major events, major LTD and total LTD were significantly correlated with reported symptoms. For the English women, all measures of stress were significantly correlated with reported symptoms. However, with one exception, stress was not significantly correlated with frequency of consultation. The exception was for the English sample where a significant relationship was found between total LTD and frequency of consultation.

The relationships between the two independent variables and the dependent variables were examined by multiple regression analyses. The rationale for this was to predict the variance in reported symptoms and consultation rates for the two samples respectively using a combination of stress variables. For the Pakistani sample major events and major LTD successfully explained 37.2% of the variance in reported symptoms. For the English sample major LTD on its own explained 27.8% of the variance in reported symptoms. While major events did explain a further proportion of the variance, it was entered later into the regression equation for the English sample, other variables such as social support being entered earlier in the analysis.

Finally, the stress variables were not successful in explaining a significant proportion of the variance in consultation rates for either sample.

Discussion

The results suggest that, though the English women experienced significantly more overall life events and long term difficulties, there were no difference between the groups with respect to major life events and major long term difficulties. The present finding of more overall life stress for the English sample is in agreement with results reported earlier in the literature (Cochrane & Stopes-Roe, 1977); the only point of departure is in the lack of difference between the group when compared with respect to severe stress.

Similarly comparable results to those reported earlier in the literature (Cochrane & Stopes-Roe,1977; Roskies et al, 1977) were found when the association between stress and symptoms was examined. Given the different measures used in earlier studies and the present work both in the assessment of psychological symptoms and life stress, the comparability of the results is reassuring.

In contrast to earlier findings, the proportion of variance in psychological symptomatology explained by life events was much higher in this study. Previous work has indicated that life events account for approximately 10% of the variance in psychological well being (Cochrane & Sobol, 1980); however, the proportion of variance accounted for by major events and long term difficulties was higher in the present work.

Although Pakistani women reported less experience of stress, these results do not justify the dismissal of the hypothesis which links migrants' psychological health with the stress encountered. The results of the multiple regression analyses clearly indicate that severe stress accounts for the greatest proportion of variance explained in psychological symptoms among Pakistanis. This lends support to the contention that stress is implicated in migrants' psychological disturbance.

In contrast to earlier work (Cochrane & Stopes Roe, 1977, 1981) where no differences were found, Pakistani women reported lower levesls of symptoms than did native women in this project. There are two probable explanations for this. First, it is possible that the different instruments used in the previous work and the present study elicited different patterns of symptoms. Second, it is possible that when a scale, such as used in previous work, contains a greater number of items concerning physical symptoms, people with physical illness and little or no emotional disorders could show up as false positives (Muller, 1971) since physical illness may or may not reflect psychological distress.

There were no difference between the groups with respect to the severity of symptoms. That is, although Pakistani women had fewer symptoms than did English women on average, the symptoms they had were of equal severity. Pakistani women also had lower rates of consultation in comparison to the English women. This may be due to the use of alternative treatment networks, but it has been suggested (Rack, 1982) that the use of traditional healers of lay networks is a supplement, rather than an alternative, to orthodox medicine. The obvious explanation is that immigrant women in this study consulted less frequently than the English women because they had less illness. However, the consultation rates for the Pakistani women were not significantly associated with the presence of reported psychological symptoms. This would therefore, suggest that there is not as direct and obvious a relationship between psychological symptoms and going to the doctor for the Pakistani women as there is for English women.

Although the present results suggest that Pakistani women have lower levels of psychological symptoms in comparison to the English women as well as lower consultation rates, the results need to be interpreted with caution. These findings are at variance with the only other two studies which have examined psychological symptoms (Cochrane & Stopes-Roe, 1981) and consultation rates (Brewin, 1980) among Pakistanis using community samples. It may be that the results differ from earlier work on account of either the differing instruments used or the particular special context of the ethnic group studied.

The major findings of the present work would suggest that the differences in the psychological health of a minority ethnic group and of native women are not a consequence of some fundamental difference between the groups, but more a consequence of their life situations. The same psychological processes underlie health and illness irrespective of ethnicity.

REFERENCES

Brewin, C. (1980). Explaining the lower rates of psychiatric treatment among Asian immigrants to the UK. *Social Psychiatry, 15,* 17-20.

Brown, G. & Harris T. (1978). *Social Origin of Depression: A Study of Psychiatric Disorder in Women.* Tavistock: London.

Cochrane, R. & Sobol, M. (1980). Life stresses and psychological consequences. In M.P. Feldmal & J. Oxford (Eds.) , *The Social Psychology of Psychological Problems.* Wiley: London.

Cochrane, L. & Stopes-Roe (1977). Psychological and social adjustment of Asian immigrants to Britain: a community survey. *Social Psychiatry, 12,* 195-207.

Cochrane, R. & Stopes-Roe, M. (1981). Psychological symptom levels in Indian immigrants to England - a comparison with natives. *Psychological Medicine,* 11, 319-327.

Mahmud, S. (1983). Life stresses, social support and psychological symptoms in Pakistani women in Britain. Doctoral dissertation, University of Birmingham.

Muller D.J. (1971). Discussion of Langener's psychiatric scale: a short screening device. *American Journal of Psychiatry, 128,* 601-606.

Rack, P. (1982). *Race, Culture and Mental Disorder* Tavistock: London.

Roskies, E., Iida-Miranda, M.L. & Strobel, M.G. (1977). Life changes as predictors of illness in immigrants. In C.P. Spielberger & I.G. Sarason (Eds), *Stress and Anxiety.* Hemisphere Publications, London.

20

Physical Handicap

Although the number of clinical psychologists working with the physically handicapped is small there has already been diversification of the settings where they work and the role that they take. Initially they were almost exclusively based in specialist rehabilitation units and providing a service only for that unit. Now they provide an area based service covering young disabled units, homes for the disabled, special care units and general hospital rehabilitation deparatments. Their role has also changed. The increasing tendency is for clinical psychologists to train other professions, such as physiotherapists and occupational therapists, in techniques of assessment and treatment, rather than work directly with patients.

The importance of psychological factors in physical handicap has long been recognized and motivation, personality, and attitudes are important determinants of whether a person adapts to his disability. These factors are being systematically investigated so that appropriate assessment and training techniques may be developed. The role of the psychologist has been to determine which variables affect the process to adaptation to disability and to determine how adaptation may be improved. They then train others in the use of these techniques, so that they may be applied to a larger proportion of patients.

The role of the clinical psychologist working with the physically handicapped is given elaborate treatment hereunder:

MONITORING THE EFFECTS OF DISABILITY

Measurement of Disability and Handicap

There is increasing emphasis on the objective evaluation of the extent of physical disability and its associated handicap. This is needed in order to provide a basis for the allocation of services, to record progress, and to predict the outcome of rehabilitation. Because of their experience in the design of assessment techniques, clinical psychologists have become involved in the development of measurement techniques for other professions.

Two types of assessment are needed. One is the measurement of physical disability, that is the loss of functions resulting from the medical condition. Examples are techniques to assess hand function (Lyle *et al.*, 1979), motor function in stroke patients (Lincoln and Leadbitter, 1979), and driving skills (Smith and Wilson, 1980).

The second type of assessment measures handicap, the social disadvantage which may result from the physical disability. For example, questionnaires have been designed to investigate the effects of memory impairment in head injury patients (Sunderland and Harris, 1980) and the effects of brain damage on personal and social life (Oddy *et al.*, 1978; Coughlan and Humphrey, 1980).

In addition, many of the assessments currently used by physiotherapists and occupational therapists are being improved by standardization of administration and scoring, such that a more objective interpretation of results may be possible. Hitherto, there has rarely been any evaluation of reliability of these measures, despite the fact that they are used by several different therapists and as measures of change. Clinical psychologists are helping to assess the reliability and validity of some of these assessments and thereby to create improved means of monitoring changes in ability, including the response to treatment.

Psychological Assessments

Psychological assessments of a more traditional type are also carried out. These are generally to answer one of three questions:

1. What is the person's level of functioning, such that appropriate guidance may be given in relation to education or employment?

2. What cognitive abilities and disabilities does this person have which may affect his rehabilitation or require specific intervention?

3. Are there psychological factors associated with the physical disability which may affect this person's response to treatment or adaptation to disability?

The assessment of overall level of functioning in relation to education or employment is generally based on the standardized test procedures used with the non-physically disabled population, for example Wechsler Adult Intelligence Scale (Wechsler, 1955), and Progressive Matrices and Mill Hill Vocabulary (Raven, 1958). Allowances are made according to the type of disability but these are rarely standardized and normative data are not usually available for the modified versions of the tests. Such data need to be collected if standard tests are to be widely used with a physically disabled population. However, the advantage of the present system is that it shows how a disabled person will compare with the general population if no allowances can be made for his disability.

Assessments of cognitive abilities and disabilities suffer less from the limitation imposed by physical disability because there is a wider variety of tests available covering the major cognitive categories. If the patient has motor speech difficulties verbal abilities may be assessed on written tasks such as the Mill Hill Vocabulary (Raven, 1958). If he is unable to write, the synonyms section of this can sometimes be carried out using a pointer. Although written forms of the comprehension and similarities test of the WAIS may not be exactly equivalent to the spoken version, they usually provide sufficient information for the referral question to be answered. Ideally, approriate normative data should be obtained. Visuospatial abilities are usually assessed on the Block Design of the WAIS or copying the Rey-Osterreith figure (Rey, 1959). However, if the patient has insufficient manual dexterity for these tasks, there are other tests available, include Cube Counting (Ratcliff, 1970). Incomplete Pictures (Gollin, 1960), and Unusual Views (Warrington, unpublished). Memory testing presents further problems. Writing answers to verbal memory tasks such as the Wechsler Logical Memory (Wechsler and Stone, 1945) is rarely used because the time from hearing to recall is longer than in oral tests. Other tests of verbal memory which are more often used are Williams Delayed Recall (Williams, 1968) and the Forced Choice Words Tests (Warrington, 1974). Visual memory tests usually involve drawing geometric forms, but there are alternatives such as the multiple choice version of the Benton Visual Retention Test (Benton, 1950), Warrington non-verbal retention test (Warrington and James, 1967), and a Forced Choice Faces Recognition. Some patients, particularly those with multiple sclerosis, also have poor visual acuity, which makes these tasks impossible. For this reason Staples and Lincoln (1981) devised a maze learning test, requiring only sufficient vision to see whether a light was on and sufficient motor control to operate a lever, to test visual memory.

Although the modifications in test procedure needed are likely to have some effect on test scores, it is usually possible to get sufficient information to be able to answer the referral question in general terms. The broad areas of difficulty may be identified but the precision and analysis of deficits used for neuropsychological investigation of patients is not generally possible in the presence of several physical handicap.

Investigation of psychological factors associated with physical disability has been extensive but has yielded relatively little of direct clinical relevance. Studies have attempted to identify psychological concomitants of disabilities. Thus, there have been attempts to identify a particular personality profile associated with a disability, such as rheumatoid arthritis or asthma. It has been suggested that these abnormal personality profiles may in some way predispose the person to a particular disease. However, the studies are generally inconclusive (Shontz, 1971) and the information gathered has not generally proved clinically useful. The one clinical situation where personality tests are occasionally used is in an attempt to differentiate organic from functional disorders, particularly in chronic low back pain patients. However, although several studies have been conducted on personality features of low back pain patients (Grzesiak, 1980), they have failed to provide an adequate means of distinguishing those with organic pathology from those without. Most psychologists use the Eysenck Personality Inventory and rating scales such as the Zung Self-rating Depression Scale (Zung, 1965), Middlesex Hospital Questionnaire (Crown and Crisp, 1970), and Goldberg General Health Questionnaire (Goldberg, 1972), in an attempt to answer the question rather than the MMPI, which was used for most experimental studies. One centre is using the Eysenck Personality Questionnaire for patients attending a spinal disorders clinic in an attempt to improve the diagnosis of patients with psychogenic problems presenting as back pain (Seal, 1979).

The other purpose of psychological assessments with patients in various disability groups has been to identify those likely to make a poor response to rehabilitation. If such people can be identified it may be possible to alter the rehabilitation programme in accordance with their difficulty. Measures of attitudes, beliefs, and mood tend to be used in this situation rather than measures of personality. In a study of patients with rheumatoid arthritis Gardiner (1980) found that those who rated themselves as 'slow, dependent, and weak' lost more time off work in the subsequent year. Since attitudes were not found to be related to the physical progression of the disease, it would suggest that such psychological variables affect the outcome of rehabilitation. Similar results were obtained with a group of chronic bronchitics (Rutter, 1976). In this study scores on the Zung Self-rataing Depression Scale (Zung, 1965) were significantly related to unemployment and poor work record whereas independent objective assessment of physical disability did not.

Another predictive variable to have been considered includes one aspect of a person's beliefs about himself, his locus of control. Brewin and Shapiro (1979) suggest that patients with an external locus of control are less likely to respond to rehabilitation than those with an internal locus of control. The implications of this suggestion were that therapists and patients should agree goals and targets which may be readily understood by the patient and let him feel that he is making progress in an objective quantifiable way. It is argued that patients who are educated to make their own decisions about their goals and their future are more likely to develop a sense of personal control and ability to change. It, therefore, seems that the predictive value of the person's locus of control is very much dependent on the nature of the rehabilitation programme in which he is engaged.

Although such measures may suggest those who will respond poorly to rehabilitation they have not been tested sufficiently in clinical practice. The type of intervention and whether it has any effect on these likely poor responders has yet to be determined. Nevertheless these approaches seem to have more direct clinical application than the examination of personality profiles.

Special Assessment Techniques

Some of the physically handicapped are too disabled for any of the assessment techniques mentioned so far to be appropriate. Those who have only very minimal movements, together with no speech, blindness, or deafness cannot be assessed on standard tasks. Special assessments have to be devised according to their disability and in general terms the questions to be answered are much more basic. For example: 'Can this person understand what is going on around him?, 'Can he learn to communicate in any way?', or 'What can he learn to do that will provide some sort of occupation or entertainment?'.

The first object is the provision of some means by which a response may be obtained. A variety of switches have been developed for disabled people to operate environmental controls or communication aids, such as a Possum typewriter. These switches can be adapted to operate other devices, such as lights, buzzers, and radios and to provide feedback of the response. Once some means of response has been established it is possible to test authority and visual comprehension to some extent by providing instructions and a response code. For example, visual matching can be assessed using a response code such as 'one press for same, two for different'. Training may be necessary on very simple items before it is possible to assess more complex tasks. If the person does not have sufficient movement to operate a switch he may be trained using biofeedback techniques. For example, increase in EMG level may be obtainable when no recordable movement is present. Such recording techniques have wider application and can provide a means of communication or can be linked to environmental controls. For example, a head injury patient may be trained to respond using EMG biofeedback and once this is done, it is possible to assess hearing threshold and verbal comprehension of instructions, and it may then be possible to establish some means of communication. Similar devices for use in assessment and treatment are reviewed by Fredilander (1980).

Special assessment techniques are also needed for particular problems associated with disability. With technial advances, driving is becoming a practical possibility for more and more disabled people. However, although the technical problems can be solved, little account has been taken so far of the effect of acquired intellectual impairment on driving skills. If the disabled person has intellectual impairment as well as motor deficits these may present difficulties returning to driving. A preliminary investigation of stroke patients (Smith and Wilson, 1980) suggests that those who have returned to driving make more mistakes on a test track than age matched controls, and that they also perform worse on some tests of intellectual function. It is hoped that it will be possible to develop a screening assessment which select patients with cognitive impairments likely to affect driving ability so that they may have adequate practical assessment and training before returning to drive.

Future Developments

Current assessment techniques are mainly concerned with measuring the extent of physical disability. A problem which is beginning to be tackled is how to measure the effect which such disabilities have on people's live. The handicap associated with a disability is probably a more useful evaluation of the effects of rehabilitation than the severity of the disability. However, even those disability measures which are available are rarely sufficiently standardized and reliable for our needs, and further work is being conducted on these.

The development of assessments is also being more oriented towards those with direct practical application. A measure of memory in multiple sclerosis patients which identifies those whose daily life is likely to be affected by the problem and for whom training is appropriate is more useful than one which is only as excellent discriminator between patients with multiple sclerosis and the general population.

Several attempts have been made to devise measures which predict response to rehabilitation. But this seems a little premature when we do not know what aspects of rehabilitation influence the course of recovery. If a particular measure predicted outcome in a particular group of patients, unless we know the effectiveness of the different component treatments, it is unlikely to be possible to use it as a predictor for another group of patients in a different hospital, with different therapists using different techniques. It is necessary first to establish what effect different treatment programmes have on promoting recovery or preventing deterioration. Predictive measures, while of interest, have not generally been applied by clinical psychologists.

General Patient Management

One of the most frequent requests to a clinical psychologist working with the physically handicapped is to advise care staff on the management of patients. The problems presented include those of patients who have difficulties in accepting their disabilities, who are uncooperative with treatment, poorly motivated, unrealistic in their aims or aggressive and disruptive. These occur at any stage between the onset of the disability and the final discharge from hospital care, in long-stay residential accommodation or in the patient's own home. Whenever the problem is presented to the psychologist it is likely that patient management in the early stages of disability will have had an effect.

Therefore, much attention is being directed towards the management of recently disabled patients.

If the onset of a disability is sudden, it may be characterized by a period of confusion, disorganization, and aggression. Psychologists have sometimes adopted a crisis management policy of the type outlined by Fordyce (1971) to help the patient and his family through this phase. This consists of providing calm stable models for the patient and his family to emulate. Also promoting performance mastery by providing carefully chosen tasks on which the patient can succeed. Patients may be aggressive, possibly because there are many punishment contingencies operating. Reinforcers which previously maintained their work and leisure activities are no longer available and instead they receive punishment, in the form of pain, physical discomfort or social disapproval, when trying to do new activities. By being aggressive, either physically or verbally, towards therapists the patient may escape from a situation which draws attention to his disability. If this is the case attempts are made to ignore the aggressive behaviour and at the same time using shaping procedures to increase participation in rehabilitation.

In addition psychologists are attempting to draw attention to other relevant aspects of acute care outlined by Michael (1970). He points out that attention and sympathy are contingent on behaviour, generally verbal, which indicates discontent, pain, and sadness. Attention is less often directed towards those who appear contented and happy, and who are quiet. The patient -- staff ratio is usually such that attention is given to those in trouble or who request care, whereas those who are coping are ignored.

Another problem outlined by Fordyce is the tendency for careers to encourage the patients to adopt a role of unquestioning obedience; being told what to do and when. In this way a pattern of strong dependency is rewarded. Since these tendencies often cannot be changed on an acute hospital ward, it is important that if they do occur they are identified and reversed as early as possible.

Once the patient has begun on a rehabilitation programme the most likely problem which may be encountered is one of poor motivation. These patients do not do as much as they are expected to do, or do not progress as well as is expected. They may also refuse to co-operate with treatment. Much of the therapist's time is spent in coping with the patient rather than using her own specialist treatment skills. Therefore, programmes are set up based on target setting with attention, rest and feedback of progress contingent on successful completion of target behaviours. There are several examples of this type of general management approach in the literature (Goodkin, 1966; Michael, 19970; Ince, 1976).

General management problems may also occur in residential settings, including the patient's own home. This may reflect a failure of rehabilitation to transfer a patient from a dependent to an independent role, a transfer which should be attempted even in those with severe physical dependence. Patients who need long-term physical care over a period of many years may have been forced into a dependent role for so many daily activities, that they cease to be as independent as they could be.

Initial work with relatives or carers may involve encouragement of patients to make progressively more of their own decisions. For example, in the early stages this may include deciding what to wear, where in the room to sit and what to eat, even though they cannot physically manage to do these things themselves.

SPECIFIC TRAINING PROGRAMMES

Specific programmes are set up to deal with individual rehabilitation problems. There are four main types:

1. Behaviour modification
2. Skills training
3. Cognitive retraining
4. Biofeedback

Behaviour Modification

If the general management principles described in the previous section are insufficient to overcome a particular behaviour problem then a specific behaviour modification programme may be set up. If progress is slow patients may become discouraged or feel that the activities they are required to do will not meet their own aims. For example, a woodworking apprentice attending a rehabilitation workshop following a head injury became uncooperative and aggressive during woodwork sessions. He became uncooperative because he considered the tasks he was being given to do were too easy, whereas the occupational therapists considered him unfit to return to work because he was show and inaccurate. A programme was designed to increase both his work speed and accuracy. A graded series of targets were devised which involved spending progressively longer on a routine woodwork task, making boxes. In addition the number of stages to be completed within the allotted time was increased. Points were awarded for the amount of work completed in the time limit, and deductions were made for specific inaccuracies, for example nail bent, corners not square. Points were exchanged for various leisure activities, and in addition a graph kept of his progress to provide additional reinforcement. His work speed increased from making one box in two half-hour sessions to eight boxes in one two-hour session. Initially, 100 per cent of points earned had to be deducted, but after te six week treatment period no deductions were necessary. Many examples of this type are quoted by Michael (1970), Ince (1976, 1980), and Fordyce (1976).

Generally psychologists using this approach have not carried out evaluations in comparison with other treatment methods. They have mainly been concerned with gaining experience in the application of behaviour modification in rehabilitation, and at best only using AB designs to evaluate the effects. Behaviour modification is becoming widely used in physical rehabilitation and further evaluation of its contribution is needed.

One major rehabilitation problem for which behaviour modification is used is in the management of chronic low back pain. Fordyce (1976) describes in detail a programme for patients with chronic low back pain with no or insufficient physical damage to account for its severity or persistence. It is based on the idea that pain behaviours may be reinforced by their consequences and over a prolonged period a whole repertoire of learned pain behaviours, including the subjective experience of pain, may be established. In other words, the patient may learn that a complaint of pain or disability leads to sympathy and help, whereas failure to complain does not. The programme aims to reverse this process by non-reinforcement of pain behaviours and reinforcement of activity. In addition, analgesics are given on a time-contingent rather than a pain-contingent basis. Results obtained by Fordyce (1976) indicate that pain behaviours may be reduced and activity increased, although in this instance no record was made of the effect of the programme on subjective pain. A pilot study by Silverman (1976) suggested that subjective pain either remained constant or improved, even though patients were doing more. Programmes of this type are being used in rehabilitation centres for low back pain and have been found to be useful. The continuous monitoring of progress means that patients may be treated on condition that they continue to improve and discharged once improvement ceases. In a group, characterized by repeatedly failing treatment and being passed from one specialist to another this ensures that therapist time is only being spent if some gains are being made. Whether the apparently good response is due to the actual treatment policy or whether it is just due to the patients being treated by someone who feels they may benefit, remains to be determined. However, chronic low back pain patients have long been a major rehabilitation problem and represent a large proportion of disabled patients so that any advance in their treatment is of significant practical benefit.

Skills Training

A large proportion of time during the rehabilitation stage involves teaching patients to perform familiar skills in different ways, such as dressing for a hemiplegic patient, or learning new skills such as propelling a wheelchair or walking with an artiifical leg. Most patients acquire these skills with practice, but if problems arise the clinical psychologist may be asked to advise on teaching methods. One of the most common reasons for failure to acquire the skill is that the patient has impaired learning ability as well as a physical disability. The task of the psychologist is to break down the skill into simple stages, with progress to the next stage dependent on successful acquisition of the previous stage. Frequent successes are ensured by keeping the stages simple and numerous. For example, in training wheelchair control the stages might be to propel a chair increasing distance in a given length of time. The difficulty of the task may be increased by restricting the available width of the route and presenting obstacles to be avoided. A similar approach may be used to train an elderly amputee to walk with an artificial leg or a stroke patient with visuospatial problems to dress.

Cognitive Retraining

Many physical handicaps have associated intellectual deficits, for example memory and reasoning difficulties in multiple sclerosis, visuospatial problems with cerebral palsy, language or perceptual problems with srokes. These cognitive deficits may be amenable to retraining. Two main approaches are used; one is to attempt to train the area of deficit, for example, by practice on perceptual spatial tasks; the other is to train the patient to circumvent the problems associated with a particular deficit, for example, training patients to use verbal instructions rather than spatial abilities, to find their way around. Which of the two is used depends to some extent on the severity of the deficit, though they can be used in conjunction with each other.

The three cognitive areas for which treatments have been developed for deficits are in language, visuospatial abilities, and memory, though others such as reasoning and sequencing have been considered. Language treatments have until recently been exclusively carried out by speech therapists, but the development of programmed instruction and verbal conditioning procedures for aphasics had led to some collaboration between psychologists and speech therapists. The efficacy of either approach with aphasic patients remains doubtful (Sarno *et al.*, 1970; Lincoln *et al.*, 1982) and this has led to the development of new treatment approaches. Visual communication using symbols or sign language has been attempted, and though the gains made are small they may be greater than those achieved by conventional methods. Melodic Intonation Therapy (Albert *et al.*, 1973) and

Brain Function Therapy (Buffery, 1977) are both based on the idea of stimulating the right hemisphere to take over language functions from the damaged left hemisphere. These have both been found useful with single cases but there seem to have been no investigations of their effectiveness compared with alternative treatment methods.

Perceptual training is a more recent development than that of language rehabilitation and most of that done by psychologists is based on the work of Diller and his colleagues (Diller, 1971, 1980). Defective visual scanning was selected for treatment. The initial aim was to make the patients aware of the difficulty and then to teach them to scan using an external stimulus which was sufficiently attractive to force the patients to turn their heads to the affected side. Diller developed a scanning machine, which requires the patient to point to a moving target. The patients has to learn to move his head when stimuli move to the left so that they come within the right visual field. Comparison of this procedure with conventional occupational therapy training indicated a beneficial effect, particularly in those with the most severe problems. Following training in scanning, treatments for spatial and sensory awareness were introduced with some patients. These consisted of matching a point touched on the patient's back with that on a manikin placed in front of the patient, and practice in estimating distances in space. Again, it was found that the treated group performed better than controls after one month's training.

Some psychologists are attempting to use these techniques with stroke and head injury patients but it is too early to judge their usefulness or effectiveness. However, it seems an area likely to develop because perceptual problems are common among stroke patients and yet are rarely identified or treated. The question yet to be answered is whether improvement acquired from training on these types of tasks is carried into performance in day to day living. It may be more appropriate to attempt retraining in real life situations or it may be that both approaches should be used to help the patient to overcome the practical difficulties associated with perceptual-spatial problems.

Two different approaches are also used in memory training. In one patients are trained in strategies to aid memory using, for example, visual imagery and mnemonic aids. Thus, Wilson (1980) attempted to train a man with memory problems, which followed a head injury, to remember the names of the staff in the rehabilitation unit using visual imagery, to remember a shopping list using an initial letter mnemonic, and to remember routes between different places using verbal cueing. The visual imagery and initial letter mnemonic produced improvements in the patient's performance, whereas the verbal cueing did not.

The alternative approach, which tends to be used with those who have more severe memory loss, is to train them to circumvent the problem. In the initial stages patients are required to tick off the days of the week and particular times of day on a well chart. This chart thus provides a reference to enable them to find out the day and time. Later, this is extended to the form of a daily diary, where events, such as activities completed in physiotherapy and occupational therapy and meals, are recorded at regular intervals throughout the day. Patients are encouraged to refer to their diary when discussing events that have happened and when planning treatment with their threapist. The planning of future events can then be incorporated into the diary. Each week the patient plans out a daily timetable in detail and is required to follow this timetable instead of asking what to do and where to go. Some patients with writing problems cannot cope with recording the information themselves, but they can be trained to refer to wall charts specifying what they should be doing and when. The benefits of this approach are that it can be easily adapted to everyday situations and is acceptable to relatives who find providing constant reminders very tedious.

Reality orientation training may also be appropriate for those with memory loss. Although mostly used with elderly demented patients, it may also be appropriate for those with similar problems associated with physical handicaps. Young disabled units often have large numbers of patients with memory problems. Reality orientation training on a 24 hour basis together with specific techniques of visual imagery and mnemonic aids might be used to help ameliorate some of their difficulties.

Biofeedback

The main type of biofeedback that has been used with the physically handicapped is electromyographic feedback for neuromuscular re-education. There are single case reports of successful treatment of a variety of clinical problems, including upper motor neurone lesions, Bell's palsy, and poliomyelitis. Some studies have compared biofeedback with alternative treatment (Brucker, 1980). In addition, Burnside *et al.*, (1979) evaluated EMG feedback in the treatment of chronic foot drop with 22 stroke patients who were residents in Social Services Old Peoples Homes. Subjects were given either twelve sessions of EMG feedback training or twelve sessions of musicle tension recording with no feedback, while all were given exercises to practise between sessions. The number of patients who improved in range of movement and gait were not significantly diffent between the groups at the end of treatment, although at six weeks follow-up the biofeedback group was significantly better. The strength ratings showed that appreciably more people in the biofeedback group improved and this was maintained at follow-up. This study suggests that EMG biofeedback is an appropriate treatment with stroke patients and gains can be made without a lengthy or elaborate treatment programme.

However, further evaluation is needed. It may be possible to make significant progress in training to alleviate foot drop thereby producing functional gain whereas training hand and arm function may require greater increase in strength before significant functional gain is obtained. In clinical practice biofeedback can be used to demonstrate improvement in EMG levels, but it only rarely produce an improvement in patients' personal independence. The question then arises whether biofeedback training is worthwhile in terms of the practical gains made, and further studies are needed on different disabilities and involving different groups of muscles. As a treatment of technique for clinical psychologists biofeedback seems likely to be useful, but continmuous monitoring of progress, using single case experimental designs, is essential.

Evaluation of Rehabilitation Techniques

Most rehabilitation techniques have developed over many years with little or no evaluation of their effectiveness. Those which have been found clinically useful have survived, but the problem is that many disabled patients improve or deteriorate independently of any intervention. It is then difficult to assess what has produced the observed changes. Such studies which have been completed have frequently had methodological faults, for example the major studies to evaluate speech therapy with stroke patients (Sarno *et al.*, 1970; Basso *et al.*, 1979). The need for evaluation of treatment effectiveness has become increasingly recognized and psychologists have become involved in both study design and in the teaching of research methods. Control group studies usually involve specific research staff and although essential do not involve many remedial therapists. On the other hand the application of single case experimental designs is a more straightforward undertaking and can be incorporated into the treatment regimes of physiotherapists, occupational therapists, and speech therapists. This latter approach at least enables therapists to identify some of the essential components of rehabilitation. However, if psychologists are to do this, then they have to ensure that psychological techniques introduced into rehabilitation do not meet with the same criticisms as earlier studies.

Adjustment to Disability

Once the rehabilitation phase is completed and the patient

has achieved his maximum level of independence, the problems referred to the psychologist tend to be those of failure to adjust to life as a disabled person. In some cases this also involves the adjustment of the spouse or relative.

The types of problem encountered include social anxieties, marital disharmony, sexual problems, over-reliance on professional help, and negative attitudes towards the self as a disabled person. Many of the techniques used by psychologists in a psychiatric setting can be directly applied to aiding the disabled in their social adjustment. For exmple, systematic desentilization can be used to help overcome anxieties about going into public places in a wheel-chair, cognitive therapy can be used to reduce negative thoughts about themselves and their disabilities, and behavioural contracting can be used for marital problems.

Group therapy, in various forms, is being used to deal with many adjustment problems. Some groups serve an educational function in order for disabled people to discuss practical problems and to share ways of solving them. Others include relatives and may have a social as well as educational function. The relatives of some disabled patients may suffer as much of the isolation and practical limitations on life as the disabled person himself. Support groups for relatives are frequently as important as those for the patients. All the groups aim to get members to rely as much on self-help as possible and to wean them, as far as is practical, from obtaining help from professional sources. The role of the psychologist in these instances has generally been to initiate the formation of the groups rather than having any direct therapeutic role within the group setting. However, since recent studies on the social and psychological consequences of brain damage (Oddy *et al.*, 1978; Coughlan and Humphrey, 1979; Kansella and Duffy, 1979) suggest that major adjustment problems do occur, a more direct therapeutic role may develop.

The one area where psychologists may take a specific therapeutic role with the long-term disabled person is by providing sexual counselling. Physical disability besides its physical effects on sexual functioning often has psychological effects as well. Disability may render a person sexually unattractive in his own or his partner's opinion. In these cases discussion of the feelings and reactions to the disability may be sufficient. In others a graded approach, similar to that outlined by Masters and Johnson (1970), can be used to overcome fears and concern about how the partners will cope. In disabilities such as stroke or head injury, there may be initial loss of sexual functioning with gradual recovery. If the couple are not aware of this, impotence in the early stages of recovery may discourage either partner from further attempts at intercourse or create anxieties which in turn result in a persistence of the problem due to psychological rataher than physical causes. A psychological approach to counselling may produce improvement even though the original problem was purely physical.

Conclusion

Clinical psychologists are involved increasingly in the management of the physically handicapped. They are involved more in primary patient care, based in the community or in residential centres, and there is room for their greater involvement in acute hospital wards and in general hospital rehabilitation units. While desirable, this wider practice should not be to the detriment of their work in specialized rehabilitation centres, for their main role is to train others in the use of psychological techniques.

One of the greatest contributions that will continue to be made by clinical psychologists is to emphasize to therapists who work with the physically handicapped, the need for accurate assessment of the value of treatment programmes, and to teach them how such assessments may be made. Thus, although not a large professional group, clinical psychologists have an important and developing role within the multidisciplinary rehabilitation team.

REFERENCES

Albert, M.L., Sparks, R.W., and Helm, N.A. (1973). Melodic intonation therapy for aphasia. *Archives of Neurology*, 29, 130-131.

Basso, A., Capitani, E., and Vignolo, L.A. (1979). The influence of rehabilitation on language skills in aphasic patients: A controlled study. *Archives of Neurology*, 36, 190-196.

Benton, A.L. (1950). A multiple choice type of the visual retention test. *Archives of Neurology and Psychiatry*, 64, 699-707.

Brewin, C.R. and Shapiro, D.A. (1979). Beliefs about the self and their importance for motivation in rehabilitation. In D.J. Osborne, M.M. Gruneberg and J.R. Eiser (eds), *Research in Psychology and Medicine, Vol. II.* London Academic Press.

Brucker, B. (1980). Biofeedback and rehabilitation. In L.P. Ince (ed.) *Behavioral Psychology in Rehabilitation Medicine.* Baltimore: Williams and Wilkins.

Buffery, A.W.H. (1977). Clinical Neuropsychology: A review and preview. In S. Rachman (ed.), *Contributions to Medical Psychology.* London: Pergmon Press.

Burnside, I.G., Tobias, H.S., and Bursill, D. (1979). Electromyographic feedback in the remobilisation of stroke patients. In D.J. Osborne, M.M. Gruneberg and J.R. Eiser (eds), *Research in Psychology and Medicine Vol. II.* London: Academic Press.

Coughlan, T., and Humphrey, M. (1980). Psychosocial problems in the rehabilitation of stroke patients. Paper presented to the Society for Research in Rehabilitation, Exeter, 10-11 July.

Crown, S., and Crisp, A.H. (1970). *The Middlesex Hospital Questionnaire Manual* Barnstable: Psychological Test Publications.

Diller, L. (1971). Cognitive and motor aspects of handicapping conditions in the neurologically impaired. In W.S. Neff (ed.), *Rehabilitation Psychology.* Washington D.C.: APA.

Diller, L. (1980). The development of a perceptual-remediation program in hemiplegia. In L.P. Ince (ed.), *Behavioural Psychology in Rehabillatation Medicine.* Baltimore: Williams and Wikins.

Fordyce, W.E. (1971), Psychological assessment and management. In F.M. Krusen, F. J. Kottke and P.M.Ellwood (eds), *Handbook of Physical Medicine and Rehabilitation,* New York: Saunders.

Fordyce,W.E. (1976). *Behavioural Methods for Chronic Pain and Illness.* St. Louis: Mosby.

Freidlander, B.Z. (1980). Automated operant methods for assessment and treatment in physical rehabilitation. In L.P. Ince (ed.), *Behavioral Psychology in Rehabilitation Medicine: Clinical Application.* Baltimore: Williams and Wilkins.

Gardiner, B.M. (1980). Psychological aspects of rheumatoid arthirtis. *Psychological Medicine,* 10, 159-165.

Goldberg, D.P. (1972). *The Detection of Psychiatric Illness by Questionnaire.* Maudsley Monograph No. 21. London: Oxford University Press.

Gollin, E.S. (1960). Development studies of visual recognition of incomplete objects. *Perceptual and Motor Skills,* 11, 289-298.

Goodkin, R. (1969). Case studies in behavioural research in rehabilitation. *Perceptual and Motor Skills,* 23, 171-182.

Grzesiak, R.C. (1980). Chronic pain: A psychobehavioral perspective. In L.P. Ince (ed.), *Behavioral Psychology in Rehabilitation Medicine: Clinical Applications,* Baltimore: Williams and Wikins.

Ince, L.P. (1976). *Behaviour Modification in Rehabilitation Medicine.* C.C. Thomas: Springfield, Illinois.

Ince, L.P. (1980). *Behavior Psychology in Rehabilitation Medicine.* Baltimore: Williams and Wilkins.

Kansella, G.J. and Duffy, F.D. (1979). Psychosocial readjustment in the spouses of aphasic patients. *Scandinavian Journal of Rehabilitation Medicine,* II, 129-132.

Lincoln, N.B., and Leadbitter, D. (1979). Assessment of motor function in stroke patients. *Physiotherapy,* 65, 48-51.

Lincoln, N.B., Pickersgill, M.J., Hankey, A.I., and Hilton, C.R. (1982). An evaluation of operant training and speech therapy in the language rehabilitation of moderate aphasics. *Behavioural Psychotherapy,* 10, 162-178.

Lyle, R.C., Stone, J., Meill, D. and Stewart, M. (1979). Abbreviation of ADL. Testing by Gutman Scaling Techniques. Paper presented at a scientific meeting of the Society for Research in Rehabilitation, Newcastle-upon-Tyne, July 1979.

Masters, W.H., and Johnson, V.E. (1970). *Human Sexual Inadequacy.* Boston: Little, Brown.

Michael, J.L. (1970). Rehabilitation. In C. Neuringer and J. Michael (eds), *Behavior Modification in Clinical Psychology.* New York: Appleton-Century-Crofts.

Oddy, M. Humphrey, M., and Uttley. D. (1978). Subjective impairment and social recovery after closed head injury. *Journal of Neurology, Neurosurgery and Psychiatry,* 41, 611-616.

Ratcliff, G. (1970). Aspects of disordered space perception. Unpublished Doctoral thesis, University of Oxford.

Raven, J.C. (1958). *Standard Progressive Matrices and Mill Hill Vocabulary.* London: Lewis.

Rey. A. (1959). *Le Test de Copie de Figure Complexe.* Paris: Editions centre de psychologic appliquee.

Rutter, B.M. (1976). Measurement of psychological factors in chronic illness. *Rheumatology and Rehabilitation,* 15, 174-178.

Sarno, M.T., Silverman, J. and Sands, E. (1970). Speech therapy and language recovery in severe aphasia. *Journal of Speech and Hearing Research,* 13, 607-623.

Seal, P.V. (1979). Early impressions from the use of the Eysenck Personality Questionnaire in patients attending a spinal disorders clinic. Lecture to the Society for Back Pain Research, London.

Shontz, F.C. (1971). Physical disability and personality. In W.S. Neff (ed.). *Rehabilitation Psychology,* Washington D.C.: A.P.A.

Silverman, L. (1976). Behavioural management of ethronic low back pain. Paper presented at course on low back pain. Rivermead Rehabilitation Centre, Oxford.

Smith, T., and Wilson, B. (1980). Personal Communication.

Staples, D., and Lincoln. N.B. ((1981). A Maze Learning Test of Memory for the use.

21

Mental Health and Value Similarity in Sweden

Introduction

The relationship between migration and mental health has been studied from three points of view (Stenius, 1983).

1. According to *social selection* theories, migration, particularly emigration, is an act which is more predictable in certain (negative) living conditions or for certain types of people, especially those with a greater disposition for psychic problems.

2. Migration is an upsetting *life event* which produces changes in most aspects of the migrants life and induces special strains in the individuals involved.

3. Many immigrants live under *social conditions* which favour the development of psychiatric problems.

In this paper the mental health and utilisation of health services of immigrants to Sweden, particularly those from Finland, are examined. The interpretations are linked more to life event and social condition theories than to the social selection theory.

In addiiton to survey and hospital case data on psychiatric problems, early retirement and sick leave statistics also reveal some aspects of psychological problems and how people cope with them. Statistics on early retirement of immigrants collected by Reinans (1986) are combined with earlier research results (Haavio-Mannila, 1984). Mental health data are related to the extent of value similarity and the familiarity of different immigrant groups to the Swedish host populations (Westin, 1984). The paper focuses on the specific situation of Finns in Sweden.

Early Retirement as a Consequence of Cultural Distance

In Sweden the official retirement age is 65 years. In 1981-82 about 1% of the 3.9 million people aged between 16 and 64 years working for pay took early retirement. Early retirement was more common among persons born abroad than among native Swedes. While foreign born persons composed 9.5% of the gainfully employed population, as many as 14.5% of persons retiring before the age of 65 years were born abroad (Reinans, 1986).

Early retirement can be looked upon as an indicator of poor adjustment to working life, since early retirement pensions are mainly given for health reasons. Diseases of muscles, skeleton and connective tissues were, in 1981-82, the most common diagnoses of those taking early retirement (38%), with diseases of the circulatory system and mental problems being the next most common causes of early retirement (17% and 17% respectively).

With the exception of Germans, all immigrant groups have higher early retirement rates than native Swedes (Table 21.1). In addition to Germans, Norwegians and Danes also have low rates of early retirement. Estonians, Poles, Turks, Finns and Hungarians were, in this respect, intermediate while early retirement rates for Yugoslavians and Greeks were very high.

The proportion of persons retiring with a psychiatric diagnosis as the main cause of retirement indicates adjustment problems more directly than does the overall retirement rate. In general this proportion is well correlated with the overall early requirement rate (Table 21.1). Exceptions are the Poles and the Turks whose proportions of people retiring for mental reasons are high compared to the oveall rate for these groups.

In earlier studies, it has been shown that the geographical and cultural distance between the country of origin and destination are good predictors of probability of becoming mentally ill in the new country. For example, according to our studies in the Vesteras psychiatric clinic and Sundby mental hospital ther were, in 1971, about 300 psychiatric patients from Denmark, Norway and other Western European countries per 100,000 population; 576 per 100,000 from Finland; 1479 from Yugoslavia; 1682 from Eastern Europe; and 1870 from Italy (Haavio-Mannila and Stenius, 1977).

The cultural difference between the country of birth of the immigrant and the Swedish culture can be measured on the basis of value similarity and familiarity as experienced by Swedes (Westin, 1984). In general, the more similarity in the values of the countries of origin and destination, according to the opinion of Swedes, the lower the early retirement rate for the immigrant group. Value similarity may be partly an expression of other similarities with regard to life conditions, standard of living, structure of health services, etc. in the two countries, not just cultural distance.

The most noticeable exception to this generalisation is the Turkish immigrant group, which has a relatively low early retirement in spite of a great perceived dissimilarity of values between them and Swedes. This may be due to several factors: Turks live together in certain areas of Sweden and, according to Murphy (1965), it is advantageous to mental health to have one's countrymen nearby in the new environment. It has also been shown that Turks get social support from their family and relatives to a higher degree than, for example, Yugoslavian

Table 21.1

Early Retirement Rate and Proportion of Retired Men and Women with Psychiatric Diagnosis According to Country of Birth, Sweden 1981-82); and Similarity of Values and Familiarity with Culture of These Countries as Experienced by Swedes, 1981 (Westin, 1984, 335-337).

Country	*New early retirements 1981-82*				
	Numbers aged 16-64	*Age-weighted rate per 1000 persons in 1980*	*Per cent due to psychiatric diagnosis*	*Value similarity 1)*	*Familiarity 2)*
Total Swedish Population	5,221,809	15	17	-	-
Germany	31,232	14	18	-	-
Norway	33,765	18	15	94	73
Denmark	35,571	18	16	91	73
Estonia	9,764	24	9	46	25
Poland	16,561	25	28	16	19
Turkey	10,553	26	27	2	5
Finland	220,412	27	18	83	59
Hungary	11,427	30	21	-	-
Yugoslavia	34,533	48	31	5	12
Greece	13,814	49	33	4	14

1. Proportion (%) of Swedes aged 18-70 years (N=1202) considering that the ethnic groups share similar values with them on issues such as children's education.
2. Proportion (%) of Swedes considering that they are familiar with the ways of life and culture of the group (i.e. they know them very well or quite well).

immigrants (Simila, 1986). Turks are devoted Muslims compared to Greek Orthodox or atheist Greeks and Yugoslavs. Religion may help them in getting along in the new environment. Finally, as a recently arrived group, Turks may not yet be sensitive to hidden discrimination in Swedish society, from which the earlier arrived Greeks and Yugoslavs, with better language skills and higher ambitions, also suffer (Jaakkola, 1983).

Mental problems as a cause for early retirement are most frequent in the culturally distant immigrant groups. Turks have lower proportions than Greeks and Yugoslavs, but differences are not as large as the total early retirement rates. Immigration into a culturally dissimilar society is a more critical life event than moving to a country in which values are relatively similar. The living conditions in a dissimilar country create more strain than those in a more similar country. The stressfulness of the migration itself and the strain experienced in the remote culture can create psychological problems which lead to early retirement. In some culturally remote ethnic groups there may be some intervening social support mechanisms, which help the immigrants to cope with these strains.

Mental Health and Use of Health Care Services among Southern European and Finnish Immigrants

A group in which the early retirement rate - both overall and due to mental problems - is relatively high, in spite of similarity in values with Swedes, is the Finnish immigrant group. This may be related to an ambivalent image of Finns, which is held in Sweden. They are, seen as both hardworking and rowdy, and this "double bind" may create mental health problems (Haavio-Mannila, 1984).

The Swedish Institute of Social Research conducted three surveys on the standard of living in 1968, 1974 and 1981 (cf. Leinio, 1984) in which Finnish and Yugoslavian immigrants were compared to Swedes matched according to age, sex and occupation. The mental health of both immigrant groups was found to be poorer than that of native Swedes.

Yugoslavian immigrant men in particular were very often registered as sick (Haavio-Mannila, 1984). Jansson and Papastavrou (1984) suggest that being registered as sick with an instruction to rest is considered by many immigrant groups to be a functional form of treatment, but it is not any more regarded as such by Swedes. In the same way early retirement, being registered sick or getting sick leave may be a preventive measure taken in order to avoid a mental or physical breakdown. Accordingly, Southern European immigrants act rationally in the cultural crisis created by the arrival in a strange country when they resort to the opportunity to take sick leave. Finns, on the other hand, have more inhibitions against utilisation of the Swedish welfare system even though they have as many or more illnesses than Yugoslavs. Both immigrant groups are hospitalized as often as comparable Swedes (Haavio-Mannila, 1984).

In connectionwith a project aimed at giving psychiatric support to immigrants in the Huddinge hospital in Stockholm, Jansson and Papastavrou (1984) compared the duration of periods of sick leave and the duration of hospital staay among Greek and Yugoslavian immigrants and natives. They also investigated whether periods of mental disorder among immigrants were more often disguised as somatic disorders, and whether immigrants were more often given sick leave certificates from physicians in private practice.

The total period of sick leave during the period in question was longer for immigrants, particularly for Yugoslavian patients. Still more pronounced was the fact that each period was longer for the immigrant groups, especially in the Greek group than among Swedish patients. However, the Greek and Yugoslavian individuals were treated for significantly less time in hospital during the observation period than were Swedish patients. Immigrant patients treated in a hospital were less often diagnosed as psychiatric patients than were the natives. However, data received from the insurance companies revealed that they suffered from psychiatric problems just as often as Swedes.

Janson and Papastavrous point out that South-Europeans, to a higher extent than Swedes, try to avoid being admitted to a psychiatric clinic out of fear of being stigmatised as mentally ill.

These studies show that immigrants have more mental health problems than Swedes even when age, sex and occupation are controlled. Southern European immigrants take advantage of the sick leave and early retirement schemes in Sweden, but they do not rely so heavily on the public health care system, because they may wish to avoid hospitalisation.

Mental Health of Finnish Immigrants

Finnish immigrants appear to have a high rate of mental problems even though the value similarity, and their familiarity, to Swedes is high. This may be related to the special features of Finnish society and language, and the relationship between Finland and Sweden in general. The historical and political position of Finland as a buffer between Eastern and Western Europe may create cross-pressures and doublebinds. Finns, who have an exacting work ethic (Jaakkola, 1983) try to cope by ploughing themselves into work, frequently over-taxing themselves and, as a consequence, falling ill.

The position of Finland is ambivalent in Sweden. On the one hand, it is distant from Sweden due to different language and a different level of economic development. On the other hand Swedes look at Finns as having fairly similar values and are familiar with their way of life and culture (Finland was part of Sweden until 1809). Finns are partly rejected by Swedes because they are not believed to be interesting newcomers, who bring colour and excitement to Swedish society. On the other hand, Finns are more accepted as immigrants than some mechanisms, which help the immigrants to cope with these strains.

Another kind of problem is the closed nature of social networks among Finnish immigrants, which time does not appear to lessen. Even the Swedish-speaking Finns in Sweden are somewhat isolated and their informal social relations were reduced after emigration.

A further ambivalence experienced by Finns in Sweden is the easiness of return migration, thanks to the geographical proximity to the home country. This creates indecision in relation to where to live. Immigrants from distant countries and political refugees have fewer choices.

Finns are seen by Swedes at one and the same time as hardworking and boisterous; close and distant. Finns may feel themselves trapped in a system of conflicting demands and expectations which they cannot satisfy. They may react in three ways: by fighting back, becoming obstreperous in various ways; by developing an inferiority complex and despising themselves and their own countrymen in a compensatory reaction, or yielding to (mental) illness, drugs, alcohol and suicide. Most of them, however, do rely on more socially constructive ways of coping.

22

Doctor's Behaviour in the Face of Patients' Non-Compliance

Introduction

Patients' non-adherence to a health regimen is a serious problem, especially in the case of out-patients who are not under the immediate control of medical staff. In many studies it was found that the percentage of persons who follow the regimen prescribed was far below 100. The compliance of Polish out-patients suffering from chronic illnesses was studied by the first author. The results showed that the numbers taking the doctors' advice varied from 42% to 93%, depending mainly on the kind of treatment recommended. When making lifestyle changes was recommended only about 50% of patients complied with doctors' advice.

Patient non-compliance is a substantial obstacle to the achievement of therapeutic goals, it potentially involves the patient in additional diagnostic and treatment procedures and is a source of professional failure for clinicians. Hence the very important problem arises, how can doctors improve patients' adherence to the regimen prescribed? There are a large number of techniques available for managing non-compliance, depending on its causes, developed within the areas of medical psychology and behavioural medicine (Anderson & Lynne, 1982; Peck & King, 1982; Zisook & Gammon 1980-81). But it would be of interest to know which forms of non-compliance management are actually applied in clinical circumstances.

Few empirical findings are available in this area (Appelbaum & Roth, 1983; Davis, 1966; Hayes-Bautista, 1976) but from these it may be concluded that, in dealing with patients' non-compliance, doctors apply only a small number of the existing techniques. What are the causes of this limitation? It has been stressed that pataients' refusal to comply could be the principal cause of doctors' professional frustration (Fedder, 1982, Zisook & Gammon, 1980-81). The authors' assumption is that frustration theory may be a useful frame of reference in studying doctors' behaviour towards non-compliance and its determinants. The aim of the present study was:

1. To examine this sphere of behaviour and compare its forms in natural clinical settings with those reported by doctors;
2. To explain doctors' attitude towards non-compliance within the framework of frustration theory (Reykowaski, 1966).

Method

The study consisted of two parts, with two different groups of physicians as subjects. The first part was designed to identify the tactics used by doctors when faced with patients' non-compliance, as observed in the natural setting of polyclinics. The second aimed at describing doctors' behaviours towards non-compliance on the basis of their own reports and ascertaining some determinants of this behaviour by identifying the subjects' habitual way of dealing with frustrating events.

The first study group was selected from among a larger group of 109 doctors on the basis of the content of tape-recorded patient visits and consisted of physicians whose interviews contained evident examples of non-compliance. In all, 30 such events were found and the relevant excerpts from the tape-recordings were transcribed. Both men and women were represented in the group, with different lengths of practice and coming from various specialist medical fields in different outpatient clinics in large Polish towns.

The second group were 60 physicians interviewed by psychologists to learn about their behaviour towards noncompliers. The group was not representative in the statistical sense but, as with the first one, was purposely heterogeneous in order to obtain a broad variety of responses. Immediately after the interview, the Rosezweig Picture-Frustration Study (RPFS) (Dunaj-Kozlowska, 1980) was applied to learn about the subjects type of habitual behaviour towards frustration.

The doctors' behaviour towards non-compliance was analysed applying the same system of categories in both groups. The system was developed by the authors a posteriorily. Altogether 11 different categories of doctors' tactics towards non-compliance were distinguished. These were:

1. Trying to determine causes of non-compliance;
2. Giving the patient information concerning the treatment to convince him that it is appropriate, explaining the rationale for the regimen;
3. Enlisting family support;
4. Replacing the medicine originally advised with another of similar efficacy but more acceptable to the patient;
5. Tolerant, indulgent dealing with the patient, allowing him to unburden himself, to express his emotions and then carrying the doctor's point;
6. Authoritarian tractics; stressing the doctor's superior position, his professional knowledge and his right to decide;
7. Using medical threat; informing the patient of the dire consequences which will certainly occur if the advice is not followed;

8. Blaming the patient for non-compliance and making him responsible for the eventual consequences;
9. Criticizing, insulting, humiliating the patient;
10. Personal tactics; treating the patient as a personal acquaintance, thus making it difficult for him to refuse the doctor's request;
11. Withdrawal, reducing the doctor's involvement in the case.

To evaluate the doctor's behaviour in the framework of frustration theory, the tactics were then divided into two large classes, according to the interpreted goal. The tactics numbered above from 1 to 5 were recognised as task-oriented, while the tactics numbered from 6 to 11 as ego-defensive.

Results

The frequency of use of various tactics when a patient failed to follow the doctor's advice is presented in Table 22.1. The greatest proportion of doctors from both groups applied medical threat.

The other tactics reported as most frequently used by the doctors interviewed were:

(i) giving medical information;

(ii) stressing the doctor's authority;

(iii) reducing his involvement in the case.

The remaining tactics were rarely mentioned. None of the doctors reported applying personal tactics or admitted blaming the patient, criticising, consulting or humiliating him. There were no significant differences between groups as to the tactics used; on the contrary a positive correlation was found between them (Spearman Rank Correlation Coefficient r = 0.62).

Table 22.1

The Frequency of Application of Various Tactics Towards Non-compliance

Kind of tactics	*Data observed (I study group)*		*Data reported (II study group)*	
	No. of cases	*% of cases*	*No. of cases*	*% of cases*
Medical threat (7)	8	28	20	34
Carrying the doctor's point in an indulgent atmosphere (5)	5	17	2	3
Authoritarian tactics (6)	4	14	11	18
Medical information (2)	3	11	14	24
Withdrawal (11)	2	7	6	10
Trying to determine causes (1)	2	7	2	3
Personal tactics (10)	2	7	0	0
Altering the regimen (4)	1	3	3	5
Blaming the patient (8)	1	3	0	0
Criticizing, insulting, humiliating the patient (9)	1	3	0	0
Enlisting family support (3)	0	0	2	3
Total	29*	100	60	100

The tactics are ordered according to their frequency in the first study group.

Figures in the brackets refer to the description in the text.

* A single case in the first study group was difficult to classify and not taken into account.

Table 22.2 shows the doctors' reaction to non-compliance grouped into two larger classes as distinguished within the frustration theory. It is evident that there were no differences between observed and reported behaviour from this point of view. The ego-defensive forms of behaviour toward non-compliance prevailed in the doctors under study.

Table 22.2

The Frequence of Task-oriented and Ego-defensive tactics

Kind of tactics	*Data observed (I study group)*		*Data reported (II study group)*	
	No. of cases	*% of cases*	*No. of cases*	*% of cases*
Task oriented	11	38	23	38
Ego-defensive	18	62	37	62
Total	29	100	60	100

In order to explore the connection between the habitual way of dealing with frustrating events and the attitude towards non-compliance, the results of RPFS were taken into account. For the purpose of this study only two types of reaction towards frustratign events were distinguished: task-oriented and ego-defensive. Of the 60 persons in our second study group, 10 were finally excluded because their RPFS results were difficult to classify from this point of view. Results for the remaining 50 are presented in Table 22.3.

Table 22.3

Type of doctors' reaction in RPFS and their behaviour towards non-compliance

The type of reaction in RPFS	*The behaviour towards no..-compliance*		*Total*
	Task-oriented	*Ego-defensive*	
Task oriented	15 (7.22)	4 (11.78)	19 (38%)
Ego-defensive	4 (11.78)	27 (19.22)	31 (62%)
Total	19 (38%)	31 (62%)	50 (100%)

$X^2 = 21.809$ df = 1 $p<.001$ $\phi = 0.66$

Kendall Q = 0.92

The table contains numbers of persons and theoretical frequencies (in brackets).

In 42 cases the doctor's own estimate of his reaction to non-complying patients agreed with RPFS results while in 8 cases there was lack of agreement. The statistical indices are high and indicate a strong connection between the attitude towards frustration and the behaviour towards non-compliant patients.

Discussion

The main aim of the study was to describe doctors' behaviour towards non-compliance, either on the basis of observation or of their own reports. Few doctors tried to ascertain the causes of non-compliance, hence the majority of responses were probably unrelated to the specific causes of the patients' poor adherence. The tactic most frequently used was medical threat and authoritarian tactics were applied relatively often. As has been reported (Anderson & Lynne, 1982; Ley, 1977; Zisook & Gammon, 1980-81) both are of doubtful effectiveness, while they also tend to worsen the patients' emotional state. On the other hand many valuable techniques of proved efficacy, elaborated in the field of behavioural medicine (Becker & Maiman, 1980; Peck & King, 1982; Zisook & Gammon, 1980-81) were quite neglected by the doctors.

What are the reasons for the doctors' low efficacy in dealing with non-compliance? One may be a lack of behavioural knowledge or interpersonal skills. However, the psychological mechanisms of the behaviour under study are probably more complex. Frustration theory provides a useful explanatory framework. When the doctors' reactions towards non-compliance were evaluated within the framework of this theory as either ego-defensive or task-oriented, it was found that the first form predominated both in the observed and reported behaviour. Moreover, the kind of tactics towards non-compliance were strongly determined by the subjects' general type of reaction to frustration as measured by RPFS.

We may conclude that patient non-compliance is perceived by the majority of doctors as a frustrating, ego-threatening event, which is accompanied by strong negative emotions. As a result, the doctor's activity is aimed primarily at defending his professional self-esteem and reducing the emotional tension. The original goal of behaviour i.e. the patient's adherence to the regimen prescribed, is postponed. This emotional arousal may also limit the doctor's flexibility and his inventiveness in looking for more effective ways of personal influence.

23

Health for All: Strategy and Targets of W.H.O.

Introduction

The World Health Organisation (WHO) is a specialised agency of the United Nations, with primary responsibility for international health matters and public health.

Throughout the Organisation, which was created in 1946, the health professions of some 160 countries exchange their knowledge and experience of health information of many kinds. WHO's main function is to act as a directing and co-ordinating authority on international health work to ensure valid and productive technical co-operation and to promote international research.

The member states of WHO have set for themselves a common goal "Health for all by the Year 2000" whereby at the end of this century all citizens of the world shall have a level of health that will permit them to lead a socially and economically productive life.

The global strategy for health for all - adopted in 1981 - represents a solemn agreement between the governments and WHO with the aim of making possible the attainment that people everywhere should have access to health services and that essential health care is planned with full community involvement.

It means that health begins at home, in schools and in factories, and that people will use better approaches than they do now for preventing disease and alleviating unavoidable disease and disability.

It means that people will realise that they have the power to shape their own lives and the lives of their families, free from the avoidable burden of disease, and aware that ill health is not inevitable.

The WHO Regional Office for Europe is one of six Regional Offices throughout the world, each with its own programme geared to the particular health problems of the countries served. The European Region has 32 active member states and it is unique in that a large proportion of them are industrialised countries with highly advanced medical services. The European programme, therefore, differs from those of other regions in concentrating on the problems associated with industrial society.

In its strategy for attaining the goal of health for all by the year 2000 the Regional Office is arranging its activities in three main areas of work: promotion of lifestyles conducive to health: reduction of preventable conditions; and provision of care that is adequate, accessible and acceptable to all.

In 1978 the International Conference on Primary Health Care, held in Alma-Ata, U.S.S.R. declared that primary health care is the key to attaining the goal of health for all by the year 2000. Primary health care is based on practical, scientifically sound and socially acceptable methods and technology. It should be made universally accessible to individuals and families in their community through their full participation and at an affordable cost on a continuing basis. Primary health care takes place at the first contact between individuals and the national health system, as close as possible to where people live and work. It is the first element in a continuing health care process, and forms an integral part of a country's health system.

The European Strategy

The European countries, with their long experience and vast resources, have a speical responsibility to the rest of the world as front-runners in exploring new avenues to solve health problems and reduce inequalities. Following the adoption in 1977 of "Health for All" as the main social target of governments and the WHO, the European Region WHO has taken important steps towards that goal with the formulation of a common health policy in 1980 and the adoption in 1984 of regional targets in support of the European regional strategy for health for all. The regional targets have been developed for the European member states through the active participation of experts and health and social institutions throughout the Region. These targets represent, therefore a common view of what could and should be health for all in Europe, and are a challenge which the member states have set for themselves. The targets and their respective strategies propose possible health improvements, possible ways of achieving these, and the means for measuring progress and evaluating efficiency and efficacy. Obviously, the methods of operation proposed by the regional targets can be implemented only by the member states themselves, and any achievement will depend on the will of the countries to orient their own policies and strategies towards a common goal such as health for all. The essential step is widespread dissemination of the message through all levels of the community from policy makers to the people, involving the mass media, the health professions, consumer groups, and the educational system. It is hoped that such dissemination could stimulate wide debate around the major issues and create the necessary conditions for change.

Pre-requisites for Health for All

In 1980 the Regional Committee for the WHO European Region approved their first common health policy, the European strategy for attaining health for all. This strategy called for a fundamental change in the countries' health developments and outlined four main areas of concern:

Lifestyles and health;

Risk factors affecting health and the environment;

Re-orientation of the health care system itself;

The political management, technological, manpower, research and other support necessary to brign about the desired changes.

Although it seemed rather ambitious to formulate specific regional targets to supplement the implementation of this strategy, since member states differ so much in socio-economic development, in health status and in political orientation, the Regional Committee in 1984 endorsed 38 regional targets that reflect common needs, priorities and values in the health systems of all member states. However, it was unanimously agreed that there could be no effective action to secure health for all without strong political and public support - not - withstanding the already high commitment from health services and health professionals alike. A high responsibility, nevertheless, lies outside the health sector. Freedom from the fear of war, adequate food and income, decent housing, safe water, sanitation and a satisfying role in society are all essential for health.

Equity in Health

Two other basic issues must also be tackled by political and social commitment. The first is to reduce health inequality among countries and among groups within countries. A second issue is to strengthen health promotion as much as to reduce disease and its consequential disabilities and handicaps. Thus a prospect for adding life to years is occasioned by ensuring the full development and the use of people's integral or residual physical and mental capacity in order to derive full benefit from, and to cope with, life in a healthy and satisfactory way. The reduction of disease and disability will add to the quality of health in life, and finally, by reducing premature deaths and thereby increasing life expectancy, will add years to life. Targets 1-12 over these two basic issues of equity in health.

Lifestyles Conducive to Health

Targets 13-17 are intimately bound up with the values, priorities and practical opportunities or constraints of specific cultural, social and economic situations affecting lifestyles. A person's particular way of life is shaped by patterns of interpersonal interaction and social learning that inter-relate with and depend upon the social environment. Thus, lifestyles shaped by experience and environmental factors are not simply individual decisions to avoid or accept certain health risks. Many lifestyles enhance health, develop physical and mental well-being, and protect the individual from the effects of stress. Other lifestyles include behaviour that may damage health. Harmful practices such as smoking or excessive alcohol consumption are sometimes ascribed to personal stress, but they often become routine habits used by a majority of people to cope with life and ease social contacts. Cultural patterns of social interaction, symbolic behaviour and tension reduction are learned in childhood and reinforced through life. Lifestyle practices are increasingly influenced by public and corporate policies that control the production of goods and promote products that may damage health. To be effective, therefore, health programmes concerned with lifestyles must deal with structural influences on behaviour as well as its specific individual components.

There are ethical issues to be considered when lifestyles policies and programmes are being devised. This means that a delicate balance must be achieved between respect for individual rights of free choice and the duty of society to promote the health of the population.

Healthy Environment

The environment of the European Region is changing rapidly in terms of demographic structure, human lifestyles, consumer goods, energy resources, methods of industrial and agricultural production, transportation, tourism and migration. All these factors can cause, and can interact to produce, impacts on health. Improvements in human environment, including the upgrading of housing, the reduction of long-standing pollution, and the provision of better working conditions involve many aspects of government at central, regional and local levels, and require well-integrated, multi-sectoral plannign and managment. The development of new technologies in the areas of energy production or chemical manufacture must be such that it minimises potential adverse effects on human health, and this requires the establishment of mechanisms for assessment, monitoring and systematic evaluation. In all countries of the Region there is widespread interest in the quality of the environment and in its influence on human health. The targets for environmental health policies number 18 to 25.

Appropriate Health Care

Over the past twenty years, there has been a massive increase in the resources allocated to health services in the Region as a whole, and technological developments in medicine have been unprecedented. As a result, the quality of life for many patients with specific physical conditions or mental illnesses has improved significantly. Despite these real achievements, however, the health of people in Europe has not progressed as rapidly as might have been expected. We are presently faced with the dilemma of what to do in an increasingly complex situation characterised by the emergence of new health problems and challenges, changing expectations, developing capabilities both within and outside the health sector, and pre-eminently finite resources. There is an increasing responsibility with the public to participate so far as possible with politicians, health planners and providers in decisions regarding financing, organising, managing and evaluating all aspects of health care. Thus the primary health care concept is as relevant for Europe as for other regions of the world. Targets 26 to 31 deal with priorities for primary health care and the quality of health services.

Health Development Support

The attainment of the targets set out in the preceding paragraphs will require a fundamental change of attitudes and working practices among politicians, health authorities, health personnel, people in other sectors, and the general public. The targets, 32-38 in this section will have to be reached much earlier than the other targets since the support measures with which they are concerned are in themselves pre-requisites for a successful health development process. Health policy formulation, the managerial process, human resource development and health technology assessment will comprise the content of the targets for health development support. In some member states health legislation may need to be strengthened, and decisive action taken to ensure that national policies are in line with community needs and are in accordance with the country's political and administrative setting.

Irrespective of the scale and type of approach which a country considers appropriate, increasing emphasis will be laid on continuous and thorough evaluation and, wherever necessary, re-programming will be undertaken according to the evidence forth-coming from the health information system and the indicators of target achievement.

Conclusion

Health for all is a challenging goal for every country in the European Region. The setting of targets provides a framework for initiating the actions necessary, stressing as they do the improvements needed in the health of the people, if they are to lead socially and economically productive lives. The Regional targets outline the contents of a European health policy which should stimulate the member states in the development of health for all policies and programmes.

The 'Health for All' movement is for the people, with the people and, above all, a movement by the people. The first task of governments is to launch the Health for All movement within their own bounds, and health authorities will have to take responsibility for leading the development necessary. Health professionals, too, have a very important role to play in health development in all countries of the Region. Their expert knowledge and the influence they have with politicians and the general public alike make them an important force in mobilising support and initiating change.

The importance of sectors other than health has been stressed throughout, and again targeting of the movement gives additional emphasis to their important and sometimes new responsibilities. Many of the major health problems facing countries today have their roots and their solutions outside national boundaries, and for that reason international co-operation is needed more than ever before. United Nations agencies and other inter-governmental organisations have an important role to play, but it is WHO that bears special responsibility in this respect. The European Region has the people, the knowledge and the resources necessary to attain health for all ; the greatest need is the will to bring all those forces more effectively to bear on prevailing problems. A joint commitment to the regional policy and setting of clear targets has created a broad movement that will foster better understanding and leave a legacy of value beyond our time.

24

Adolescent Services

The Adolescent Period — A Definition

Adolescence is often defined as the 'growing up period between childhood and maturity' (Graham and Rutter, 1976). However, this simple definition conceals a number of issues which require more detailed elaboration. In the first place problems arise in the selection of the criteria adopted to delineate the end of childhood or the beginning of adulthood. The major physical changes of puberty are usually taken to indicate the starting point for adolescence. In particular the onset of menstruation in girls and the appearance of public hairs in boys are used to signify the beginning of puberty and the end of childhood. However, the choice of these events is to some extent arbitrary since these two easily observable changes from only a small part of the complex bodily modifications taking place around this time.

Similar difficulties arise in defining the upper limit of adolescence. Clearly a number of criteria could be adopted, for example the attainment of physical or emotional maturity or simply arrival of the statutory age at which adult responsibilities can be taken on (e.g. voting, marriage, etc.).

A second problem in the definition of the adolescent period arises from the considerable variability in the age at which individuals achieve developmental milestones. Accordingly, the age period described as adolescence may vary markedly from one individual to the next (Tanner, 1973).

Whilst the above difficulties in defining the adolescent period might appear academic, obvious practical difficulties may arise in the planning of services such as day care or in-patient facilities for adolescent patients where arbitrary age limits need to be set. For example, an adolescent unit accepting youngsters between the ages of 12 and 17 may contain individual patients who are at very different stages of development (pre-pubertal, pubertal, or post-pubertal) and who consequently need to make quite different psychological adjustments. Such problems have given rise to the suggestion that placement should be made on biological rather than chronological grounds and that rigid age limits should be abolished (Court, 1976, paragraph 11.9 p. 166).

However, for the purpose of simplicity in this chapter the age period from 11 to 19 years will be considered.

Health Needs of the Adolescent

In terms of physical illness, adolescents place far fewer demands upon the health service than younger children. Instead, the major health problems for adolescents lie within the social and behavioural sphere (Court, 1976). This fact presumably reflects the major developmental tasks of the adolescent period where the young person is striving to become independent from his or her family, beginning to form relationships with the opposite sex and also beginning to make major decisions about life ahead, for example in terms of education and employment. Traditionally adolescence has been viewed as a time of 'storm and stress' (Hall, 1904). Furthermore, some writers have suggested that a steady progress in development during this period is a sign of abnormality (Freud, 1952; Geleard, 1961). However, recent research has suggested that these views of adolescence may be misguided. Contrary to early speculation younger adolescents, at least, do not show increased evidence of psychological disturbance when compared with child or adult populations (Rutter *et al.*, 1976) nor do the *majority* of adolescents show the marked feelings of alienation and conflict with parents so often reported in literature (Douvan and Adelson, 1966; Bandura, 1972; Rutter *et al.*, 1976; Fogelman, 1976). Nevertheless, although some problems of adolescence are not necessarily more numerous than those of childhood in a number of respects they appear to differ in nature from those of earlier years. An example of this is that depression (Rutter *et al.*, 1976), suicide (Shaffer, 1974; Tyler, 1978), and attempted suicide (White, 1974) become more common in adolescence.

Other problems which have been reported to occur more frequently in adolescence are school refusal (Rutter *et al.*, 1970), anorexia nervosa (Crisp, 1967; Kendell *et al.*, 1973; Crisp *et al.*, 1976), drug dependence (Connell, 1976), and alcohol dependence (O'Connor, 1977). In addition, since in adolescence the young person is becoming sexually mature some problems (unwanted pregnancies, venereal disease, difficulty in sexual functioning) may occur as a result of this increased sexual activity (Schofield, 1973; Farrell, 1978). Finally, the incidence of some rarer psychiatric disorders such as schizophrenia (Rutter, 1972), manic depressive psychosis (Anothony and Scott, 1960), and obsessional compulsive states (Black, 1974) have been shown to increase in the adolescent period.

The wide ranging social and behavioural problems of adolescence described above bring young people into contact with many different agencies both within and outside the health service. For example, an adolescent who fails to attend school may be referred to the school psychological service, whilst another whose anxiety is expressed in physical symptoms may be referred to an appropriate hospital department for further investigation. Young people who break the law may have their first contacts with the police and juvenile courts. Subsequently they may be placed in care with the Local Authority and later maintained in a community home. Others with problems of drug addiction and fears of unwanted pregnancy who are afraid or unwilling to seek help through the family GP or hospital service may seek help from voluntary agencies. Youngsters whose parents are concerned about their behaviour may be taken to their general practitioner and subsequently referred to the child and adolescent psychiatric service; older adolescents may be referred to the adult psychiatric service. Table 24.1 lists some of the varied settings to which young people with psychological problems may be referred.

Traditionally, clinical psychologists specializing in adolescent problems have worked in psychiatric settings such as residential adolescent units. However, it is clear that any developing clinical psychology service for adolescents must establish close links with the wide network of agencies in health, education, and social services to which adolescents are referred.

The progress that clinical psychologists have made in this direction is documented in the remaining sections of this chapter.

Development of Clinical Psychology Service for Adolescents

Although numbers of clinical psychologists in the health service have increased rapidly over the last 20 years (from 198 in 1962 to 795 in 1978 in England and Wales) the profession is still a relatively small one. Consequently the development of specialized services has only been possible in recent years. Nevertheless, individual clinical psychologists have been working with adolescents over quite a long period of time even though it has not been possible always to organize separate adolescent psychology services in the way envisaged by the Trethowan Report (1977).

It is difficult to trace the beginnings of this work with adolescents. However, unlike the educational psychology service which began independently with the appointment of the first local authority psychologist in 1913 and the establishment of the London Child Guidance Training Centre in 1928 the work of clinical psychologists with adolescents had its beginning in the

Table 24.1

Settings to which Adolescents with Psychological Problems may be Referred

1.	**Health**
	(a) Health centres, general practice
	(b) Hospital departments of child and adolescent psychiatry: out-patient, in-patient, and day-patient
	(c) Hospital departments of adult psychiatry
	(d) Other hospital departments, e.g. paediatrics, dermatology, wards admitting suicidal adolescents
	(e) Child guidance clinics administered by NHS
	(f) Special hospitals
	(g) Youth treatment centres
2.	**Education**
	(a) Child guidance clinics administered by local authority departaments
	(b) Schools and units for maladjusted children (day and residential)
	(c) Other special schools
3.	**Social Services**
	(a) Observation and assessment
	(b) Community homes
	(c) Community schools
4.	**Voluntary Agencies**
	For example, Brook Advisory Centres, Grapevine Young People's Advisory Service, Samaritans

establishment of child and adolescent psychiatric services within the NHS. The development of these services began following the National Health Service Act of 1946 which required the Regional Health Service Boards to provide medical services both in-patient and out-patient for children suffering from 'mental illness and maladjustment' (Howellis, 1965). As new in patient and day patient and out-patient facilities for adolescents were opened psychologists' posts were established to service these units.

In some cases posts were established to cover both child and adolescent services, in other cases posts were created specifically for work with adolescents, for example in adolescent in-patient units. By 1972 there were 257 beds for adolescents in such units and by 1974—436 beds (Court, 1976).

At the same time as these developments were taking place in the NHS demand for educational psychology services was also increasing. Following the Underwood Committee recommendation in 1955 educational psychologists were working in child guidance clinics and the school psychological service and these services provided an alternative source of help for disturbed adolescents. Furthermore, some older adolescents were being seen by clinical psychologists working in adult psychiatric settings and in the special hospitals.

However, during the 1970s a number of developments began to take place which led to a reappraisal of child and adolescent psychological services. The first of these was the reorganization of the health service which gave rise to increasing demands for the services of clinical psychologists.

A second development was the publishing of the Trethowan Report (DHSS, 1977) which recommended that clinical psychology services should be organized on an area basis and that individual psychologists should be made available to social service and education departments (para 5.3.9). In addition, this report suggested that clinical psychologists should become more closely involved in primary care settings with general practitioners (para 5.3.2).

The third influence was the Court Report published in 1976. This underlined the important role played by psychologists in the assessment and treatment of children and adolescents and recommended an expansion of the numbers of psychologists working in this field. Furthermore, it emphasized the advice giving role of psychologists to other professional workers.

Implicit in all these developments was the need for more extensive services. Clinical psychologists were being requested not only to see more children and adolescents but also to work in diverse settings (community homes, special schools, local authority hostels, community health centres). In addition they were being called upon to provide support for an increasing number of other professional groups inclouding nurses, social workers, child care staff, and teachers.

From the results of a Division of Educational and Child Psychology (DECP) inquiry carried out in England and Wales (BPS, 1978a) it was clear that some of these influences were already having some impact on the work of clinical psychologists in health service settings. Table 24.2 and 24.3 list some of the settings in which these psychologists were working together with the professionals with whom they had contact.

Table 24.2

Percentage of Health Service Psychologists working in various Settings with Children and Adolescents (N=91)

1.	Child Psychiatry Departments in Hospitals	86.6%
2.	Paediatric Departments	24.1%
3.	Subnormality Hospitals	43.5%
4.	Child Guidance Clinics	22.9%
5.	Special Day Schools	19.0%
6.	Community Health Centres	13.2%

Figures taken from 'Psychological Services for Children', *Bulletin of The British Psychological Society* (1978a) 31, 11-15.

Table 24.3

Percentage of Health Service Psychologists having contact with Various Professionals (at least monthly contact)

1.	Psychiatrist	85.0%
2.	Other hospital doctors	60.7%
3.	Social Services Field Workers	52.3%
4.	Teachers	51.7%
5.	Educational psychologists	47.1%
6.	Speech therapists	39.0%

Figures taken from 'Psychological Services for Children', *Bulletin of The British Psychological Survey* (1978a) 31, 11-15.

However, it was also clear that some of the recommendations of these reports could not be fully implemented. For example, the findings of the DECP inquiry that many of the NHS psychologists worked with children and adolescents through the age groups 0-19 years probably reflected the fact that in some localities there were too few psychologists to specialize solely in adolescent psychology services. This problem was met in some areas by one psychologist taking special responsibility for this service even though he/she was working with children of other age groups.

The DECP inquiry also showed that there was increasing liaison and cooperation between educational psychology and child psychology groups. However, with regard to the relationship between the two professional groups of psychologists the Court Report had made two controversial recommendations. First, this report suggested that the professions of educational and clinical psychology should be combined to form an integrated child psychology service. The second recommendation was that the distinction between child guidance clinics and child psychiatric hospital services should be dropped and that both should be reorganized as part of an integrated Child and Adolescent Psychiatry Service. These suggstions were not met favourably by many educational and clinical psychologists and in 1978 the BPS voiced a number of objections to these recommendations in its comments to the Report (BPS, 1978b). As a result of some of these issues and the need for increasing co-operation between the two professional groups dealing with children and adolescents, the Professional Affairs Board of the BPS set up a working party to consider the future of psychological services for children and adolescents. At the time of going to press this body has still to make its final recommendations.

It is clear that clinical psychology services for adolescents are at an interesting stage of development. Although many areas are not yet able to support the specialized grouping of adolescent services headed by a principal psychologist envisaged by the Trethowan document the demand for such services exists. In the present economic climate a rapid expansion of services is obviously impossible. However, it is important to note that a number of psychologists have begun to extend their work with adolescents ina number of ways. For example, some have begun to work in association with social service departments or in community health settings. Moreover, some posts are being established which are jointly funded by health service and local authority. More detailed discussion of the role of a clinical psychologist in these settings will be left until the next section.

The Role of the Clinical Psychologist in Adolescent Services

Traditionally in child and adolescent psychiatric services the psychologist was seen as having mainly an assessment function. For example, the psychologist's contribution to the multi disciplinary team would be to carry out psychometric assessment with the individual child or adolescent, whilst other workers would have the responsibility of assessing the family situation (Howells, 1965). However, in recent years a number of developments have effectively changed this rather limited role.

In the first instance, there has been substantial growth in the body of psychological knowledge concerning effective treatment methods. Moreover, in the last fifteen years or so psychologists have been responsible for the evolution of a number of sophisticated assessment procedures often involving direct observation of behaviour. These developments in assessment methods have enabled more detailed formulations of clinical problems to be made together with a closer monitoring of treatment progress. Inevitably this has led to an important role for psychologists in the treatment of adolescents.

Secondly, psychologists have become increasingly involved in indirect treatment methods by the transmission of their skills to other professional workers such as teachers, social workers, and child care staff. An examination of Table 24.4 shows that amongst all grades of child clinical psychologists below Principal level (field workers) the greatest proportion of time was spent in *indirect* treatment methods. Perhaps this has arisen partly from the impracticalities of carrying out individual treatment in the face of increasing demand for psychological services and partly froma growing emphasis on the interactive nature of the problems of children and adolescents.

A third developmetn arises from the involvement of some psychologists in the wider aspects of the policy and planning of treatment environments.

Treatment with Individuals

It is possible in the limited space available to give a detailed account of treatment methodologies with adolescent youngsters. However, it is possible to draw attention to some issues underlying therapy and to illustrate these by specific examples.

Adolescent problems are of a multifactorial nature. Accordingly, different factors may produce and maintain the same problem behaviour in different youngsters. For this reason it is not possible to apply psychological treatments to a particular problem in a 'cookbook fashion'. Many psychologists adopt

Table 24.4

Sessions worked by Clinical Psychologists in Child and Adolescent Services on Various Categories of Work

Category of work	*Principles (Full and part-time) (N = 17)*		*Field workers (full and part-time) (N = 66)*	
	Mean no. of sessions	*Per cent of total time*	*Mean no. of sessions*	*Per cent total time*
Direct treatment	4.09	14.6	5.52	19.1
Indirect treatment	2.96	10.6	5.87	20.3
Assessment, etc.	5.08	18.1	5.31	18.4
Planning	3.89	13.9	2.71	9.4
Administration	2.41	8.6	2.42	8.4
Data collection	2.44	8.7	1.14	3.9
Professional development	2.41	8.6	1.57	5.4
Training	3.57	12.7	3.10	10.7
Other	1.18	4.2	1.23	4.3
Total	28.03	100.0	28.87	100.0

Figures taken from Psychological Services for Children in England and Wales, DECP (1980).

what has been termed an 'applied scientist' approach to clinical problems (Davidson, 1977). Fundamental to this approach is (1) a careful and objective description of the problem, (2) a detailed formulation of the problem (that is setting up hypotheses concerning the origins and maintenance of the problem), and (3) a systematic testing of the hypotheses through treatment inventions the effects of which are closely monitored.

One of the important stages in this process is the formulation of the clinical problem. It is often tempting in clinical practice, when a presenting problem is one for which effective treatment methods have been found, to embark upon treatment without an adequate clinical formulation. However, such a short cut may be misguided. A practical example of this issue arose in an out-patient clinic held by the author to which a sixteen year old boy was referred with problems obsessional handwashing and cleaning rituals. These rituals had persisted for several months and were taking up much of the young man's time so that he was in danger of losing his job as a lorry driver's mate. He was extremely reluctant to talk about his problems but clearly was very distressed so that it was tempting to embark upon a programme involving response prevention (Meyer *et al.*, 1974) and flooding (Marks *et al.*, 1975) as quickly as possible. However, a detailed analysis of the problem over a number of sessions revealed that the young man had been experiencing a great deal of anxiety concerning his first experiences of sexual attraction towards a young woman staying in his parent's home. His high level of anxiety had given rise to a number of physical symptoms including increased frequency of urination which he had interpreted as a sign of veneral disease. His excessive handwashing and cleanliness was an attempt to protect his family from his 'infection' and was maintained by anxiety reduction. He had had no sexual experience and his knowledge concerning sex was extremely limited. Figure 24.1 gives a simple formulation of the problem. This anecdotal example illustrtaes how a premature programme using response prevention and flooding would have been both time consuming and costly. In this case rapid progress was achieved and complete elimination of the compulsive handwashing within three sessions which focused upon (a) an explanation of his physical symptoms; (b) factual information concerning sexual functioning and sexual relationships.

A similar emphasis on the detailed formulation of clinical problems has been given by Slade (1982) in the case of adolescent anorexic behaviour. In this model the eating problem of the anorexic patient is viewed not as the primary disorder but as a 'secondary adaptation to a more general set of psychological problems'. Using this formulation one of the most important goals of treatment is to enable the anorexic girl to establish sources of satisfaction other than dieting. Accordingly this view would support the notion expressed by some writers of the misguided nature of treatment methods which have placed central attention on weight gain as the main goal in therapy for anorexic patients (Bemis, 1978).

The wide ranging problems of adolescents include anxiety, depression, difficulties in interpersonal relationships, delinquent behaviour, sexual problems, drug taking, heavy drinking, and attempted suicide. These problems differ in nature from those of childhood and reflect some of the developmental tasks of the adolescent period. Undoubtedly one of the major tasks for the adolescent is to gain independence from the family. However, some young people may suffer considerable anxiety in taking steps towards independence whilst others may find that their independent actions bring them in conflict with the police or school authorities. A fundamental aim of therapy then is to aid the young person to gain independence by developing their problem solving skills in a way that will allow them to avoid undue psychological distress.

Such an approach was adopted by Yule and his colleagues (Yule *et al.*, 1980) in behavioural treatment of a twelve-year old boy with school refusal problems which had developed following a period of ill-health and a subsequent hospitalization. Significant factors were fears of academic failoure linked to high academic goals, decreased performance at school prior to school refusal due to high anxiety and loss of concentration, later phobic avoidance of school and school friends and specific anxiety associated with inability to explain his absence to school friends. Successful treatment involved increasing the youngster's coping strategies by training in relaxation skills, graded exposure in imagination and in real-life, lowering in academic goals (moving into a lower stream at school), rehearsal and role-playing to enable him to explain his absence to his school friends. Similar approaches to the treatment of school phobia have been described by psychologists working in educational settings (Blagg, 1977; Galloway, 1980).

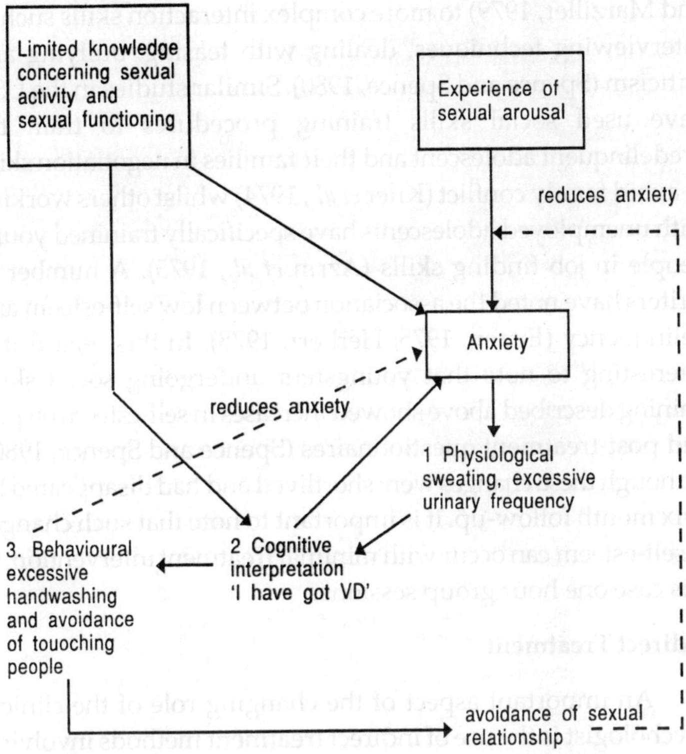

Fig. 24.1 Clinical formulation of obsessional handwashing in a 16-year-old male adolescent

A second example of treatment as a training in problem solving skills arises in the treatment of young offenders. It has been argued that delinquent behaviour of some youngsters arises because the young person has not learnt appropriate ways of responding in some social situations. A youngsters may, for example, use aggressive behaviour to obtain a desired goal in the absence of any other alternative behavioural strategy. An interesting approach to treatment of delinquent behaviour has been developed by a number of psychologists who have been carrying out social skills training programmes with young offenders in a community home setting. Such programmes have included training in a range of skills from quite specific behaviours such as eye contact and head movements (Spence and Marziller, 1979) to more complex interaction skills such as interviewing techniques, dealing with teasing, bullying and criticism (Spence and Spence, 1980). Similar studies in the USA have used social skills training procedures to train the predelinquent adolescent and their families in negotiation skills to avoid family conflict (Kifer *et al.*, 1974) whilst others working with unemployed adolescents have specifically trainined young people in job finding skills (Azrin *et al.*, 1975). A number of writers have noted the association between low self-esteem and delinquency (Eitzen, 1975; Herbert, 1978). In this regard it is interesting to note that youngsters undergoing social skills training described above showed increases in self-esteem on pre- and post-treatment questionnaires (Spence and Spence, 1980). Although these changes were shortlived and had disappeared by a six month follow-up, it is important to note that such changes in self-esteem can occur with minimal treatment intervention, in this case one hour group sessions.

Indirect Treatment

An important aspect of the changing role of the clinical psychologist is the use of indirect treatment methods involving transmission of skills to parents, nurses, teachers and child care staff. Particularly influential in this respect are the writings of some American psychologists (Tharp and Wetzel, 1969; Patterson, 1974). In this country examples of this approach are to be found within social service settings. For instance, one group of workers have investigated the feasibility of the implementation of a behavioural treatment programme for enuresis by child care staff within a community home setting. The incidence of bed wetting is reported to be particularly high amongst children in residential homes (Stein and Susser, 1967; Yule and Raynes, 1972). Moreover, such a problem may impose considerable restrictions on fostering or return to parents. There are obvious advantages of findings a successful treatment method for enuretic youngsters living in such residential settings.

A group of 39 children in 34 children's homes took part in the study; 19 in a treatment group and a further 20 in a no-treatment control group. The children's homes ranged from small family units to larger residential establishments. Most children slept in dormitories and only one of the children had his own room. Treatment involved the regular use of an enuresis alarm over a number of weeks. The alarm consists of two metal gauze detector pads which are assembled on the bed at night and connected to an alarm box which is placed at the side of the bed. Urination during the night causes the alarm to ring and the child to awaken. Although this form of treatment is extremely successful in out-patient settings (see, for example, Taylor and Turner, 1975) difficulties could clearly arise in community homes where there are a multiplicity of staff caring for children and where other children in a dormitory could easily be disturbed. The study, therefore, set out to examine the effectiveness and the feasibility of carring out this treatment programme within a community home setting (Jehu *et al.*, 1977).

To ensure adequate compliance with treatment instructions house-parents were asked to make sure that youngsters got up and went to the toilet when the alarm sounded. They were also asked to help remake the bed, reset the alarm, and keep a record of wet and dry nights.

As a result of treatment all but one of the children in the treatment group ceased to wet the bed at night whereas youngsters in the control group did not improve significantly. The mean duration of treatment was 12 weeks. It is interesting to note that some youngsters were also reported to have improved more generally in their behaviour. Moreover, staff reported minimal disruption in the homes and expressed an enthusiasm to use the treatment method again with other enuretic children.

Such a study clearly indicated one way that psychologists might usefully provide a behaviourally oriented support service to help residential staff in the management of children with difficult behaviour problems. Another example arises from the social skills training programme described earlier where attempts are now being made to involve child care staff in the teaching of social skills to youngsters in community schools (Spence and Marziller, 1979).

Psychologists have also been involved in a consultant role in other aspects of social service work. For example, a number of local authorities have been operating family placement schemes for children who would otherwise be placed in a community home school (Hazel and Cox, 1976). In Birmingham some psychologists have been involved in giving advice to foster parents on how to deal with problems of management of these sometimes difficult youngsters (Druce, 1977).

More extensive examples of this approach can be seen in those units that have adopted a social learning theory philosophy such that the whole units is run along behavioural lines. One psychologist has described the setting up of such a regime within Youth Treatment Centres (YTC) (Reid, 1981). YTCs are units which were initially set up to provide special long term treatment facilities for disturbed adolescents who could not easily be contained within the community home system and youngsters who had committed serious offences and were detained under Section 53 of the Children and Young People Act, 1933 (Cawson and Martell, 1975). There are now two such units in the country, the units are under the direct control of the DHSS and act as an extension to the secure units already providing for difficult boys within the community homes system.

Reid (1981) has listed some of the problem behaviours of the young people referred to these units. As can be seen in Table 24.5 these behaviours are wide ranging and provide a sizeable problem for any institution attempting to provide a comprehensive treatment programme.

Table 24.5

Problem Behaviours of Young People Referred to a Youth Treatment Centre (from Reid, 1981)

1. **Major offence behaviours** Murder Manslaughter Armed robbery Sexual assaults Arson	5. **Behavioural excesses** Physical violence (persons and property) Self-mutilation (head banging, wrist slashing, overdoses) Verbal violence
2. **Minor offence behaviours** Theft Take and drive av'ay Burglary Prostitution	6. **Institutional problem behaviours** Hostages Sit in/barricades Sexual behaviour Violence Attempted escapes
3. **'Clinical' problems** Obsessional rituals (e.g. washing, dressing, thoughts) Enuresis Faecal smearing Anxiety	7. **Problems of generalization** Self-help skills Job skills - interview behaviour, work skills, etc. Family conflicts Deviant peer group Absondings
4. **Behavioural deficits** Limited intellectual ability Lack of educational attainment Lack of social skills (verbal and non verbal) Lack of survival skills (e.g. self-help budgeting, etc.)	

In Glenthorne Youth Treatment Centre the clinical psychologists act mainly in an advisory capacity whilst the 'front-line' therapists are group workers coming from the teaching, nursing, and child care professions.

The main goal of treatment is to establish through reinforcement, modelling, and instruction, behavioural competence in social, educational, vocational, and self-care skills. In addition, attempts are made to modify those disruptive behaviour that have often brought youngsters to the centre in the first instance.

Initially, all young people entering the YTC are admitted into the assessment unit which is run as a point economy system. Here young people earn points for achieving specified goals. Accordingly, this unit allows a detailed assessment to be made of the youngsters' level of functioning. From here allocation is made either to one of the secure units or to an open unit or hostel. As the youngster progresses to lessening degrees of security, fewer prompts are given by staff and more reliance is given to naturally occurring contingencies (e.g. verbal approval, self-control). In addition, youngsters are able to spend increasing amounts of time outside the centre and practise developing skills in the 'real world'. Great emphasis is placed on the flexible design of individual programmes, direct observation, and detailed monitoring of achievement goals by staff (Reid, 1981).

Although this centre is in its early stages of development the treatment approach which emphasizes the acquisition of positive problem solving skills appears to be extremely promising.

Policy and Planning

In an article concerning the development of 'community psychology' one psychologist has described the importance of a multilevel approach within clinical psychology services. Three levels are described: (1) working with clients individually or in groups; (2) working with staff in order to help larger groups of clients; and (3) working with managers in monitoring policy and planning (Bender, 1979). The involvement of some psychologists in the setting up oof total treatment environments has given rise to their participation in the policy and planning of such institutions (Brown, 1977; Brown and Sawyer, 1978; Reid, 1981). For example in the YTC described earlier the principal psychologist has become the Programme Director with a line management function and responsibility for the overall treatment programme of the institution, staff recruitment, and staff training (Fig. 24.2). An important part of this new role for psychologists is the undertaking of careful research investigations into the effectiveness of different types of policy and provision for young people (see for example, Cornish and Clarke, 1975). Such studies provide a firm factual basis upon which policy and planning decisions can be made.

Future Progress of Clinical Psychology Services For Adolescents

Previous sections have outlined some of the psychological needs of adolescents and have pointed to some of the contributions of clinical psychologists working in different health and social service settings. It is clear that although psychological services for adolescents are at an early stage of development there is considerable potential for increasing the application of psychological skills and knowledge in this field. It is worthwhile in this concluding section, therefore, to consider avenues for future development of the service.

(1) The high rates of suicidal behaviour in adolescents are well known (Morgan *et al.*, 1975; Tyler, 1978). Many adolescents make repeated attempts at taking their own lives. Furthermore, some young people learn that this behaviour is one effective, if drastic, way of obtaining help. At least one study has noted that once referred such children take up quite a large proportion of psychiatric services, since they are more likely to be admitted into hospital, once in hospital they are more likely to remain there for longer and once discharged they are more likely to be sent for further institutional care or treatment than children referred with other problems (Mattson *et al.*, 1969). Suicide and depressive behaviour in young people becomes therefore one of the major health concerns of the adolescent population.

Close liaison with casualty departments and early intervention through the establishment of crisis counselling services may enable psychological services to prevent the repetitive cycle of suicide attempts and psychiatric hospital admission for some of these young people. In particular utilization of cognitive behaviour therapy methods currently proving useful in the treatment of depression in adult populations (Blackburn *et al.*, 1981) may equip young people with strategies which would enable them to deal more effectively with future depressive episodes.

(2) No mention has been made in the earlier sections of this chapter of the effects of physical illness on young people. In the USA some psychologists have established counselling services for such patients and for the terminally ill. One counselling

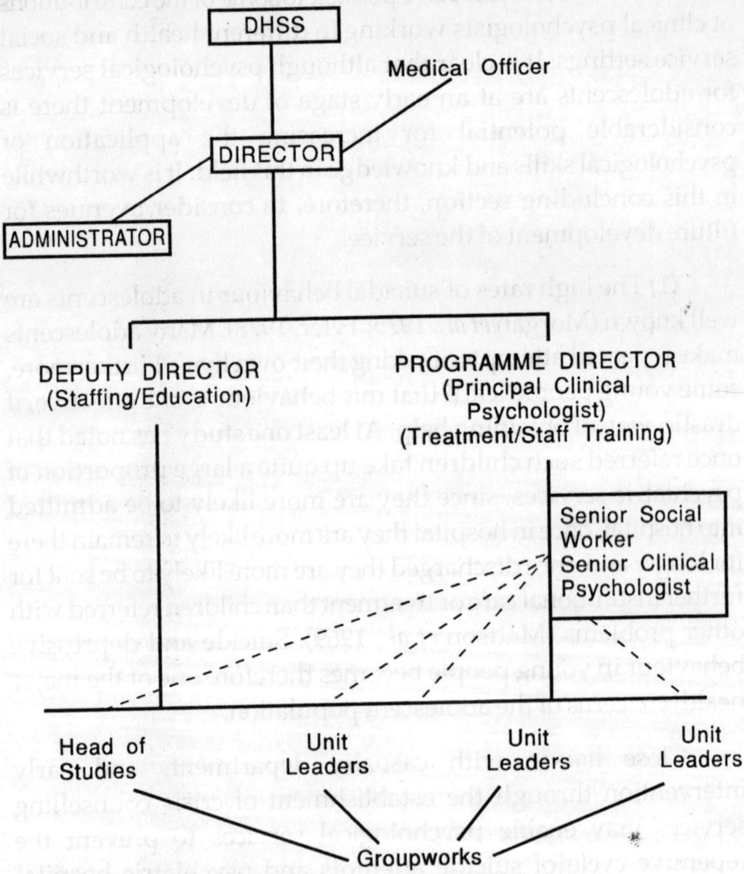

Fig. 24.2 Glenthorne Youth Treatment Centre

service for terminally ill adolescents was set up recently in this country (Kuykendall, 1981). Preliminary investigations in Liverpool (Edwards, 1982) suggest that this may be a useful area for future development. This type of counselling service for adolescents with serious illnesses and for their parents could well be offered as part of an adolescent clinical psychology service.

(3) Reference was made earlier to the number of young women who face unwanted pregnancies. Although overall rates for illegitimate birth and abortions in yooung women (11-19 years) have stabilized in recent years, the number of abortions of younger adolescents (11-15 years) has continued to rise (Court, 1976). In this respect it is interesting to note that a recent article commenting on the clinical psychology servicing of an obstetrics and gynaecology department paid particular attention to the need for termination counselling for young girls in this setting (Broome, 1980).

(4) As many young people find it easier to seek help from bodies not associated with home or school, a fourth potential area for liaison work exists in the field of voluntary services. Clinical psychologists specializing in the psychological treatment of sexual problems, problem drinking and drug addiction may well be able to offer a specialist support service in such settings.

(5) Finally, many clinical psychologists have already established close links with GPs and community health centres. Such developments are also important for adolescent services where early identification of psychological problems may prevent compulsory hospitalization at a later stage. In such setting some psychologists have established self-help groups for young people (for eating problems, see Caswell, 1976) whilst others have become involved in the use of family therapy (for reviews, see Minuchin, 1974; Skynner, 1976). Clearly this type of service could well extend in the future.

However, it is perhaps important to add a few cautionary remarks to the above suggestions for the future development of clinical psychology services for adolescents. In the first place, as noted earlier, problems of adolescents are wide ranging, encompassing difficulties within the social, psychological, vocational and medical domains. Youngsters may have problems adapting in the family, in the school, or at work and these problems may bring the young person into contact with many different professional agencies. Any development of clinical psychology services must take into account the provision made by other agencies for adolescent problems and clear links should be developed both at the level of policy and planning and at a more personal level between one professional and another.

Secondly, it is not sufficient simply to demonstrate that there is a need for increased services and then to supply that need. The establishment of new services should be closely monitored and their effectiveness ascertained. Furthermore, there is an overriding need for more research into adolescent problems, a fact that was noted recently by the SSRC by the establishment of a special fund to promote research in this area (Schaffer and Hargreaves, 1978).

In a number of ways the problems of adolescents have been neglected in health service provision. The setting up of more effective services for both prevention and treatment may ensure the avoidance of later crises in adult life.

Select Bibliography

Anthony, J., and Scott, P. (1960). Manic-depressive psychosis in childhood. *Journal of Child Pshchology and Psychiatry*, 1, 53-72.

Bandura, A. (1972). The stormy decade. Fact or fiction? In D. Rogers (ed.) *Issues in Adolescent Psychology*, 2nd ed. New York: Appleton-Century-Crofts.

Bemis, K. (1978). Current approaches to the etiology and treatment of anorexia nervosa. *Psychological Bulletin*, 85, 593-617.

Bender, M.P. (1979). Community psychology: When? *Bulletin of The British Psychological Society*, 32, 6-9.

Black, A. (1974). The natural history of obsessional neurosis. In R. Beech (ed.) *Obsessional States*. London: Methuen.

Blackburn, I.M., Bishop, S. Glen, A.I.M., Whalley, L., and Christie, J.C. (1981). The efficacy of cognitive therapy in depression: A treatment trial using cognitive therapy and pharmcotherapy, each alone and in combination. *British Journal of Psychiatry.* 139, 181-189.

Blagg, N. (1977). A detailed strategy for the rapid treatment of school phobics. *British Association of Behavioural Psychotherapy Bulletin,* 5, 70-75.

British Psychological Society (1978a). Psychological services for children. *Bulletin of The British Psychological Society,* 31, 125-127.

British Psychological Society (1978b). The Society's comments on the Report of the Court Committee on Child Health Services. *Bulletin of The British Psychological Society,* 31, 157-160.

Broome, A.K. (1980). Clinical psychology within obstetrics and gynaecology. *Bulletin of The British Psychological Society,* 33, 357-359.

Brown, B. (1977). Gillbey House: A token economy management scheme in a residential school for adolescent boys in trouble. *British Association of Behavioural Psychotherapy,* 5, 79-89.

Brown, B.J. and Sawyer, C.E. (1978). Uses and abuses of psychologists — Some alternatives for psychologists working in social services departments. *Bulletin of the British Psychological Society,* 31, 218-222.

Caswell,G. (1976). A study to compare the effectiveness of the behavioural modification of eating habits with dietary advice to overweight adolescent girls. Unpublished M.Sc. Thesis, Leeds.

Cawson, P., and Martell, P. (1975). Children referred to closed units. DHSS Research Report No. 5. London: HMSO.

Coleman, J.C. (1980). *The Native of Adolescence.* New York: Methuen.

Connell, P. (1976). Clinical aspects of drug misuse. In M. Rutter and L. Hersov (eds), *Child Psychiatry: Modern Approaches.* Oxford: Blackwell Scientific Publications.

Cornish D.B., and Clarke, R.V.G. (1975). Residential treatment and its effects on delinquency, London: HMSO.

Court, S.D.M. (1976). *Fit for the future: The report of the Committee on Child Health Services,* London: HMSO.

Crisp, A.H. (1967). Anorexin nervosa. *Hospital Medicine,* I, 713-718.

Crisp. A.H., Palmer, R.L., and Kallucy, R.S. (1976). How common in anorexia nervosa? *British Journal of Psychiatry,* 128, 549-554.

Davidson, M. (1977). The scientific/applied debate in psychology: A contribution *Bulletin of The British Psychological Society*, 30, 273-278.

Division of Educational and Clinical Psychology (1978). Psychological Services for Children. *Bulletin of The British Psychological Society*, 31, 11-15.

Douvan, E., and Adelson, J. (1966).*The Adolescent Experience.* New York: Willey.

Druce, N.R. (1977). Social learning approaches to professional fostering and treatment with security. In Behavioural Approaches to the Treatment of Delinquent Adolescents. Unpublished manuscript: Tennal School.

Edwards, G. (1982). A study of adjustment and illness related anxieties in adolescents with cystic fibrosis in relation to communication and denial within the family. Unpublished M. Psychol, dissertation, University of Liverpool.

Eitzen, D.S. (1975). The effects of behaviour modification on the attitude of delinquents. *Behaviour Research and Therapy,* 13, 295-299.

Farrell, C. (1978). *My Mother Said,* London: Routledge and Kegan Paul.

Fogelman, K. (1976). *Britain's Sixteen Year Olds.* London: National Children's Bureau.

Freud, A. (1952). Adolescence. *Psychoanalytic Study of the Child,* 13, 255-278.

Galloway, D. (1980). Problems in the assessment and management of persistent absenteeism from school. In L. Hersov and I.Berg (eds). *Out of School* Chichester: Wiley.

Geleard, E.R. (1961). Some aspects of ego vicissitudes in adolescence. *Journal of The American Psychonalytic Association,* 9, 394-350.

Graham, P. and Rutter, M. (1976). Adolescent disorders. In M. Rutter and L. Hersov (eds) *Child Psychiatry: Modern Approahes.* Oxford: Blackwell Scientific Publications.

Hall, G.S. (1904). *Adolescence, its Psychology and its Relations to Psychology, Anthropology, Sociology, Sex, Crime, Religion and Education,* Vols. I and II. New York: Appleton.

Hazel, N., and Cox, R. (1976). First report of the Special Family Project. Kent Social Services Department.

Herbert, M. (1978). *Conduct Disorders of Childhood and Adolescence: A Behavioural Approach to Assessment and Treatment.* Chichester:

Wiley.

Howells, J. (1965). Organisations of Child Psychiatric Services. In G. Howell (ed.), *Modern Perspectives in Adolescent Psychiatry*. Edinburgh: Oliver and Boyd.

Jehu, D., Morgan, R.T.T., Turner,R., and Jones, A. (1977). A controlled trial of the treatment of nocturnal enuresis in residential homes for children. *Behavioural Research and Therapy,* 15, 1-16.

Kendell, R.E., Hall, D.J., Hailey,A., and Babigan, H.M. (1973). The epidemiology of anorexia nervosa. *Psychological Medicine,* 3, 200-203.

Kennedy, P., Krietman, N., and Ovenstone, I. (1974). The prevalence of suicide and parasuicide (attempted suicide) in Edinburgh. *British Journal of Psychiatry,* 124, 36-11.

Kifer, R.E., Lewis, M.A. Green, D.R., and Phillips, E.L. (1974). Training predelinquent youths and their parents to negotiate conflic situations. *Journal of Applied Behaviour Analysis,* 7, 357-364.

Kuykendall, J. (1981). Personal communication.

Marks, I.M., Hodgson, R., and Rachman, S. (1975). Treatment of chronic obsessive-compulsive neurosis by in vivo exposure. *British Journal of Psychiatry,* 127, 349-364.

Meyer, V., Levy, R., and Schnurer, A. (1974). The behavioural treatment of obsessive compulsive disorders. H.R. Beech (ed.). *Obsessional States.* London: Methuen.

Mattson, A., Seese, L.R. and Hawkins, J.W. (1969). Suicidal behaviour as a child psychiatric emergency. *Archives of General Psychiatry,* 20, 100-109.

Minuchin, S. (1974). *Families and Family Therapy,* London: Tavistock.

Morgan, H.G., Pocock, H., and Pottle, S. (1975). The urban distribution of non-fatal deliberate self-harm. *British Journal of Psychiatry,* 126, 319-328.

O'Connor, J. (1977). Normal and problem drinking among children. *Journal of Child Psychology and Psychiatry,* 18, 279-284.

Patterson, G.R. (1974). Interventions with boys and conduct problems: Multiple settings, treatments and criteria. *Journal of Consulting Psychology,* 42, 471-481.

Reid, I. (1981). The development and maintenance of a behavioural regime in a secure treatment centre. In M.P. Feldman (ed.)

Development in the Study of Criminal Behaviour, Volume I: The Prevention and Control of Offenders. London: Wiley.

Rutter, M. (1972). Childhood schizophrenia reconsidered. *Journal of Autism and Schizophrenia,* 2, 315-337.

Rutter, M., Graham, P., Chadwick, O., and Yule, W. (1976). Adolescent turmoil: Fact of Fiction *Journal of Child Psychology and Psychiatry,* 17, 35-56.

Rutter, M. Tizard, J., and Whitmre, K. (1970). *Education, Health and Behaviour.* London: Longman.

Schaffer, H.R., and Hargreaves, D. (1978). Young people in the society: A research initiative by the SSRC. *Bulletin of The British Psychological Society,* 31, 81-94.

Schofield, M. (1965). *The Sexual Behaviour of Young People.* London: Longman.

Schofield, M. (1973). *The Sexual Behaviour of Young Adults.* London: Allen Lane.

Shaffer, D. (1974). Suicide in Childhood and Early Adolescence. *Journal of Child Psychology and Psychiatry,* 15, 275-291.

Shaw, C., and Shelkun, R. (1965). Suicidal adolescents and children. *Psychiatry,* 28, 157-168.

Skynner, R. (1976). *One Flesh Separate Persons.* London: Constable.

Slade, P. (1982). Towards a functional analysis of anorexia and bulimia nervosa. *British Journal of Clinical Psychology,* 21, 167-179.

Spence. S.H., and Marziller, J. (1979). Social skills training with adolescent male offenders: I— short term effects. *Behavioural Research and Therapy,* 17, 7-16.

Spence, A.J. and Spence S.H. (1980). Cognitive changes associated with social skills training. *Behaviour Research and Therapy,* 18, 265-272.

Stein, Z.A., and Susser, M, (1967). The social dimensions of a symptom: A socio-medical study of enuresis. *Social Science and Medicine,* 1, 183-201.

Tanner, J.M. (1973). *Growing Up. Scientific American,* 229, 35-42.

Taylor, P.D., and Turner, R.K. (1975). A clinical trial of continuous intermittent and overlearning 'bell and pad' treatments for nocturnal enuresis. *Behavioural Research and Therapy,* 13, 281-293.

Tharp, R.C., and Wetzel, R.J. (1969). *Behaviour Modification in the Natural Environment*. New York: Academic Press.

Trethowan, W.H. (1977). *The Role of Psychologists in the Health Services*. London: HMSO.

Tyler, M. (1978). Advisory and counselling services for young people. DHSS Research Report No. 1, London: HMSO.

White, H.C. (1974). Self poisoning in adolescents. *British Journal of Psychiatry*, 124. 24-35.

Yule, W., Hersov, L., and Treseder, J. (1980). Behavioural treatments in school refusal. In L. Hersov and I. Berg (eds) *Out of School*. Chichester: Wiley.

Yule, W., and Raynes, N.V. (1972). Behavioural characteristics of children in residential care in relation to indices of separation. *Journal of Child Psychology and Psychiatry*, 13, 249-258.

25

In Vitro Fertilisation: A Psychosocial and Development Study

Introduction

In vitro fertilization (IVF), management of frozen embryos and embryo transfer have progressed from science fiction to scientific medical reality, outstripping legal and moral frameworks. New directions have arisen for infertile couples bringing with them various physical and psychological questions regarding the development of children conceived by these means.

There have also been concerns regarding ethical and moral issues. Yet there has been no scientific follow-up of a significant group of such children. This study is particularly concerned with the following factors:

Biological issues querying increased congenital abnormalities including mental retardation.

Parent issues exploring positive and negative factors such as parental reasons to have children, unsuccessful resolution of marital problems or psychological conflicts including infertility that may resurface at certain stressful periods and influence the couple's relationship and/or parenting capacity. These issues can be further confounded if donor sperm or ae used and if this is kept a secret.

Issues of the child, looking at the possibility of these children being seen as special in many ways other than those related to their manner of conception and made vulnerable to unreal concerns or expectations, affecting the parent/child relationship and later the child's interactions with peers and teachers. Failed parental expectations and the child's internalizations of parental issues can greatly affect the child's self-esteem and self-control.

Family issues are concerned with possible stressful effects that fertility, the desire to have children and the intrusive nature of the infertility management, particularly the IVF management, may place on the marital and sexual relationships of the couples as well as distrupting their socio-familial life. If unresolved these conflicts may be displaced on to the children and inhibit parent/child communication regarding IVP origins. These issues can be enhanced by the exploitation, demands and expectations as a result of publicity.

More general issues are concerned with the importance of a better understanding by medical practitioners of the couples, the consequences of intervention and procedures, in order that adequate counselling and intervention can be provided from the beginning of the programme. It is important to determine whether there is a significant risk of physical pathology or psycho-pathology pertinent to children and their families.

With these concerns in mind, we felt it important that we see these families. As an initial step we studied the first group of children to be conceived through the Monash University IVF Programme. While recognising the need for a more extensive study, this group was clinically evaluated in order to determine whether or not they presented clinical concerns which might call into question theclinical justification for IVF conception.

Method

The first 52 children born from the Monash IVF programme received paediatric evaluation at 6 weeks and after 10 months of age. One child died at 4½ months and one family with twins refused follow-up. Thirty-three of these children were seen by a psychologist and a child psychiatrist and had psychosocial and developmental assessments between 1 and 3 years of age - the majority between 12 and 20 months. These children were basically selected in order of presentation to the paediatrician, with any bias going towards those about whom he was concerned. Because of various logistic reasons some of the 49 children were not seen for psychosocial evaluations. A review of these cases by the paediatrician revealed no current concerns about developmental problems at the 12 month evaluation and he did not consider any of them to be at risk for such problems (Spensley et al, 1986, for information on paediatric assessments). The psychosocial evaluation consisted of:

A parent interview regarding their child, themselves, their marriage and their experience of the IVF Programme. This included parental perceptions of problem issues concerning the child, parental assessment of their child's developmental status, history of current and past psychiatric problems and contacts with psychiatric facilities (Mushin et al, 1985 and 1986, for more details).

Administration of the Bayley Scales of Infant Development to the children. This instrument was chosen as it is well researched and standardised and commonly used in Australia for developmental evaluation of children in the age range seen. In one child the McCarthy Scales of Development were administered because the Bayley only goes up to 30 months of age.

Observations of family functioning and interactions in the interview setting. Evaluators also noted congruency between their observations and parental perceptions.

Population Studied

Children - Nineteen boys and fourteen girls, including six sets of twins, with a mean age of 17 months were included in the study.

Parents - The age of the parents was, as expected, above average. The mean age of mothers was 33 and of fathers 36. The cause of infertility was indiopathic in 26%; and 18% were due to factors in the male partners, this being the percentage of children conceived with donor sperm. The remainder of cases had medically diagnosed factors in the female partner. Sixty per cent conceived at the first IVF cycle and 8% required four or five attempts. All couples were married.

Method of delivery - Nine births were normal vaginal delivery, nine were forceps, one was breech, one was vacuum and thirteen were caesarian sections.

Results

Five children were considered by their parents to have significant problems with behaviour. In all of these families, problems could be related to parent/child international difficulties where parents had adapational problems. No significant marital problems were reported. Two mothers described significant depression following child birth but depression had spontaneously resolved by the time they were seen. There were no cases of child neglect or abuse and none of severe disturbance in the child's ability to relate to others.

Twelve of the 33 couples seen for psychosocial evaluations reported issues concerning the IVF programme. Five had concerns regarding staff communication and support and four had concerns over collection of sperm. Other issues, such as difficulty with travel,were reported. Three couples felt that IVF had altered their perception of the child. Despite the concerns, none of the couples reported strong negative feelings towards the programme. It will be important to follow up couples who were unsuccessful in conceiving in order to ascertain their perception of the programme.

Factors Relating to the Birth

There was a high rate of caesarian section (37%). This is

greater than twice the expected rate. In addition, the incidence of pre-term children was approximately four times the expected rate and that of very low birthweight children, below 1500 gm, was greater than ten times that expected in the population at large. The incidence of twin births was twenty times that found in the general population. These factors, particularly those relating to prematurity, seem to be the main ones influencing IVF children at this early stage in their development.

Severe Physical and Psychosocial Problems

If both physical and psychosocial findings are considered together, four families were noted to have issues of significant clinical magnitude. In three of these families the children had a significant physical problem. One had severe congenital heart disease requiring surgical correction and periods of hospitalisation. Two children had significant neurological problems acquired in the perinatal period. These last two children were in the very low birthweight group. In the fourth family, three were significant mother/child international problems, with the mother having difficulties in adapting to her parenting role and interfering with the child's attempts to explore the environment. These four children showed significant developmental delays on the Bayley Scales.

Less Severe Clinical Conditions

Apart from the three children with physical problems, ten were reported to have physical features of a less severe nature. These included colic (30%) and asthma (12%). A number of mild conditions, such as eating and sleeping problems, occurred in less than 10% of the children seen. Two of the families reported some mild problems of adaptation to parenthood. These findings are in line with the occurrence of such conditions in the general population (Thomas, 1981, Williams and Phelan, 1975). Forty eight per cent of the children had neonatal jaundice. If the pre-term group is discoused, 23% are left in this group, a percentage comparable with figures for the general population of new born children (Maisels, 1982). On follow-up one child was found to have an asymptomatic congenital defect. This was not considered to be of clinical concern.

Psychosocial Development

The Bayley Scales of Infant Development were administered to 32 of the 33 children seen for psychosocial assessment. The means were well within the expected normal range. Only one child had significantly low Mental Development Index (MDI) and three other children had low Physical Development Indicies (PDI). The child with the very low MDI also had a very low PDI. These four children were the ones referred to in the section on severe conditions. Paediatric follow-up of these children some months alter showed that the child with congenital heart disease was making good progress and the child with the international problems had significantly improved. As can be seen, most developmental delays were in the physical-motor areas. Given the low birthweight, the high number of twins, and some bias towards seeing children over whom the paediatrician had expressed some concern, the range of findings do not indicate reasons for concern. Most of the children, 31 out of 32, showed social development within the accepted range. The child given the McCarthy Scales of Intelligence also scored well within the expected range in both intellectual and social skills.

Discussion

While the study did not have a control group it is considered that the above findings are consistent with what might be expected of a group of 33 children and their parents. Studies such as that of MacFarlane and co-authors (1971) point to figures of 33% for sleep and feed disorders and 58% and 44% for "bad temper attacks" in boys and girls respectively. Colic is reported in about one third of the children. Thus there is no data at present to indicate an increased incidence of minor behavioural problems in the children at this stage in their development. This is supported by positive results in the assessment of social skills on the Bayley. It is thus considered that, given a sample bias towards problem families and high incidence of premature birth and twins the findings do not support the hypothesis, postulating an increase in physical and psychosocial problems in children born by IVF conception. It is recognised, however, that longitudinal controlled studies will be necessary to address many of the issues raised. Issues of identify and sexuality will not be evident until the children ae older, nor will the nature of their relations with teachers and peers.

Future Issues

The present study employed a small sample population without a control group and was undertaken at an early stage of development. In order to understand fully the effects of IVF on children and families, it will be necessary to undertake a longitudinal study with a variety of relevant control groups. The population needs to be studied at various stages of development. The focus should be at two levels - the evaluation of significant pathology and the study of particular differences in developmental, interactive and family parameters. Focus should be placed on the children, their needs and their rights. Such investigations may also add to the understanding of infertility and its significance, by evaluating how infertile couples manage as parents and how these children develop. From a management point of view, such findings may indicate whether or not it is important for these couples to have resolved conflicts about their infertility prior to having children. Thus the question of screening prospective parents should be reviewed.

Such investigations would also clarify whether or not these families have greater difficulties in resolving problem issues should they occur, and if so, whether undue focus on IVF issues serves to inhibit problem resolution. Another important area is that of the child's perception of IVF conception, i.e. what it means to the child to be told of such origins. As the children develop, social, peer and sexual issues (including their own fertility or infertility) will become more prominent, as will the effects on the family of community anxieties.

REFERENCES

Macfarlane, J.W., Allen, L. & Honzik, M.P. (1971).A developmental study of the behaviour problems of normal children between 21 months and 14 years. In M.C. Jones, N.Bayley, J.W. McFarlane & M.P. Honzik (Eds). *The Course of Human Development*. Zerox College Publications: Waltham, Mass.

Maisels, M.J. (1982) Jaundice in the newborn. *Paediatrics in Review*, 3, 305-319.

Mushin, D.N., Barreda-Hanson, M. & Spensley, J., (1986) In vitro fertilization children: early psychosocial development. *Journal of In-Vitro Fertilization and Embryo Transfer* (in Press).

Mushin, D.N., Spensley, J. & Barreda-Hanson, M. (1985). Children of the vitro fertilization. *Clinics in Obstetrics and Gynaecology*, 12, December.

Spensley, John C., Mushin, D. & Barreda-Hanson, Maria (1986). The children of IVF pregnancies: a cohort study. *The Australian Paediatric Journal*, 22, 285-289.

Thomas, D.B. (1981). Aetiological association in infantile colic - an hypothesis. *The Australian Paediatric Journal*, 17, 292-295.

Williams, H.E. & Phelan, P.D. (1975). *Respiratory Illness in Children*. Blackwell Scientific Publications, Melbourne: Australia.

26

Psychological Symptomatology and Health Beliefs

Introduction

An individual's cultural and ethnic background are of importance in the clinical setting in the sense that how illness is perceived, experienced and coped with is based on how sickness is understood in that culture. The cultural interpretations individuals place on their symptoms have been shown to influence the perceived intensity and expression of pain (Diller, 1980); the way symptoms are presented (White, 1982); the attributions placed on the illness (Abrahamson *et al*, 1961) and subsequent help-seeking behaviour (Carstairs & Kapur, 1976).

Cultural influences on symptomatology are epitomised in the form of culture-bound syndromes which are very specific, localised interpretations and manifestations of illness. There are also more general national differences of culturally appropriate expressions of distress encoded in symptoms that have symbolic meanings within their cultural context: the French are said, for example, to place great emphasis on the liver (Herzlich, 1973), American Blacks on the blood and Iranians on the heart and blood (Helman, 1985).

It has already been illustrated that many ethnic communities present differential symptom patterns, but does the same supply to 'psycho-atric' patients (patients presenting with psychological problems or a psychiatric illness)? To be more specific, doAsian 'psycho-atric' patients in Britain present symptoms differentially from indigenous patients? The evidence from China and Taiwan, for example, would strongly suggest that 'psycho-atric' patients present with somatic symptoms more often than Western pataients (Kleinman and Good, 1985). There is also evidence, however, to suggest that 'psycho-atric' patients generally present with many somatic complaints (Bridges and Goldberg, 1985); though it is believed that developing countries have a higher rate of somatic presentation (Lloyd, 1986).

What is meant by somatisation is essentially a coded message, whereby the individual having problems in various areas of life chooses consciously or unconsciously to convey these in bodily terms. The aim is presumably to obtain relief both from the physical complaints and from the underlying difficulty.

This paper describes a preliminary study carried out by the author comparing the symptoms of 50 Asians (25 Punjabi Sikhs; 25 Pakistanis) and 50 English born patients at four General Practitioner clinics in Birmingham. The study aimed to assess if Asian patients presented a psychological problem with physical symptoms more often than did English patients and, if this was the case, whether GPs were making a diagnosis of the patients' physical illness more often than of the psychological distress.

Four family practitioners in a central area of Birmingham consented to their patients being interviewed by the author. From each of the two English and two Asian GPs, 25 patients were interviewed, matched for sex and ethnic group, as far as possible.

The main part of the interview comprised administering the Langner 22-item questionnaire. With Asian patients, a culturally validated version of the Langner was used either in Punjabi or Urdu (Cochrane et al, 1977). Patients were further asked about their presenting symptoms and how many visits they had made to their G.P. for the same complaint.

Scores from the Langner-22 questionnaire indicated whether the patient had any psychological problems. This was compared with the patients' presenting symptoms to assess if the symptomatology and psychological state were concordant. The GPs were also asked to complete a diagnostic sheet for each patient requesting details of the patients' symptoms, the diagnosis and whether they felt the patient had any psychological problems.

A comparison of the two independent measurements (from patient and doctor) was used to indicate whether ethno-cultural differenes existed:

(a) Whether Asian patients presented with more somatic and psychosomatic symptoms compared with English patients;

(b) Whether the GP had a differential rate of diagnosing psychological problems in Asian and English patients;

(c) Whether there was a relationship between the patients' presenting symptoms, their Langner score and the doctor's diagnosis. In other words, would a doctor diagnose an Asian patient presenting with a somatic (or psychosomatic) symptom but with a high score on the Langner as having a psychological or non-psychological problem any more or less often than an English patient with the same symptoms and the same Langner score?

Results

Before describing the results, it is important to define the interpretations placed on (a) somatic, (b) psychosomatic, and (c) psychological symptoms;

(a) Symptoms were classified as 'somatic' when the patient was presenting with physical symptoms with clear bio-physica lorigins; e.g. a twisted foot; industrial or domestic burns to the skin; viral infections, etc.

(b) A 'psychosomatic' symptom was classified as one where the patient was complaining of vague physical symptoms which could have either a physical or psychological aetiology: eg skin rshes, headaches, overall muscular-skeletal pains.

(c) Symptoms were classified as 'psychological' when the patient described them in purely psychological terms without any physical component: eg anxiety, depression, stress, nervousness, etc.

Results

The data reveal that a comparable number of Asian and English patients presented with somatic symptoms. The results differed markedly, however, for psychosomatic and psychological presentations. Of the 50 Asian born, 20 presented with psychosomatic symptoms; 28 with somatic and 2 with psychological symptoms. With the English born, the figures are 10 with psychosomatic, 33 with somatic and 7 with psychological symptoms ($x^2 = 6.52$, 2 df, $p<0.51$).

A similar pattern emerges when patients' presenting symptoms ae cross-tabulated with GP's diagnoses. Whereas of the 10 English patients presenting psychosomatically, 5 were diagnosed as having a psychological problems, of the 20 Asian patients presenting psychosomatically, only 7 were diagnosed as having a psychological problem.

Inconsistencies also arose between the patient's Langner scores and the recognition by the GP of psychological problems when Asian and english patients were compared. There was a good match between Langner non-cases and the GP's recognition of non-psychological problems for both groups of patients. GPs were not, therefore, misdiagnosing non-psychological patients as "cases". With those English patients scoring highly on the Langner, once again GPs are accurately recognising the psychological origins of their problems. Where the GP's recognition of psychological problems comes into question is with those Asian patients who score highly on the Langner. Of the 30 Asian patients classified as cases by the Langner scale, only 9 were recognised as such by the GP ($x^2 = 0.212.1$ df NS), whereas of the 14 English patients scoring 7 and above on the Langner scale, 10 were recognised as having a psychological problem ($x^2 = 7.36$, 1 df, $p<0.01$).

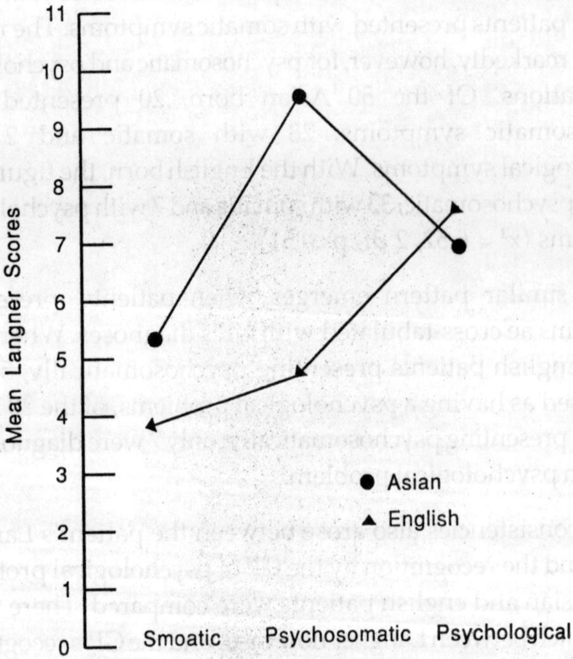

Fig. 26.1 Interaction between ethnic group and presenting symptoms on Langner scores

For a more complete analysis of the relationships between Langner scale scores and other variations, a two-way analysis of variance was undertaken using ethnic group and presenting symptoms as the main effect. As a diagrammatical interpretation of the 2-way ANOVA shows (Figures 26.1) Asian patients scored more highly on the Langner than English patients, except for psychological symptoms, where they scored fractionally lower. An interesting point which the figure reveals quite clearly is the very high Langner score of Asian patients presenting psychosomatically. Certainly, one implication of this is that Asian patients with 'psycho-atric' problems were manifesting them psychosomatically. A more typical trend is shown with English patients and Langner mean scores, with gradual increase in scores from somatic through psychosomatic to psychological symptomatology.

Discussion

The findings of this study can be discussed with reference to ethno-cultural factors pertaining to traditional health beliefs and aetiologies that may explain the greater psychosomatic presentation of psychological problems by Asian patients.

It is important, however, to understand the concepts the Asian patient has concerning the aetiology and attributions of 'psycho-atric' problems before any insight can be gained into symptomatology and health beliefs. On the Asian subcontinent, but in India specifically, mental illness is thought to be caused by one of three main factors (Weiss et al, 1986):

(a) Firstly illness can be caused by an imbalance of body humours, a view subscribed to for some 3000 years and forming the basis of the Asian medical system. Illness, according to this theory, can be caused by eating foods with a constitution that might cause an excess of heat or cold in the body. Alternatively, an imbalance can be caused by an exposure to extreme of temperature.

(b) Mental illness is also thought to be caused by another person's wish to cause harm through sorcery or magic - a concept, again, that is adhered to by different nationalities (Helman, 1985).

(c) Finally, mental illness is believed to be caused by gods who become angry after they are treated irreverently, or by supernatural powers as punishment for breaking a taboo or cultural rule.

Clearly, an individual's health beliefs are culturally determined. Health beliefs are not *ad hoc* transitory notions of illness and disease, but are part of a rigid, structured, medical system which defines clinical reality. Similarly, the way the individual explains his/her illness (the explanatory model) is strongly related to ethno-cultural health beliefs influencing illness presentation, illness-behaviour and help-seeking behaviour (Nations et al, 1985).

Turning then, to the cultural influences which may determine the greater psychosomatisation of Asian patients, the first explanation to be considered concerns the concept of locus of controls or the extent to which patients believe they have control over their illness. It can be argued that Asians feel they are, in many instances, responsible for their own illness, through having violated a taboo, angered a god or by having eaten the wrong type of food. As such, they have brought the the illness upon themselves. One purpose of somatisation, therefore, could be a mechanism for the denial or repression of the existence of a psychological problem.

In contrast, studies on the health beliefs of British working-class women have shown that ill-health is thought to come about either through environmental factors, such as the weather, through hereditary, family and individual susceptibility, or by germs, viruses and infections (Helman, 1985).

The point being emphasised here, then, is that these differential interpretations of illness and disease, and the amount of control the individual feels they have, will often result in differences in illness-presentation and help-seeking behaviour. These points may be reflected in the greater numbers of Asian 'psycho-atric' patients presenting psycho-somatically.

Another insight into lay beliefs is the way illness is expressed. In Britain, for example, somewhat over-generalised and vague mechanistic interpretations are often attributed to physical and mental ill-health: "I feel run down", "my batteries need charging", "I had a nervous breakdown", "I'm on the mend". Contrast this with the metaphore likely to be used by Asians: *"Mera dil dukh da he"* (my heart hurts) for "I am depressed". Although a somatic presentation is used, it is not the same as the vague mechanistic interpretations, previously cited as being typical of English patients. Whereas the latter example is a cultural interpretation of depression, the heart being regarded as the seat of the emotions, the former illustration is an example where responsibility is shifted from the individual by analogising illness with mechanical failure.

These expressions of health and ill-health have implications not only for the individual but also for the clinician. Whereas one could say with some certainty that a clinician would not misunderstand an English patient's "I am heart-broken", the same could not be said for an Asian patient's "my heart hurts". There are also practical reasons why Asian patients may present psychological problems somatically. The first, and most obvious, concerns the language barrier. If patients have difficulty in articulating their complaints because they are unable to clearly express themselves, it may be that presenting somatically reduces that difficulty. The responsibility is placed on the clinician to define and ascribe illness. In fact, in the traditional Asian health setting, it is the role of the healer to tell the patient what is wrong with them and not vice versa (Carstairs & Kapur, 1976). Alternatively the Asian patient may present with a somatic symptom, believing the clinician as a bio-medic treats bio-physical ailments only.

Implications

There are several important points to consider for the clinician who is dealing with Asian patients, issues which have a direct bearing on the patients' compliance with treatment regimens and with clinical outcome.

Although language can often be a barrier between the clinician and the patient, it has to be remembered that many Asians have been resident in Britain for ten years or more, so their grasp of English is often better than they care to admit. Holding a dialogue with an Asian patient may be difficult, but not impossible. Given the interactional nature of the clinician-patient encounter, it becomes clear how attributions are important to each. For the patient distressed by bodily or psychological feelings, a causal explanations provides some control of them. Furthermore, causal explanations indicate forms of lay and medical consultations that may also be pursued to control the discomfort.

For the clinician, illness attributions are important precisely because they reveal the meanings patients attach to those symptoms or disabilities which hey bring to the consultation. It is this meaning of illness that determines, in turn, the patient's illness behaviours, coping responses and clinical outcome. Effective communication requires that the patient's conceptions of illness be explored and differences from the clinician acknowledged, interpreted and, if possible, resolved.

It must be difficult for any practitioner to by-pass conventional medical explanations and treatment programmes for the sake of getting the patient's whole-hearted agreement and compliance. How, for example, would one begin to help an Asian patient who is tense and anxious because he or she feels that a relative in India is making life extremely difficult through actively wishing him or her harm. This belief may be further strengthened in the patient's mind through a series of ill-fates.

Conventional relaxation programmes may help overcome physical symptoms of stress and anxiety but would do little for the underlying problem. To try and convince the patient that there is no evidence that a relative is bearing a grudge might seem a natural step, but one which overlooks a cultural milieu where it is believed that one individual can have a malevolent impact on the life-events of another. A more positive approach would be to accept the patient's explanatory model and to incorporate it in the treatment process.

The suggestion here, then, is that despite these conflicting ideas about illness causation between clinician and patient, successful treatment may still be accomplished. By eliciting the patient's ethno-cultural, patho-psychological ideas, the clinician and patient can then discuss, negotiate and co-operate for a successful outcome. Questions such as: What do you feel may be causing your problem?". "How do you feel the illness is affecting you?" and "What do you feel might be of benefit?" are possible ways of gaining insight into the patient's explanatory model.

REFERENCES

Abrahamson, J.H., Mayett, F.G.H. & Majola, G.C. (1961). What is wrong with me? *South African Medical Journal, 19,* 690-694.

Bridges, K.W. & Goldberg, D.P. (1985). Somatic presentation of DSM III psychiatric disorders in primary care. *Journal of Psychosomatic Research, 29,* No. 6, 563-569.

Carstairs, G.M. & Kapur, R.L. (1976). *The Great University of Kota: Stress, Change and Mental Disorder in an Indian Village.* Hogarth: London.

Cochrane, R., Hashmi, F. & Stopes-Roe, M. (1977). Measuring psychological disturbance in Asian immigrants to Britain. *Social Science and Medicine, 11,* 157-164.

Diller, A. (1980). Cross-cultural pain semantics. *Pain, 9,* 9-26.

Helman, C.G. (1985). *Culture, Health and Illness.* John Wright: Bristol.

Herzlich, C. (1973). *Health and Illness: A Social Psychological Analysis.* Academic Press: London.

Kleinman, A. & Good, B. (Eds) (1985). *Culture and Depression: Studies in the Anthropology and Cross-Cultural Psychiatry of Affect and Disorder.* University of California Press: Berkeley.

Lloyd, G.G. (1986). Review article: Psychiatric syndromes with a somatic presentation. *Journal of Psychosomatic Research, 30,* No. 2, 113-120.

Nations, M.K., Camino, L.A. & Walker, F.B., (1985), "Hidden" popular illnesses in primary care: residents recognition and clinical implications.

Index

E

F

H

I

M

□□□